OHIO

OFF THE BEATEN PATH®

OFF THE BEATEN PATH® SERIES

FIFTEENTH EDITION

OHIO

OFF THE BEATEN PATH®

JACKIE SHECKLER FINCH

Essex, Connecticut

All the information in this guidebook is subject to change. We recommend that you call ahead to obtain current information before traveling.

Globe Pequot

An imprint of Globe Pequot, the trade division of
The Rowman & Littlefield Publishing Group, Inc.
4501 Forbes Blvd., Ste. 200
Lanham, MD 20706
www.rowman.com

Distributed by NATIONAL BOOK NETWORK

Maps by The Rowman & Littlefield Publishing Group, Inc.

British Library Cataloguing in Publication Information available

ISSN 1539-8196

ISBN 978-1-4930-7757-1 (paper)
ISBN 978-1-4930-7758-8 (electronic)

∞™ The paper used in this publication meets the minimum requirements of American National Standard for Information Sciences—Permanence of Paper for Printed Library Materials, ANSI/NISO Z39.48-1992.

To my parents, Smiley Jack and Margaret Poynter, for instilling in me the desire to travel. And to my first traveling buddies: my sisters, Elaine Emmich, Jennifer Boyer, Juliette Maples, and Jeanine Clifford; and my brothers, Jim Poynter and Joe Poynter.
My gratitude to my family for their encouragement:
Kelly Rose; Sean Rose, Crystal, Breylon, and Garrett Christian; Stefanie, Will, Trey, and Arianna Scott; and Logan Peters. And a special remembrance to my husband, Bill Finch, who taught me to value every day on this earth.

—Jackie Sheckler Finch

OHIO

Toledo
NORTHWEST OHIO
Cleveland
NORTHEAST OHIO
Akron
Mansfield
Lima
Canton
WEST CENTRAL OHIO
EAST CENTRAL OHIO
Newark
Columbus
Dayton
Lancaster
SOUTHWEST OHIO
SOUTHEAST OHIO
Cincinnati

Contents

About the Author

An award-winning journalist and photographer, Jackie Sheckler Finch has covered a wide array of topics, from birth to death, with all the joy and sorrow in between. She has written more than two dozen travel guidebooks and has had articles published in numerous magazines and newspapers. She has been named the Mark Twain Travel Writer of the Year by Midwest Travel Journalists Association a record six times—in 1998, 2001, 2003, 2007, 2012, and 2023—and is a member of the Society of American Travel Writers.

One of her greatest joys is taking to the road to find the fascinating people and places that wait over the hill and around the next bend.

Acknowledgments

Thanks to the Ohio Division of Travel and Tourism, the Ohio Department of Natural Resources, and the Ohio Historical Society for providing supplemental information and materials about many of the places described in this book. Their cooperation made researching Ohio Off the Beaten Path a productive and enjoyable endeavor.

I'm grateful to Greta Schmitz and the friendly and professional staff at Globe Pequot for allowing me the pleasure of revising this book.

Introduction

When I was a child, my parents loved to pile all of us kids in the station wagon and take off for a weekend drive. Usually Mom did the driving and she didn't have any particular destination in mind. We would just drive through the countryside and along the rivers, stopping at little roadside stands and mom-and-pop stores to pick up pickled bologna, crackers, cheese, and other goodies for lunch at a roadside park. That was my first introduction to my birth state, probably a big part of why I became a travel writer and why I keep Ohio so close to my heart. I hope you'll come along on a trip off the beaten path with me to see some of the wealth that Ohio has to offer.

"The Mother of Presidents," Ohio Claims Eight U.S. Presidents

Ohio, known as "The Mother of Presidents," has been the birthplace of seven U.S. presidents: Ulysses S. Grant (Point Pleasant), Rutherford Hayes (Delaware), James Garfield (Orange Township, now Moreland Hills), Benjamin Harrison (North Bend), William McKinley (Niles), William Howard Taft (Cincinnati), and Warren G. Harding (Corsica, now Blooming Grove).

When William Henry Harrison was born (in Virginia), there were no states, only 13 colonies. He claimed Ohio from the time it became a state, and Ohio claims him. During his presidential campaign, he used the buckeye as his symbol because of its association with Ohio. Harrison's supporters often wore necklaces made from a string of buckeyes, and he carried a cane created from a buckeye tree and was said to always carry a buckeye nut in his pocket. Ohio residents have been called "buckeyes" since the mid-1800s. The buckeye was named the Ohio state tree in 1953.

As America's ninth president, William Henry Harrison gave an 8,445-word inauguration speech—edited by Daniel Webster—for an hour and 45 minutes in cold rain without a hat, overcoat, or gloves. He caught a cold that developed into pneumonia and died just 31 days after taking office.

John Tyler then became the first vice president to succeed to the presidency, serving from 1841 to 1845.

The next Ohioan in office was Civil War hero Ulysses S. Grant, the 18th president. The Republican served two terms from 1869 to 1877. He supported amnesty for Confederate leaders and civil rights for African Americans. He also signed legislation establishing Yellowstone National Park as America's first national park and proclaiming Christmas a national holiday.

Another Ohio Republican, Rutherford B. Hayes, served as the 19th president from 1877 to 1881. He signed a bill in 1879 allowing female attorneys to argue cases before the

Ohio is an excellent state to explore—it has breathtaking natural beauty, a rich historical heritage, countless fine restaurants, and varied and unique overnight lodging. *Ohio Off the Beaten Path* exposes the reader to Ohio's best—from rolling pastoral farmland to rugged wooded cliffs and gorges, from restored canal towns and gristmills to country inns and working historical farms. After years of researching and traveling the state, I can only conclude that Ohio offers a wealth of opportunities for recreation, for appreciating the history that shaped its present and future, and for pleasurable excursions to suit any tastes or interests.

Most of the destinations described in this book, be they historical, culinary, or recreational, are located away from interstate highways and major

U.S. Supreme Court. He also held the first Easter Egg Roll on the White House lawn, a tradition that continues to this day.

James A. Garfield, another Ohio Republican, was the 20th president. Six months after taking office, he was shot on July 2, 1881, and died 79 days later of a ruptured splenic artery aneurysm following sepsis and bronchial pneumonia. Most historians and medical experts now believe that Garfield probably would have survived his gunshot wound if doctors at the time had known to practice safety measures to prevent infections.

Benjamin Harrison, the grandson of former president William Henry Harrison, became the 23rd president from 1889 to 1893. The Republican signed the Sherman Anti-Trust Act, the oldest of all U.S. anti-trust laws.

Another Ohio Republican, William McKinley, served as the 25th president from 1897 to 1901. He increased the size of the United States by annexing Puerto Rico, Guam, the Philippines, and Hawaii. During his second term, McKinley was shot at the Pan-American Exposition in Buffalo, New York, on September 6, 1901. He died of gangrene and blood poisoning from the wound on September 14, 1901.

William Howard Taft, another Ohio Republican, served as the 27th president from 1909 to 1913. He launched eighty antitrust suits against some of the nation's largest corporations. He was also the first president to throw out the ceremonial first pitch at a baseball game (in 1910) and the first president to be buried in Arlington National Cemetery (in 1930).

The last Ohio president—so far—was Warren G. Harding, a Republican who served as 29th president from 1921 to 1923. Harding hosted the first international strategic arms limitation talks at the 1921 Washington Naval Conference and was the first president to ride to his inauguration in an automobile.

The Ohio Statehouse has named six House and two Senate hearing rooms in honor of Ohio's eight presidents.

metropolitan areas—an indication of our preference for scenic roads and picturesque towns and villages (traveling by interstate highway just does not provide the enjoyment of winding through forests and cresting hills on a narrow, two-lane country road). To take full advantage of *Ohio Off the Beaten Path*, you might find it handy to have an Ohio highway map. TourismOhio will mail you a travel guide with an Ohio map at no charge if you call (800) BUCKEYE (282-5393). TourismOhio can also provide another valuable service—confirmation of specific information on thousands of sites and attractions around the state.

Although every effort has been made to ensure that addresses, phone numbers, rates, hours, and seasons of the places described in this book are accurate at the time of publication, establishments do change owners or hours of operation, relocate, and even close. For this reason, I advise taking advantage of the state's toll-free service to verify important information before making that two- or three-hour drive. Another excellent resource is TourismOhio's website, ohio.org, which includes links to hundreds of other Ohio tourism websites.

Whether spending a week, a weekend, or just an afternoon traveling to a new destination, you will probably find, as I did, that Ohio's friendly people and splendid countryside make any trip that much more rewarding. And if you have yet to experience the state's historic and recreational opportunities, I believe you will be impressed and amazed by all Ohio has to offer.

Ohio Facts

- **Nickname:** Buckeye State
- **Capital:** Columbus
- **Population:** 11,780,000
- **Admitted to Union:** Ohio became the 17th state when it was admitted on February 19, 1803.
- **Major Cities and Populations:** Columbus, 906,528; Cleveland, 367,991; Cincinnati, 308,935; Toledo, 268,508; Akron, 189,347; Dayton, 137,571
- **Famous Residents:** William Henry Harrison, Ulysses S. Grant, Rutherford B. Hayes, James Garfield, Benjamin Harrison, William McKinley, William Howard Taft, Warren G. Harding, Harriet Beecher Stowe, James Thurber, George A. Custer, Johnny Appleseed, Doris Day, Jack Nicklaus, Steven Spielberg, Neil Armstrong, John Glenn, Charles Goodyear, John D. Rockefeller, Thomas Edison, Clark Gable, Bob Hope, Langston Hughes, Woody Harrelson, Rob Lowe, Paul Newman, Annie

Oakley, Roy Rogers, Martin Sheen, Dean Martin, Drew Carey, LeBron James, Sarah Jessica Parker, Maya Lin

- **Travel Information:** Contact TourismOhio at (800) BUCKEYE (282-5393) or ohio.org.
- **State Parks:** Contact Ohio State Parks at (614) 265-6561, or ohiodnr.gov.
- **State Song:** "Beautiful Ohio"
- **State Rock Song:** "Hang on Sloopy"
- **State Wildflower:** White trillium
- **State Flower:** Red carnation
- **State Bird:** The cardinal
- **State Tree:** The buckeye
- **State Animal:** White-tailed deer
- **State Motto:** "With God All Things Are Possible"

Northeast Ohio

Cuyahoga Valley

Tranquil, stream-fed Chippewa Lake provides the setting for an outstanding country dining establishment, the ***Oaks Lakeside***. Eight acres of tall trees surround this rambling former estate, which rests a stone's throw from the water. Railroad industrialist J. F. Townsend remodeled this former farmhouse in 1914, using it to entertain such captains of industry as J. Pierpont Morgan. Townsend dubbed the place Five Oaks for the semicircle of oak trees that graced the front of the home at the time.

Don Casper and Al Hitchins purchased the Medina County property in 1961 and earned a reputation for an innovative menu and an impressive kitchen. In the summer of 2004, Johnny and Audrey Pollizi joined with Don's family to maintain the family's tradition of gracious elegance and outstanding cuisine. Now a third generation of the Don Casper family—Don's three nieces: Bonnie Casper Drushal, Cheryl Casper Iaquinta, and Holli Stille Boylan—are continuing the tradition. Each of the six dining areas has its own distinct character, and the large

NORTHEAST OHIO

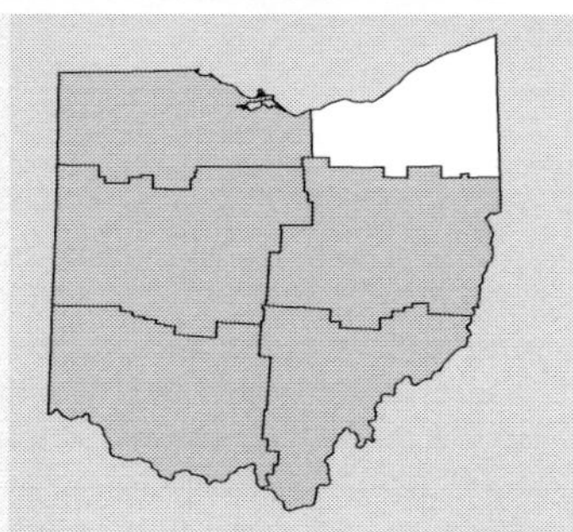

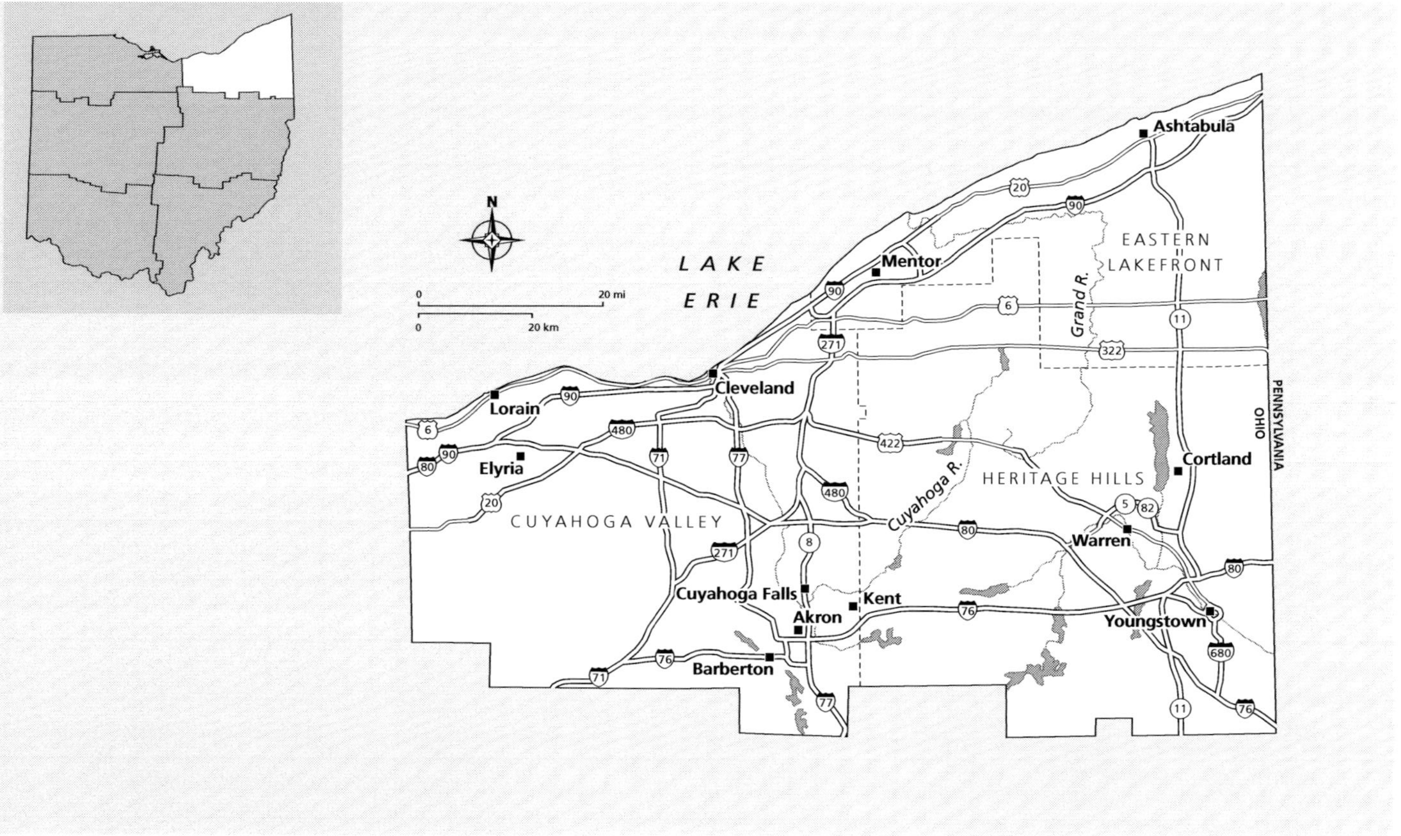

windows allow a view of the spacious patio—a perfect spot for a cocktail or after-dinner drink—and the gazebo at water's edge.

Dinner at the Oaks Lakeside includes dishes such as veal marsala, pan-seared duck breast, dry-aged strip steak with pinot noir sage butter, filet mignon, and grilled chicken spinach alfredo with pappardelle pasta. Seafood fans can choose from rosemary grilled salmon, South African lobster tail, Alaskan king crab legs, and steamed scampi.

A fine dinner salad distinguishes a quality restaurant from an ordinary one, and an Oaks Classic salad comes brimming with mixed greens, toasted pecans, dried cranberries, citrus vanilla vinaigrette, and Danish blue cheese. A nice variety of appetizers includes baklava brie with orange ginger glaze, thyme, dill crackers and bread sticks; herbed truffle fries with barbecue balsamic reduction, and sauerkraut balls with Santa Fe mustard and plum sauce. The lodge's luxurious desserts include fallen chocolate souffle with vanilla bean ice cream, pecan and cranberry bread pudding topped with caramel whiskey sauce, and chocolate brownie parfait topped with whipped cream. From the fresh flowers and stylish decor (the lodge has won several awards for interior design) to the culinary expertise, the Oaks Lakeside rates high marks.

BEST ATTRACTIONS

- Oaks Lakeside
- Hickories Museum
- Allen Memorial Art Museum
- Crawford Auto-Aviation Museum
- Rock & Roll Hall of Fame and Museum
- Hale Farm and Village
- Blossom Music Center
- Akron Art Museum
- Stan Hywet Hall & Gardens
- Perkins Stone Mansion
- John Brown House
- Kent State University Museum
- Youngstown Historical Center of Industry and Labor
- Butler Institute of American Art/Arms Family Museum of Local History
- Mill Creek MetroParks
- The Welshfield Inn
- Rothenbuhler Cheesemakers
- Burton Sugar Camp and Log Cabin
- Century Village Museum
- Richards Maple Products
- Alpine Valley Ski Area
- Holden Arboretum
- Lake Metroparks Farmpark
- Debonne Vineyards
- Grand River Cellars

birthplaceof aluminum

We have Charles M. Hall to thank for a world full of aluminum siding and aluminum everything else. Born in Thompson on December 6, 1863, Hall moved with his family to Oberlin. Along with a country full of scientists, he had been trying to find a cheap way to make aluminum; Hall did his experiments in an old woodshed while still in high school.

Hall attended Oberlin College, where he continued to experiment. Eight months after graduating, the 22-year-old discovered the process he and the others had been seeking. After a patent dispute with a French scientist claiming the same invention, Hall secured capital from Andrew Mellon and built what became the American Aluminum Company. Hall died in 1914, leaving a substantial bequest to Oberlin College.

The Oaks Lakeside is at 5878 Longacre Ln., Chippewa Lake; (330) 769-2601, (800) 922-5736; theoakslakeside.com. Open Wed through Sat from 4 p.m. to 9 p.m., Sun from 11 a.m. to 3 p.m. Live entertainment is offered Thur and Fri evening June through Aug.

Medina County is also the location of a unique annual occurrence—Ohio's equivalent of the swallows returning to Capistrano. Each year in mid-March, about 75 turkey vultures come home to roost in trees by the cliffs and caverns of Whipp's Ledges near Hinckley. With clocklike regularity, the buzzards have returned to this summer home for more than 150 years. Hinckley townspeople mark the occasion with celebrations on the first Sunday after March 15, when a "buzzard breakfast" is served.

The architect was Arthur Oviatt; the owner, Arthur Lovett Garford. The result of their vision: one of the finest residences in northeast Ohio, now the ***Hickories Museum***.

Construction on this massive 19-room stone-and-shingle home began in 1894 and cost Garford $100,000. On the large corner lot stand many of the original shagbark hickory trees from which came the name Hickories.

Within the walls of the Hickories Museum are Tiffany-style windows, 6 fireplaces, 12 built-in seats, and approximately 60 carved faces. Features are the grand staircase, pier mirrors, a Gothic chapel, and a bull moose head given to Garford by Teddy Roosevelt. An opulent Victorian bathroom as well as a restored master bedroom and guest room can be seen on the second floor.

Garford was a young banker when he hopped on a newfangled high-wheeled vehicle, the bicycle. A rough ride on the bike's hard seat launched a new career for A. L.—he invented a padded bicycle seat, which made him a millionaire. His interests would grow to include such diverse items as golf balls, telephone parts, lighting fixtures, and steel; he also became involved in car and truck manufacturing, mining, and publishing.

The Hickories Museum is at 509 Washington Ave., Elyria; (440) 322-3341; lchs.org. Open for tours Wed through Fri, at 1 p.m. or by appointment. Admission: adults $5, children (ages 13 to 18) $3; children (ages 6 to 12) $2.

Founded in 1917, the ***Allen Memorial Art Museum*** at Oberlin College is ranked as one of the finest college or university collections in the nation. Cass Gilbert designed the original building; he also designed four other buildings for Oberlin College between 1907 and 1931. The museum's contemporary addition, designed by Robert Venturi, opened in 1977.

The museum's collection consists of some 11,000 objects from ancient Egypt to contemporary America. Collection highlights include Dutch and Flemish paintings of the seventeenth century, European art of the late 19th and 20th centuries, and contemporary American art. Of particular note are the Mary A. Ainsworth collection of Japanese woodblock prints, the Charles Martin Hall collection of Islamic carpets, the Joseph and Enid Bissett collection of modern European paintings, and a comprehensive collection of Old Master prints, including Rembrandt and Dürer. The museum also has a growing collection of African and African-American art. In addition to the galleries, a number of sculptures can be found on the museum's well-manicured grounds. Be sure to tour the Frank Lloyd Wright home on the grounds—built in 1950, this is an example of the compact Usonian houses he created for middle-class families.

The Allen Memorial Art Museum is at 87 N. Main St., Oberlin; (440) 775-8665; amam.oberlin.edu. Open Tues through Sat, 10 a.m. to 5 p.m.; Sun, 1 to 5 p.m. No admission charge. Tours of the Frank Lloyd Wright Usonian House are offered the first Sunday of each month from April through Nov, noon to 5 p.m. Admission is $10 for adults.

Take the high road or take the low road, but those wishing for a wee bit of Scotland in Ohio should take to the road on the fourth Saturday every June to celebrate the ***Ohio Scottish Game Weekend*** in Oberlin. Visitors can enjoy the colorful Scottish games and the traditional dress in the parade of clan tartans. In addition there is a competition between the pipe and drum corps. The event is held in Oberlin. Visit ohioscottishgames.com for information.

One of the best car collections you'll find is the ***Crawford Auto-Aviation Museum*** in Cleveland. The collection tells the history of technological as well as stylistic changes and developments in the auto industry. With some 150 cars in the collection, the vehicles range from the famous to the obscure, from a Model T to a modern Jaguar. For example, the visitor can admire a rare 1897 Panhard et Lavassor, which was the first automobile to enclose the passenger area and protect the occupants from the elements. The car enthusiast can also view the 1982 Indy car driven by Ohio's own Bobby Rahal.

Since car manufacturing is now centered on a few dominant companies, many people may not know just how many small automotive manufacturers existed in the early 1900s. The Crawford Auto-Aviation Museum highlights the remarkable number of carmakers that were located in the Cleveland area.

Between 1898 and 1931 more than 80 makes of cars were produced here, including the Winton Bullet. Alexander Winton was the leading automotive pioneer in Cleveland, selling his first car in 1898. The Winton Bullet held the land-speed record in 1902 and is on display in the museum.

Along with the car collection, the museum also features bikes, motorcycles, and aircraft. The centerpiece of the aviation collection is a 1912 Curtiss Hydroaeroplane, which was once piloted by Cleveland aviator Al Engel.

This museum is part of a larger complex, the Western Reserve Historical Society's University Circle. This campus-like setting also houses a history museum in a turn-of-the-twentieth-century mansion. A visitor to this museum can go on a mansion tour and view a costume collection and various special displays. Also nearby is the renowned Cleveland Museum of Art. The Western Reserve Historical Society's library is one of the best genealogical resources in the nation.

The Crawford Auto Aviation Museum is located at 10825 East Blvd., Cleveland; (216) 721-5722; wrhs.org. Open Thurs noon to 8 p.m.; Fri, Sat, and Sun, 10 a.m. to 4 p.m. Admission: adults $15; seniors $13; children (ages 3 to 12) $8. Parking in the museum lot costs $8 for the first two hours and $1 for each additional 30 minutes with a daily maximum of $15.

The ***Dittrick Museum of Medical History*** presents the medical history of Cleveland and the Western Reserve. Exhibits trace advances in diagnostic technology from the stethoscope to the X-ray machine.

Visitors inspect an array of early surgical instruments, bloodletting tools, and the museum's collection of microscopes. Also featured are two complete and furnished doctors' offices, one from 1880 and the other from 1930.

The Dittrick Museum of Medical History is on the third floor of the Allen Memorial Medical Library at 11000 Euclid Ave., Cleveland; (216) 368-3648; artsci.case.edu. Open Fri, 10:30 a.m. to 4 p.m.; Sat, noon to 4 p.m. No admission charge.

Critics have and will continue to debate the location of the birthplace of rock & roll, but there's no debate that Cleveland has provided a home for rock for the ages with the outstanding ***Rock & Roll Hall of Fame and Museum***. The spectacular $92 million facility overlooks Lake Erie. Designed by renowned architect I. M. Pei, the 150,000-square-foot building consists of bold geometric forms and dramatic spaces anchored by a 162-foot tower.

Rock fans of all ages will discover memorabilia from all phases of rock & roll, from its birth in the 1950s to its explosion in the 1960s and its evolution to the present. Among the highlights of this most extensive collection are John Lennon's Sgt. Pepper uniform and the Rickenbacker guitar he used at the Shea Stadium concert, the black leather stage outfit Elvis wore during his 1968 "comeback" TV special, Tina Turner's "Acid Queen" costume from the movie *Tommy*, Jim Morrison's Cub Scout uniform, and Jimi Hendrix's handwritten lyrics to "Purple Haze." The original recording equipment from Sam Phillips's Memphis Recording Service is on display, along with Janis Joplin's psychedelic Porsche convertible.

Music plays throughout the museum, except in the actual top-floor Hall of Fame. Film and video presentations trace the history of rock and offer snapshots of its various incarnations and tangents. If you are or ever have been a fan of rock & roll, this is a must-see.

The Rock & Roll Hall of Fame and Museum is at 1100 Rock and Roll Blvd. (East Ninth St.), Cleveland; (216) 781-7625; rockhall.com. Open daily, 10 a.m. to 5 p.m. (until 9 p.m. on Thurs) from Jan through June. From July through Aug open daily 10 a.m. to 5 p.m., Thurs through Sat until 9 p.m. Admission: adults $35; children (ages 6 to 12) $25.

Looking for an unusual tour or for a unique setting for lunch or dinner? Then be ready to board the **Goodtime III**. This 1,000-passenger boat offers two-hour sightseeing tours Tues through Sun and has provided a great way to see Cleveland since 1958. As you cruise by, your guide will help you learn more about the area. The boat offers indoor and outdoor seating so you can tour even if the weather is not perfect. Along with sightseeing you can also enjoy a box or buffet lunch. Dance cruises and happy hour cruises sail on Fri, dinner cruises on Sat, and brunch cruises on Sun.

Goodtime III is at 825 E. 9th St. Pier, Cleveland; (216) 861-5110; goodtimeiii.com. The summer sailing schedule runs from June 15 through Labor Day; limited sailings in May and Sept. Tours are available Tues through Sun

north olmsted to and from

Talk about "necessity being the mother of invention!" The mayor of North Olmsted was given one week's notice that the railway connecting his community with Cleveland was calling it quits. Mayor Charles Seltzer had until midnight February 28, 1931, to find a way to get 150 of his constituents to work.

His solution: that North Olmsted start a municipal bus line, the first in Ohio. The city council concurred, and they all scrambled to purchase two used buses and two sets of license plates and hire two drivers. At 5 a.m. March 1, two freshly painted red-and-white coaches hit the road, changing Ohio transportation history.

Rock & Roll Hall of Fame Honors Great Musicians

Several teens in the audience began to chuckle when the film narrator said, "Imagine there was a time in America when there was no rock and roll."

For these youngsters, there never was such a time. Rock & roll has always been a part of their lives. So the Rock & Roll Hall of Fame and Museum must have been a real eye opener for them. After the short film ended, I saw the young people avidly reading information in the exhibits and commenting on how much music has changed. They even giggled at Elvis' flamboyant jumpsuit and the video of a Baptist preacher denouncing Elvis as an evil influence in a 1956 sermon.

The Rock & Roll Hall of Fame and Museum has something to interest everyone.

"We have 5,000 to 8,000 visitors a day and 85 percent of them are from out of town," a tour guide told me. "It is Cleveland's biggest attraction." Which leads to the question—why Cleveland?

Alan Freed was a Cleveland DJ who coined the term "rock & roll" and hosted the first rock concert here in 1952. Cleveland was also the first place north of the Mason-Dixon Line where Elvis played.

When the idea for a Rock & Roll Hall of Fame initially came about, Cleveland leaders were among the first and most enthusiastic in lobbying Hall of Fame officials to bring the museum to their fair city. Cleveland overwhelmingly beat all rivals in a *USA Today* poll, earning more than 100,000 votes over its nearest rival.

In addition, 660,000 people signed petitions to bring the museum to Cleveland. The city's civic and business leaders worked together to provide the necessary financial support to make the museum not only a reality but also a stunning showcase for the history of rock & roll.

Cleveland was selected as the site for the museum in 1986, with a groundbreaking in 1993 and opening in 1995. Located on the shores of Lake Erie, this museum designed by I.M. Pei is a real beauty. A futuristic composition of bold geometric forms and dynamic cantilevered spaces, it is anchored by a 162-foot tower supporting a dual-triangular-shaped glass "tent" that extends at its base onto a 65,000-square-foot plaza, making a dramatic main entry facade.

"In designing this building," Pei has said, "it was my intention to echo the energy of rock & roll. I have consciously used an architectural vocabulary that is bold and new."

The $92 million structure was funded through a public-private partnership that included the State of Ohio, City of Cleveland, Cuyahoga County, Cleveland-Cuyahoga County Port Authority, and Cleveland area and music industry corporations and foundations.

The original concept for the museum and archive dedicated to rock & roll was initiated in 1983 when several music industry leaders created the Rock & Roll Hall of Fame Foundation. Their goal was to honor the men and women who made significant contributions to this musical style.

In 1986, they began inducting individuals. The museum was built to house the Hall of Fame, so they are two distinct entities.

The first-year Hall of Fame roster included Chuck Berry, James Brown, Ray Charles, Sam Cooke, Fats Domino, Everly Brothers, Buddy Holly, Jerry Lee Lewis, Elvis Presley, and Little Richard. Artists become eligible for the Rock & Roll Hall of Fame 25 years after the release of their first commercial recording. The process of nominating inductees each year is based on the artist's "influence and significance to the development and perpetuation of rock & roll." Ballots are then sent to about 900 performers, historians, and music industry professionals. Those nominees who receive the most votes are inducted. The Hall of Fame typically welcomes five to seven artists each year.

For the museum itself, leave plenty of time to visit. The constantly changing museum has so much to see, read, and hear. For starters, there's the fashion of Sgt. Pepper, Jimi Hendrix's handwritten lyrics and the patchwork jacket from his final concert appearance, Janis Joplin's psychedelic wardrobe, and a dazzling Tina Turner costume designed by Gianna Versace. Other objects of interest include John Lennon's grammar-school report card, Buddy Holly's high school diploma, David Bowie's "Ziggy Stardust" jumpsuit, Bruce Springsteen's outfit from the cover of "Born in the U.S.A.," a shirt John Mellencamp wore on his "Scarecrow" tour, and autographed drumsticks from Kenny Aronoff.

Then there are the musical instruments—enough to delight any music lover. You can see Duane Eddy's Gretsch guitar, Eddie Cochran's 1955 Gretsch, Duane Allman's 1959 Gibson Les Paul, Dickey Betts' 1954 Les Paul gold top, Lead Belly's 12-string acoustic guitar, Louis Jordan's tenor saxophone and Robbie Robertson's 1958 Fender Stratocaster. Exhibited items are rotated over time, so many visitors return to see and hear what is new.

Several theaters take visitors on a cinematic journey through rock & roll history, including Dick Clark's American Bandstand in the RMS Theater and a 14-minute film in the Elvis exhibit. An exhibit called Part of the Machine: Rock & Pinball showcases rocked-out pinball machines with popular performers and bands. At the Rock & Roll Radio exhibit, you can hear sound clips from famous rock & roll DJs from different eras and regions.

Before the museum opened, experts predicted fans would need about two and a half hours to wander through the musical lesson. They were sure wrong. "We've found that most people stay closer to four hours or even the entire day," a guide told me before I left. "Once they get here, people are often surprised at all there is to see and they stay longer than they expected."

For details: rockhall.com

at noon and 3 p.m. for $30 for adults; $15 for children (ages 5 to 12). Two-hour lunch cruises are $49.95 for adults; $39.95 for children (ages 5 to 12). Friday and Saturday dinner and city lights cruise: adults $79.95. For the luncheon or dinner and city lights cruise, be sure to call ahead for reservations. Ask about departure times for the evening cruise. A smoke-free and vape-free vessel.

For more cruising and dining, board the **Lady Caroline**. Buffet lunches, brunches, and dinners are part of the sightseeing experience aboard this pleasure cruise. You glide by the "Flats" and parks, and view the Cleveland skyline while munching on a wide variety of salads, entrees, and desserts. There are outdoor observation decks so you can enjoy the sun or stars during your approximately two-hour voyage. The dining areas are enclosed so that a bit of foul weather won't put a damper on the dining experience. When you call for information, you might want to ask about the *Lady Caroline*'s special events. You might enjoy one of their theme cruises, or have the staff plan something special for a birthday or anniversary.

The *Lady Caroline* is located at 1153 Main Ave. (on the West Bank of the Flats), Cleveland; (216) 696-8888, (800) 837-0604; ladycaroline.com. Sails Apr through Dec. Lunch cruises: Mon through Fri, noon; Sat, 11 a.m.; Sun, 1 p.m. Dinner cruises: Mon through Thur, 7 p.m.; Fri and Sat, 7:30 p.m. Lunch cruise prices: $54.95; children (age 2 to 11) $39.95. Free for children younger than 2. Sunset dinner cruise prices: Tues through Thur, $64.95 per person; Fri and Sat, $89.95 per person. Sunday brunch prices: $64.95; children (age 2 to 11) $49.95. Free for children younger than 2. All cruises include unlimited buffet, coffee, tea, or iced tea, and musical entertainment.

The North Union Colony of Shakers was established here in 1822 and thrived for 67 years. This unique religious group of more than 200 people stressed social justice, freedom, and equality of men and women. They built their own school and cared for orphans. They farmed and sold their apple products, herbs, and high-quality, simple handmade furniture. When the community declined, the Shakers' property was sold to a real estate company and developed to become Shaker Heights.

ALSO WORTH SEEING

Great Lakes Science Center, Cleveland

Cleveland Museum of Art

Cleveland MetroParks Zoo

Children's Museum of Cleveland

Twins Day Festival

You'll be seeing double, but that's to be expected if you visit Twinsburg for the annual Twins Day Festival. What better place than Twinsburg to host a national gathering of those special siblings we call twins?

Matched sets of brothers and sisters come from all over the nation to gather for this celebration of duality. Infants and oldsters and in-betweeners all attend. Some are so close in looks and dress, down to the hat, the socks, or the tie tack, that you have to wonder how even their mothers and fathers tell them apart.

Triplets, quadruplets, and beyond are also welcome. To add to the fun of celebrating these look-alikes, there's a parade, a fireworks display, arts and crafts, food, of course, and even a golf tournament (with identical twins on the course, keeping the scoring straight could be a challenge).

The Twins Day Festival is held first weekend in August in Twinsburg. For more information call (330) 425-3652 (or get your twin to call) or visit twinsdays.org.

The ***Shaker Historical Museum*** occupies a Tudor-style mansion facing Horseshoe Lake. The Shaker Historical Society presents exhibits about the Shakers, the development of Shaker Heights by the Van Sweringen brothers, as well as seasonal displays, programs, and events. The museum shop offers books, herbs, candles, cards, and Shaker-style boxes and carriers.

The Shaker Historical Museum is located at 16740 S. Park Blvd., Shaker Heights; (216) 921-1201, (800) 860-6078; shakerhistory.org. Open Wed through Fri, 11 a.m. to 5 p.m., and Sat and Sun, noon to 5 p.m. Admission: $5 donation.

Pigs, ponies, and a gaggle of geese are likely to greet visitors to the ***Stearns Farm***. The Parma Area Historical Society, mostly with a lot of volunteer labor, has saved a little chunk of rural Ohio and preserved the Stearns Farm in the midst of urban growth. The Stearns family built the farmhouse in 1855. When the Gibbs family bought the farm, they added a second house in 1919. A barn, which is tilting a little to the west, is home to an unlikely vehicle collection: a 1948 fire engine and a horse carriage once used by President William McKinley. The collection of farm animals delights visiting children, and volunteers sell feed so you can offer a treat to one of these four-legged inhabitants. There are also a variety of special events at the farm throughout the summer months, such as ice-cream socials and antiques markets.

Check out the Stearns County Store, where you can buy gifts, homemade crafts, old-fashioned candy, ice cream, and beverages. Items from the past are displayed on store shelves, giving the store a museum feel.

The Stearns Farm is at 6975 Ridge Rd., Parma; (440) 845-9770; stearnshome stead.com. Open Sat from 11 a.m. to 2 p.m. Admission and parking are free but donations are welcomed.

The Western Reserve region of Ohio was "reserved" for settlers moving west from Connecticut after the American Revolution. One of those settlers, Jonathan Hale, relocated his family in 1810, establishing a farm in the rolling acreage of what is today northern Summit County. The Hale property remained in the family until the death of Miss Clara Belle Ritchie, great-granddaughter of Jonathan, in 1956. She willed the farm to the Western Reserve Historical Society, stipulating that it be opened to the public so that as many people as possible could "be informed about the history and culture of the Western Reserve."

The history and culture of the region are faithfully preserved at the working ***Hale Farm and Village***. Guides in period clothing help transport the visitor back to 1848. You will meet Jacob and Hannah Meredith, who will tell you about their prosperous dairy farm and life at their household in the mid-1800s. You can also chat with the village founder and the town gossip to learn even more about the flavor of the place and the time. The color and scents of the mid-nineteenth century are reflected in the gardens and in the arts on display around the village. You can watch glassblowing, spinning, weaving, candle and basket making, and even try your hand at making bricks.

Hale Farm and Village is in the 32,000-acre Cuyahoga Valley National Park at 2686 Oak Hill Rd., Bath; (330) 666-3711, (800) 589-9703; wrhs.org. Open June through Aug, Wed through Sun, 10 a.m. to 5 p.m.; Sept and Oct, Sat and Sun, 10 a.m. to 5 p.m. Admission: adults $15; children (ages 3 to 12) $8.

Cuyahoga Valley National Park follows the Cuyahoga River for 22 miles between Akron and Cleveland. The park offers numerous hiking, nature, and bicycle trails, scenic overlooks, and picnic areas.

The Towpath Trail follows the historic route of the Ohio & Erie Canal, which was built between 1825 and 1832. This canal provided a transportation link between Cleveland, on Lake Erie, and Portsmouth, on the Ohio River, and opened Ohio to the eastern United States. Prior to the canal, Ohio was a sparsely populated wilderness, where travel was difficult and the shipping of crops was nearly impossible.

Today hikers, joggers, and cyclists follow the same route once used by "canawlers." Locks and related structures are still visible, as you travel through forests, fields, and wetlands brimming with wildlife.

Information about all the recreational opportunities and programs at this vast park are available at the six visitor centers: Canal Exploration Center, Boston Store, Hunt House, Happy Days Visitor Center, Frazer House, and

TOP ANNUAL EVENTS

Medina Ice Festival
Medina, Feb
(330) 722-6186
mainstreetmedina.com

Burton Pancake Breakfast
Burton, Mar
(440) 834-4204
pancaketown-usa.com

Geauga County Maple Festival
Chardon, Apr
(440) 332-7055
maplefestival.com

Strawberry Festival and Craft Bazaar
Jefferson, June
(440) 576-0133
jeffersonchamber.com

Ohio Scottish Game Weekend
Berea, June
ohioscottishgames.com

Lorain International Festival
Lorain, June
loraininternational.com

Festival of the Fish
Vermilion, June
(440) 967-4477
vermilionohio.com

Shakespeare at Stan Hywet
Akron, July/Aug
(330) 836-5533
stanhywet.org

Civil War Weekend
Bath, Aug
(330) 666-3711, (800) 589-9703
wrhs.org

Twins Day Festival
Twinsburg, Aug
(330) 425-3652
twinsdays.org

North Ridgeville Corn Festival
North Ridgeville, Aug
(440) 218-9802
nrcornfest.org

Vintage Ohio Wine Festival
Kirtland, Aug
(440) 466-4417
visitvintageohio.com

Woollybear Festival
Vermilion, Sept
(440) 967-4477
vermilionohio.com

Mantua Potato Festival
Mantua, Sept
(330) 352-6099
mantuapotatofestival.org

Grape Jamboree
Geneva, Sept
(440) 466-5262
grapejamboree.com

Ashtabula County Covered Bridge Festival
Jefferson, Oct
(440) 576-3769
coveredbridgefestival.org

Peninsula Depot. Or you can call (216) 524-1497 or visit the website at nps.gov/cuva. For information on the Cuyahoga Valley Scenic Railroad, call (330) 439-5708 or go to cvsr.com.

Winter sports in the park include sledding, ice-skating, and cross-country skiing. Two complete ski centers, ***Brandywine*** in Sagamore Hills and ***Boston***

Mills in nearby Peninsula (both at 800-875-4241), serve downhill skiers with complete ski shops, lifts, instruction, and equipment rentals.

Nestled in 800 acres of rolling hills between Akron and Cleveland is one of America's premier outdoor cultural and entertainment complexes, ***Blossom Music Center***. The summer home for the renowned Cleveland Orchestra, Blossom also attracts audiences for performances that range from jazz to rock & roll.

The nation's top artists take the stage in the innovative pavilion, a fan-shaped open-air structure seating 5,281. Its enormous roof rises 94 feet above the stage level (it's the largest shingled area in the country), creating a sound chamber requiring little or no electronic amplification for those seated in the pavilion.

Four acres of lawn on the gentle hillside provide outdoor seating for an additional 13,500 patrons. A unique computerized sound system has a delay feature that transmits the sound from speakers at precisely the moment the sound from the stage reaches the lawn audience, creating near-perfect listening conditions.

Artists perform almost every evening during the June-through-September season. A full-service restaurant is open on all concert nights. For information and a schedule of coming attractions April through September, you can phone the center at (330) 920-8040 or visit livenation.com.

The ***Akron Art Museum*** originally was housed in an 1899 Italian Renaissance–style structure that once served as the Akron post office. In 2007 the museum opened its new, magnificent Coop Himmelb(l)au–designed building just south of the original. This ultramodern structure provides a compelling contrast with the original museum. The permanent collection boasts more than 3,000 works from the mid-1800s to the present. Much of the collection is dedicated to contemporary painting and photography. Works by photographers Robert Frank, Margaret Bourke-White, and Harry Callahan are featured, along with the contemporary art of Andy Warhol, Frank Stella, and Carrie Mae Weems. The Myers Sculpture Court is an outdoor venue for large-scale sculpture as well as concerts during the spring and summer months. The museum also hosts traveling exhibitions throughout the year.

The Akron Art Museum is at One S. High St., Akron; (330) 376- 9186; akronartmuseum.org. Open Wed, Fri, and Sat, 11 a.m. to 5 p.m.; open to 8 p.m. on Thurs. Admission: adults $12; seniors $10; students $8. Free admission on Thurs.

Constructed at an estimated cost of $2 million, Frank A. and Gertrude Seiberling's ***Stan Hywet Hall*** in Akron took four years to build and was completed in 1915. Frank Seiberling founded the Goodyear and Seiberling rubber companies, and this lavish 65-room mansion gives testimony to the personal wealth amassed by industrialists in that era.

Considered to be one of the finest examples of American Tudor revival architecture, Stan Hywet is patterned after three Tudor estates in England, with elements of each incorporated in the design of the structure. As is typical of Tudor buildings, windows, doors, chimneys, and roof peaks are asymmetrical and appear randomly placed. The name Stan Hywet means "stone quarry" in Anglo-Saxon, a reference to the sandstone quarry once located on the original 3,000-acre estate.

Molded plaster ceilings and hand-carved oak walls, both commonly used in English Tudor residences, can be found throughout the Seiberling home. The Seiberlings went to considerable trouble to make Stan Hywet as faithful as possible to the Tudor style; they concealed telephones behind wall coverings and installed 23 working fireplaces, even though the building is equipped with central heating. They also built a rope elevator for hauling firewood from the basement to the upper floors.

Formal balls and other social functions were held in the large music room, which has three massive crystal chandeliers, 16 wall sconces, and a second-floor balcony for a small orchestra. The formal dining room seats 40, and an oil-on-canvas mural above the oak walls depicts Chaucer's Canterbury Tales. Rare American chestnut, a type of wood that's no longer available because of devastating blight, lines the walls of the billiard room.

The Seiberlings removed the paneling and fireplace from a room in an English manor house scheduled for demolition and installed these materials in the second-floor master bedroom. Also in their bedroom is an original Tudor canopy bed, ca. 1575. Throughout the tour, guides point out many of the outstanding pieces in the Seiberlings' priceless collection of antiques.

Formal gardens, woodlands crisscrossed with paths and trails, and splendid shrubbery surround Stan Hywet Hall. Clear stream water pours over

stanhywet/ shakespeare

The owners of the impressive Stan Hywet Hall were well known for their love of music and the performing arts. That love continues as the estate hosts Shakespeare at Stan Hywet each July.

Outdoor performances are held in the early evenings on the grounds of the great hall. Generally the performances are held on two consecutive weekends in July. The grand mansion and grounds also are the setting for other special activities, including art shows and teas on the terrace featuring period music and entertainment. For information on Shakespeare and other special events at Stan Hywet, call (330) 836-5533.

a stone waterfall in a cool pond in the tall trees just behind the Seiberling mansion.

Stan Hywet Hall and Gardens is at 714 N. Portage Path, Akron; (330) 836-5533, (888) 836-5533; stanhywet.org. Open Apr through Dec, Tues through Sun, 10 a.m. to 6 p.m. Admission for guided manor house tour: adults $21; children (ages 3 to 17) $10; children (ages 2 and under) free. Admission closes at 4:30 p.m.

From Stan Hywet Hall, take Portage Path south for a drive past many fine old Akron homes and estates. If you continue south to the intersection of Copley Road and South Portage Path, you will find two museums.

The mansion of Colonel Simon Perkins was constructed adjacent to the historic Portage Path at Akron between the years 1835 and 1837. The home is an example of the Greek revival style, which had great influence on architecture during the early settlement of the Western Reserve. Built of native sandstone on the brow of a hill, the ***Perkins Stone Mansion***, with its two-story portico, overlooks the city of Akron. Through the years, it has become recognized as one of the most imposing homes of northern Ohio.

Colonel Perkins was born to General and Mrs. Simon Perkins at Warren, Ohio, in 1805. His father organized the Western Reserve Bank in 1813, and, in connection with Paul Williams, founded the village of Akron in 1825.

Colonel Perkins, who served in the Ohio legislature and was an active promoter of the Cleveland, Zanesville & Cincinnati Railroad, purchased 115 acres of land on this site in 1832 for $1,300. Perkins and his wife, sister of the future governor of Ohio, David Tod, resided in Warren before moving to Akron in 1835. While the mansion was under construction, they lived in a small frame house, now known as the ***John Brown House***.

Surrounded by more than 10 acres of beautiful grounds, the mansion today contains some of its original furnishings, as well as items connected with the early history of Summit County. Situated on the grounds are the original carriage house, a combination summer kitchen and laundry built in 1890, the original well—dug through 40 feet of sandstone—and a visitor center, previously the Perkins' woodshed.

Across the street is the John Brown House, so named to commemorate the residency of that abolitionist leader from 1844 to 1854. At the time, Brown was associated with Colonel Simon Perkins in the sheep and wool business. The original frame structure, to which several additions have been made, is believed to have been built around 1830. Inside is an exhibit that explains the importance of the canal to the development of Akron, as well as a replica of a canal boat captain's cabin.

Both museums are operated by the Summit County Historical Society, 550 Copley Rd., Akron; (330) 535-1120; summithistory.org. Self-guided tours are available Wed through Sat, from 1 to 3:30 Apr through Dec. Admission (to both museums): adults $8, children (under 18) $2, and senior citizens $4. Guided tours are by appointment only.

Kay and Donna Vaughan have been farming in the Hartville area since the 1960s, and both quit their teaching jobs in the '70s to farm full-time. By 2000 their children had joined the operation, they purchased a 140-year-old barn and refurbished it, and the Maize Valley Farm Market opened for business. In 2005 the next expansion created what is now known as the ***Maize Valley Market, Winery and Craft Brewery***. The craft brewery was added in 2014.

Today the Vaughan family farms 750 acres, including 200 acres of fruits and vegetables. Super-sweet corn and juicy tomatoes grow alongside cantaloupes, watermelons, peppers, green beans, squash, strawberries, raspberries, and blueberries.

allfiredup inbarberton

The unusually named Ohio Columbus Barber was a premier match maker, but he was not one involved in pairing couples for romance. No, Barber and his company, Diamond Match Company, made fire-starting matches, a quarter billion a day during the company's heyday.

Barber came from a family of match makers: His father made them, too, and peddled them. The younger Barber founded Diamond Match in 1880, and his success resulted in the creation of a new town, Barberton, which he conceived and promoted. He was known during his day as the "Match King."

The winery produces a crisp, dry, fruity Riesling, and a medium-bodied Chambourcin, a spicy dry red with hints of black cherries and raspberries balanced by soft tannins and toasted oak. The Maize Valley cabernet sauvignon is aged in American oak barrels and features rich currant and black-cherry flavors. The winery has come up with some unusual names, such as Hanky Panky Pink, a slightly sweetened wine made from the Catawba grape with a citrus finish. Among other selections, try the red table wine known as Red Neck Red, the sparkling White Wedding, or one of the many fun fruit wines produced here. The Mad Cow with its light fruity white flavor is a nod to the family's former farm where they owned about 130 cows. Money from selling the cows was used to start the current business. "The days of 4 a.m. milking are now long gone," the family says. The wines are already winning regional awards.

The Vaughans often stage special events at the winery, everything from a performance by an Elvis-tribute artist to hot-air balloons. The winery has live music every Saturday from 6 to 8:30 p.m. Fall harvest time means corn mazes and that the Pumpkin Cannon is locked and loaded—be sure not to park down range, or plan on a trip to the nearest carwash. Wagon rides around the property are popular with visitors, as is the petting pasture for younger guests.

The Tasting Room Café is a great place for a quick bite or a relaxing lunch or dinner. Menu choices vary and are made fresh with local produce. Menus vary but the fresh baked pies are always popular.

The Maize Valley Market, Winery and Craft Brewery is at 6193 Edison St. NE (OH 619), Hartville; (330) 877-8344; maizevalley.com. Open Mon through Sat 11 a.m. to 9 p.m.; Sun, noon to 7 p.m.

Heritage Hills

Founded with an initial gift from Jerry Silverman and Shannon Rodgers, the ***Kent State University Museum*** opened its doors in 1985. Silverman and Rodgers, New York dress manufacturers, donated 4,000 costumes and accessories, almost 1,000 pieces of decorative art, and a 5,000-volume reference library. Today the collection consists of more than 20,000 pieces representing the major world cultures.

Highlights of the collection include the black velvet evening cape, trimmed with a band of crystals, worn by Joan Crawford at Truman Capote's Black and White Ball. Another favorite is the eighteenth-century English silk dress, in a style typical of the Spitalfields silk-weaving district in London. There's a magnificent uniform of the Chinese Imperial Palace Guard worn at the end of the Manchu dynasty around 1900 and a fancy blue silk ball gown from the French couture house of Balenciaga, ca. 1958.

A second gift to the museum was the Tarter/Miller collection of more than 200,000 pieces of collectible glass. A distinctive part of this collection is the Vaseline glass, so called because of its unusual yellow-green color. The recent acquisition of the Paige Palmer Collection of Ohio art pottery includes exquisite examples of Roseville, Weller, and Rookwood pieces.

The Kent State University Museum is in Rockwell Hall on the corner of East Main and South Lincoln Streets on the Kent State University campus at 515 Hilltop Drive, Kent; (330) 672-3450; kent.edu/museum. Open Tues through Sat, 11 a.m. to 5 p.m. Sun, noon to 5 p.m. Admission: adults $6; seniors $5; students and children (ages 5 to 18) $4; children younger than 5 free. Free admission on Sundays.

The history of the Mahoning Valley is the history of the iron and steel industries. Deposits of black coal suitable for blast furnaces were discovered near Youngstown in 1845, and by the 1850s the Valley was one of the nation's centers of iron production. As technology advanced, the Valley switched to steel production; the Ohio Steel Company, the area's first steel company, was organized in 1892.

Steel mill jobs attracted immigrants from eastern and southern Europe, as well as African Americans from the South. Working conditions for these laborers were appalling—typically 12-hour days, six or even seven days a week, in an environment of heavy machinery, poisonous gases, and open vats of molten steel. These conditions eventually led to the formation of the United Steelworkers of America in 1936.

Youngstown's steel production and employment soared during the middle of the twentieth century, peaking in 1973. But just four years later, "Black Monday" hit the area on September 19, 1977, with the closing of Youngstown's Sheet and Tube's Campbell Works. Global changes in the steel market, labor-management disputes, and a depletion of high-grade ores all contributed to the death of the Valley's steel industry.

The ups and downs of this pivotal industry are presented at the ***Youngstown Historical Center of Industry and Labor***. The museum's permanent exhibit, By the Sweat of Their Brow: Forging the Steel Valley, uses videos, artifacts, photographs, and reconstructed scenes to tell the story of steel in the valley.

The Youngstown Historical Center of Industry and Labor is at 151 W. Wood St., Youngstown; (330) 941-1314, (800) 262-6137; youngstownohiosteelmuseum .org. Open Wed through Fri, 10 a.m. to 4 p.m.; Sat, noon to 4 p.m. Admission: adults $7; children (ages 6 to 12) $3.50; free for children 5 and under.

In a city best known for steel and other heavy industry, Youngstown's ***Butler Institute of American Art*** houses an outstanding permanent collection of more than 10,000 works. From the earliest Limner painters of the colonial period through contemporary masters, the Butler Institute features representative works by Benjamin West, John Singleton Copley, Winslow Homer, Thomas Eakins, Martin Johnson Heade, and Mary Cassatt.

Specialty collections include western art by the likes of Albert Bierstadt, Frederic Remington, and Victor Higgins, and an expansive group of marine paintings featuring the works of Fitz Hugh Lane, Edward Moran, William Bradford, and Alfred Bricher. The Lester F. Donnell Gallery of American Sports Art features paintings, sculpture, drawings, and prints of all things sporting, including works by George Bellows, John Steuart Curry, Red Grooms, Robert Riggs, and Roy Lichtenstein.

Founded in 1919 by industrialist Joseph G. Butler Jr., the Butler Institute is housed in a classic building, the first structure built in the United States specifically to house a collection of American art. Additions to this historic edifice in the 1930s and 1960s preceded the impressive West Wing addition in 1987 and the Beecher Center for Art and Technology in 2000. These postmodern structures, awash in marble and partially lit by soaring skylights, brings to 20 the number of galleries at the Butler Institute.

The Butler Institute of American Art is at 524 Wick Ave., Youngstown; (330) 743-1107; butlerart.com. Open Tues through Sat, 11 a.m. to 4 p.m.; Sun, noon to 4 p.m. No admission charge.

Just down the road from the Butler Institute is another Youngstown treasure: the early twentieth-century mansion of Wilford and Olive Arms, Greystone, now the ***Arms Family Museum of Local History***. The three main rooms on the first floor of this elegant mansion preserve the Arms' way of life; their family portraits, furniture, china, glassware, silver, linens, Oriental rugs, and objets d'art are still in place.

On the lower level, a large exhibition room depicts pioneer life in the region, with a collection of farm and household tools, implements and utensils, antique toys, and Native American relics. Second-floor exhibits explore the more recent history of the Mahoning Valley through photographs, costumes, and artifacts.

Period gowns adorn mannequins throughout the museum, and the table setting in the dining room changes periodically to rotate the display of china, crystal, and silver. Special exhibits here include toys and dolls, costumes and accessories, political memorabilia, and works of art.

The Arms Family Museum of Local History is at 648 Wick Ave., Youngstown; (330) 743-2589; mahoninghistory.org/arms-family-museum. Open Tues through Sun, noon to 4 p.m. Admission: adults $7; senior citizens $6; children (3 to 18) $5.

One of Ohio's greatest regional parks offers visitors more than 4,400 acres of streams, lakes, gardens, woods, meadows, and wildlife. It's Mahoning County's ***Mill Creek MetroParks***, and it features 21 miles of roads and 15 miles of foot trails through truly spectacular scenery. Hiking, picnicking, and boating are popular pastimes on Lake Newport and Lake Glacier.

The central feature of the park is picturesque Mill Creek. Many pioneer industries developed along the creek, and relics still remain to be discovered by visitors. Lanterman's Mill operates today as it did in the early 1800s, grinding corn, wheat, and buckwheat via power driven by a 14-foot oak waterwheel. The mill had ceased operation in 1888, only to reopen a century later. A covered bridge stands just south of the mill and is one of the scenic highlights of the park.

Downstream from the mill is the start of the Gorge Trail. Mill Creek borders one side of this 2-mile trail; a massive wall of sandstone forms the other boundary. The trail takes hikers past a stunning waterfall.

More than 40,000 flowering bulbs announce the arrival of spring each year at the Fellows Riverside Garden. As summer arrives, a spectacle of colorful annuals takes over. The wooded setting of the shade garden is a showcase for ornamental plants that thrive in low light. Other park highlights include a golf course, tennis courts, miniature golf, an ice-skating rink, ball fields, and basketball courts.

Mill Creek Park is at 810 Glenwood Ave., Youngstown; (330) 702-3000; millcreekmetroparks.org. Open during daylight hours.

The Packard automobile may be a thing of America's past, but its history is preserved at the ***National Packard Museum***. The museum is located in the community of Warren, and its mission is to document and tell the story of the Packard family, the Packard Electric Company, the Packard Motor Car Company, and the innovations they created. The museum has several wonderfully restored Packards, and plenty of displays and Packard memorabilia, as well as changing exhibits. Bring your camera. Photography is not only allowed, it's encouraged.

The National Packard Museum is at 1899 Mahoning Ave. NW, Warren; (330) 394-1899; packardmuseum.org. Open Tues through Sat, noon to 5 p.m.; Sun, 1 to 5 p.m. Admission: adults $10; senior citizens $8; children (ages 7 to 12) $5.

Jacob Welsh and his daughter traveled from Boston, Massachusetts, in 1811 to the Western Reserve area of northeast Ohio. Mr. Welsh donated 50 acres of his land on which to build a church, parsonage, and cemetery. In addition, he agreed to provide the nails and glass for the church if his neighbors would call the area Welshfield, in honor of his family.

Built in the 1840s by Alden J. Nash and originally called the Nash Hotel, the ***Welshfield Inn*** served as an Underground Railway station for slaves escaping from the South to Canada. Stagecoaches traveling between Cleveland and Pittsburgh also frequently stopped here for food and overnight accommodations.

In 2007 the inn was purchased by the proprietors of the Gamekeepers Taverne in Chagrin Falls, Bass Lake Taverne and Inn in Chardon, and the Allegheny Grille in Foxburg, Pennsylvania. After extensive renovation and restoration, the Welshfield Inn was purchased by the Driftwood Restaurant Group and reopened in November 2007.

Although lodging is no longer offered here, the tradition of serving delicious cooking has been maintained by the new owners. The menu at the Welshfield Inn features such popular options as seared sea scallops with three cheese and chive risotto; cedar planked salmon with sweet corn salsa and maple brussels sprouts; crispy pork loin schnitzel with asparagus and hand-mashed potatoes with lemon hollandaise; and panko chicken parmesan with roasted San Marzano sauce, fresh basil, spaghetti, asiago, parmesan and

Romano cheese. On Fridays, the inn offers the popular beer-battered fish fry with all-you-can-eat cod, fries, and coleslaw for $14.99. Specialty side dishes include Maine lobster macaroni and cheese and Maine lobster risotto. The Inn also offers cocktails, beer, and wine.

The large dining room with a fireplace contains an eclectic mix of bentwood chairs and wooden tables; browns, greens, and other earth tones predominate, and fresh flowers dress up each table. One of the smaller dining rooms, called Peddlers Parlor, has Early American decor with antiques, Quaker lace tablecloths, and seasonal flowers. On the front porch, lawn furniture creates a friendly, informal atmosphere under the tall columns. Also under the porch roof is a huge wooden sled named Snowbird capable of carrying 20 to 30 people.

The Welshfield Inn is on OH 422, 14001 Main Market Rd., Burton; (440) 834-0190; thedriftwoodgroup.com. Open Tues through Thurs, 11:30 a.m. to 8 p.m.; Fri and Sat, 11:30 a.m. to 9 p.m.; and Sun, 10 a.m. to 9 p.m.

Approximately 16,000 Amish live in Geauga County, making it one of the largest Amish communities in the country. Wearing the traditional dark, solid-colored clothing and rejecting modern conveniences such as electricity and automobiles, the "plain people" strive for a simple farming life. Merchants in Middlefield, Ohio, provide hitching posts for their Amish customers.

The Schaden family has a most unique and charming business. They are the owners of the ***End of the Commons General Store*** in picturesque Mesopotamia.

Ken Schaden, once a frequent customer, gave up a corporate position with extensive international travel requirements to purchase the store in 1982 and spend more time with his wife, Margaret, and their 11 children. The Schadens sell more than 800 products in bulk to area Amish families, most arriving at the store in horse-drawn buggies. As its name indicates, the store sits at the end of a parklike commons, surrounded by 30 historic homes, the oldest of which was built in 1816.

When they purchased the store and began to clean out the old storage areas, they found hundreds of items related to the store's and the town's history. Today visitors find on display old clothes, shoes, a barber chair, a post office, a player piano, and many things of bygone days. Penny candy still lines shelves by the checkout counter (yes, it is still just a penny), where slots and boxes of the old post office remain. In summer, hand-dipped ice cream is dispensed from a window where stamps once were sold. Amish families who host church services in their homes buy pounds and pounds of bologna and cheese here and also bake lots of bread and goodies with the unusual flours they find here in suitable quantities. The Commons Cafe serves lunch and dinner daily.

In 2010, an additional 5,000 square feet was built to bring together the Schaden's 1940-era gas station and hardware store.

The End of the Commons General Store is at 8719 OH 534, Mesopotamia; (440) 693-4295; endofthecommons.com. Open Mon through Fri, 8:30 a.m. to 8:30 p.m.; Sat, 8:30 a.m. to 6 p.m.

Mid-February through mid-April is a special time in Geauga County—maple syrup season. Those first February thaws start the sap flowing, and farmers throughout the county use special taps and buckets to drain the sap from their sugar maple trees. Once collected it is boiled and evaporated, with 30 to 60 gallons of sap needed to make one gallon of maple syrup. Smoke rising from area sugarhouses means syrup production is underway.

The ***Burton Sugar Camp*** is the only municipally owned sugar camp in the country. In a 10-acre park in the center of Burton at 14590 E. Park St., sap from the park's 1,500 sugar maples is boiled into syrup in a rustic log cabin. The cabin is open daily from late Feb through Apr, and maple syrup products are sold on weekends from May through the middle of Dec. Call (440) 834-4204.

At the south end of Burton's town square is ***Century Village***—18 restored buildings that provide a glimpse of the Western Reserve in the 1800s. The Blacksmith Shop, built in 1822, has an impressive complement of smithy tools and equipment. For a look at upper-middle-class life in the region, the Boughton House is furnished with pieces typical of the 1840s. The B&O Railroad built the Aultman station after the Civil War, and next to it sits a 20-ton B&O caboose. Guides from the Geauga County Historical Society conduct one-and-a-half-hour tours of the village.

Century Village is on the town square in Burton at 14653 E. Park St.; (440) 834-1492; centuryvillagemuseum.org. Open May through Oct, Sat with free guided tours at 11 a.m., 1 p.m., and 3 p.m. Generous donors have provided funds for free guided tours.

The annual ***Geauga County Maple Festival***, held on the last full weekend in April, takes place in Chardon, 10 miles north of Burton. Parades, maple syrup contests, a quilt and afghan show, competitions in pancake flipping and eating, wood chopping, rooster crowing, and beard shaving with an ax are just some of the activities at this yearly celebration. For more information, check the website at maplefestival.com.

Many of the Amish operate dairy farms, and they bring their milk to the ***Rothenbuhler Cheesemakers*** to be manufactured into Swiss cheese. The cheese plant, founded as a cooperative in 1956 by twenty-five area farmers, is one of the largest producers of quality Swiss in the U.S., with an output of more than 20 million pounds annually.

Visitors are invited to view a film which carefully describes each step in the cheese-making process. A tour of the cheese house museum features Old World carvings from Switzerland, antique cheese-making equipment, Amish artifacts, and historical photos. Be sure to stop in the Cheese Chalet Shop, where fresh sausages, homemade breads and pastries, Geauga County maple syrup, plus a wide selection of fine cheeses are available for purchase. A light lunch of soup, sandwiches, muffins, pie, and ice cream is served.

Rothenbuhler Cheesemakers is on OH 608 at 15815 Nauvoo Rd., Middlefield; (440) 632-5228, (800) 327-9477; rothenbuhlercheesemakers.com. Open Mon through Sat, 9 a.m. to 5:30 p.m. No admission charge.

The king of maple products in Geauga County has to be Paul Richards, of ***Richards Maple Products***—his family has been in the business since 1910.

Paul purchases tens of thousands of gallons of syrup annually from area farmers, syrup that he transforms into pure maple spread (similar to honey butter), maple sugar, maple cream (a fudgelike concoction available with or without black walnuts), maple candy, and of course, three grades of maple syrup. All of these are produced without the use of preservatives.

Richards Maple Products also sells a wide selection of gift boxes containing endless combinations of their various products. Catalogs of gift box selections are available by mail.

Richards Maple Products is at 545 Water St. (US 6, west of the central business district), Chardon; (440) 286-4160; richardsmapleproducts.com. Open Mon through Fri, 9 a.m. to 6 p.m.; Sat, 9 a.m. to 4 p.m. The company also has a second location at 7955 Euclid Chardon Rd., Kirtland, (216) 331-8503.

You can return home from your visit to ***Fowler's Milling Company*** with a taste of the 1800s. The mill was established in 1834 by Milo and Hiram Fowler and has been operating for almost all the years since. Currently the millstones grind corn and wheat. You can purchase their stone-ground flours in traditional cloth bags and do some scratch baking. The mill also offers a variety of baking mixes, pastas, and gift items.

Fowler's Mill is at 12500 Fowlers Mill Rd., Chardon; (440) 286-2024; fowlers-mill.com. Open Mon through Fri, 10 a.m. to 5 p.m. From Thanksgiving through Christmas also open Sat 10 a.m. to 5 p.m. and Sun noon to 4 p.m.

From late November to the middle of March, skiers hit the powder at the ***Alpine Valley Ski Area***. This complete ski resort has six slopes and a backwoods trail, high-powered lighting towers for night skiing, and a 10,000-square-foot rental shop with 1,400 pairs of skis. Their Professional Ski Instructors of America (PSIA) ski school offers both private and group lessons. After a strenuous day on the slopes, a blazing fire in the lodge's fireplace lures skiers there to unwind. The lodge offers a great view of the slopes, as well as a full-service cafeteria, a pizza shop, and a pub called Chaser's.

The Alpine Valley Ski Area is on US 322, 4 miles east of Chesterland at 10620 Mayfield Rd.; (440) 285-2211, (440) 729-9775 (ski reports); alpinevalley ohio.com.

Eastern Lakefront

The ***Holden Arboretum***, one of the world's largest arboreta, encompasses 3,600 acres of wooded trails, ponds full of ducks and geese, fields, and deep ravines. Dedicated to increasing knowledge of the plant world, Holden has five primary nature trails, which take visitors past the maple collection, renowned for its beauty when the leaves change color in the fall; the conifer collection of pines, firs, spruces, and junipers; and the wildflower garden, where a showcase of Ohio's flora can be enjoyed.

The lilac and rhododendron gardens and crabapple and shrub collections are other examples of the many and varied exhibits in this vast nature preserve. Nature walks and frequent lectures are offered at the arboretum, as are memberships. Membership entitles you to free admission to the grounds, cross-country skiing privileges, and discounts on courses, lectures, and gift shop purchases. Bird-watching and wildflower walks are popular at Holden, and the arboretum has summertime nature discovery sessions as well as special programs for children on subjects such as animal communication.

The Holden Arboretum is at 9500 Sperry Rd., Kirtland; (440) 946-4400; holdenfg.org. Open Tues through Sun 9 a.m. to 5 p.m. Admission: adults $20; children (ages 3 to 12) $14.

Picture, if you will, a giant tomato plant with vines as thick as your waist, fruit 6 feet across, and leaves up to 12 feet long. The stuff of science fiction? No, science, not science fiction. These are features of the creative Great Tomato Works at ***Lake Metroparks Farmpark***. The Farmpark is an outdoor museum where city folks can learn about and learn to appreciate agriculture—the source of our food supply. The number of farmers among us has declined from more than 90 percent in 1800 to less than 3 percent today. Relatively few Americans have ever met a farmer, let alone understand what he or she does.

Try your hand milking a cow, or just enjoy the 235 acres of fields and forests. Two miles of easy walking roads cross the property, and wagon rides are also offered. You'll discover more than 50 breeds of livestock including cattle, sheep, goats, pigs, and poultry, plus orchards, gardens, and vineyards. You'll leave knowing the difference between strip cropping and contour plowing, and perhaps having seen the planting, cultivating, or harvesting of fields of hay, oats, rye, wheat, corn, and barley.

Lake Metroparks Farmpark is at 8800 Euclid Chardon Rd. (US 6), Kirtland; (440) 256-2122, (800) 366-3276; lakemetroparks.com/parks-trails/farmpark. Open Tues through Sun, 9 a.m. to 5 p.m. Admission: adults (ages 12 and up) $8; senior citizens $7; children (age 2 to 11) $6.

After a day exploring the Lake Metroparks Farmpark or the Holden Arboretum, you might want to relax with a night's stay at ***Rider's Inn***. Rider's Inn has offered hospitality to Ohio visitors since 1812, when Joseph Rider opened it as a stagecoach stop for those heading to the Western Reserve and beyond. The inn provided a different kind of hospitality prior to the Civil War, as it served as a stop on the Underground Railroad, offering safe haven to fleeing slaves. The inn also was briefly a hot springs spa and was reputed to offer yet another kind of hospitality to thirsty drinkers during Prohibition.

The new owners purchased the inn in 1988 and refurbished the eleven guest rooms. Some of the guest rooms have private baths, but others share facilities so if you have a preference, be sure and ask when you are making reservations. The Innkeeper's Suite and Suzanne's Suite (named after Joseph Rider's third wife) have some of the Riders' original furnishings. Guests have a gathering room to enjoy and are served a continental breakfast in bed.

Along with the accommodations, the inn also houses Mistress Suzanne's Dining Room, featuring fish and game recipes from the colonial period as well as more traditional dishes. You also can enjoy a game of darts in the English-style pub or just sit and sip your favorite beverage by the old stone fireplace. The pub has live music every Tues, Fri, and Sat. The innkeepers enjoy outdoor activities, including boating and sailing, and are happy to introduce their guests to the many sporting and cultural activities in the area.

Rider's Inn is located at 792 Mentor Ave., Painesville; (440) 354-8200; riders inn.com. Rates: $110 to $125 per night. The restaurant is open for lunch and dinner Tues, Wed, and Thurs, noon to 10:30 p.m.; Fri and Sat noon to 11 p.m.

The Debevcs have made wine for family and friends for three generations, but it wasn't until 1970 that Tony Sr. and Tony Jr. decided to convert some of their farm acreage into a commercial vineyard. ***Debonne Vineyards*** produced its first bottle for sale in 1972, and near-constant expansion has taken place ever since. Winemaker Tony Jr. oversees production from 100 acres of vineyard.

Guests at Debonne sample the more than 40 varieties of Debevc wine—14 white wines, 12 reds, 4 blush wines, 10 fruit and specialty wines, and three ice wines—in a Swiss-style A-frame chalet with a large fireplace, burgundy tablecloths, and weathered barn-board siding on the inside walls. Visitors may also sit under the covered patio during warm weather, and snacks such as cheese and sausage and homemade bread are served. Regional bands perform on Wed and Fri evenings and Sat afternoons.

Tours of the winery take place hourly, or as needed, with members of the Debevc family explaining the various steps in winemaking, from grape crushing and filtering to aging and bottling. Debonne holds 100,000 gallons of wine in various stages of fermentation in the cellar and bottled for sale. Debonne is also the first Ohio winery to open a micro-brewery, Double Wing Brewing Co., with its distinctive double wing airplane on the label.

Debonne Vineyards is off OH 528 and Griswold Road at 7840 Doty Rd., Madison; (440) 466-3485, (800) 424-WINE; debonne.com. Open Mon and Tues, noon to 6 p.m.; Wed noon to 8 p.m.; Thurs noon to 9 p.m.; Fri and Sat, noon to 10 p.m.; Sun noon to 8 p.m. Shorter hours in Dec and Jan.

Acres of vineyards can be seen throughout eastern Lake County, and five minutes from Debonne is another winery invested in by the Debevc family and two other area families, ***Grand River Cellars***. After driving past the rows of grapevines, you reach a modern building at the edge of a cool forest. Its Riesling, Chardonnay, Cabernet franc, and pinot grigio all benefit from the care taken in the vineyard to produce a quality Ohio wine. A second label was created, Stonewood Vineyards, to represent the sweeter side of wine tasting. Stonewood labels market to the palates of those who enjoy sweeter blends as well as distinct Concord wine found in the Wine Hound Red and Niagara wine found in the White Fox. The winery also offers a large range of appetizers, grilled sandwiches, and a diverse dinner menu.

Grand River Cellars is at 5750 S. Madison Rd. (OH 528), Madison; (440) 298-9838; grandrivercellars.com. Open Mon and Tues noon to 6 p.m.; Wed noon to 8 p.m., Thur noon to 9 p.m., Fri and Sat noon to 10 p.m., and Sun noon to 8 p.m. Kitchen and bar close 30 minutes before closing.

His Majesty's Bed and Breakfast has three guest rooms located in a historic home in Madison. The Queen's Cottage is a charming home, built

HELPFUL WEBSITES

Ohio Division of Travel and Tourism
ohio.org

Destination Cleveland
thisiscleveland.com

Cleveland Plain Dealer
cleveland.com/plaindealer

Mahoning County Convention and Visitors Bureau
youngstownlive.com

in 1861, and located on the village square. The three rooms in the Queen's Cottage—The Queen Anne, The Queen Elizabeth, and The Royal Suite—are ornate with a Victorian theme, and one room features a whirlpool tub. All rooms have private baths.

A full-course breakfast is included with your stay. In addition, the proprietors will be happy to create a package for you, steer you to local wine tastings, or make reservations for that perfect night of dinner and dancing.

The Queen's Cottage is located at 25 Park St., Madison; (440) 221-1758; hismajestys.com. Rates: $149 to $179 per night.

Places to Stay in Northeast Ohio

AKRON

Berrodin Bed & Breakfast
814 Bloomfield Ave.
(330) 775-7405
berrodinbb.com

Blu-Tique Hotel, A Tribute Portfolio Hotel
1 S. Main St.
(330) 983-4905
blu-tique.com

O'Neil House Bed & Breakfast
1290 W. Exchange St.
(330) 867-2650
oneilhouse.com

797 Residence & Suites
797 E. Market St.
(330) 617-5777
797suites.com

CLEVELAND

Clifford House Bed & Breakfast
1810 W. 28th St.
(216) 589-0121
cliffordhouse.com

Emerald Necklace Tearoom & Inn
18840 Lorain Rd.
(440) 333-9100
emeraldnecklaceinn.com

Glidden House
1901 Ford Dr.
(216) 231-8900
gliddenhouse.com

Hotel Indigo Cleveland Downtown
651 Huron Rd. E.
(216) 377-9000
ihg.com

Metropolitan at The 9, Autograph Collection
2017 E. Ninth St.
(216) 239-1200
Marriott.com

Stone Gables Bed & Breakfast
3806 Franklin Blvd.
(877) 215-4326
stonegablesinn.com

Tudor Arms Hotel Cleveland
10660 Carnegie Ave.
(216) 455-1260
Hilton.com

University Circle House
1575 E. 108th St.
(216) 282-4344
universitycirclehouse.com

Wallace Manor Bed & Breakfast
4724 Franklin Blvd.
(216) 961-6298
wallacemanor.com

MADISON

His Majesty's Bed & Breakfast
25 Park St.
(440) 221-1758
hismajestys.com

The Lost Pearl Bed & Breakfast
4194 Dayton Rd.
(440) 299-8301
thelostpearl.com

PAINESVILLE

Quail Hollow Resort & Conference Center
11080 Concord-Hambden Rd.
(440) 497-1100
quailhollowresort.com

Rider's Inn
792 Mentor Ave.
(440) 354-8200
ridersinn.com

Steele Mansion Inn & Gathering Hub
348 Mentor Ave.
(440) 639-7948
steelemansion.com

WARREN

The Grand Resort
9519 E. Market St.
(330) 856-1900
thegrandresort.com

Places to Eat in Northeast Ohio

AKRON

Alexander Pierce Restaurant
797 E. Market St.
(330) 529-2003
alexanderpiercerestaurant.com

D'Agnese's at White Pond Akron
566 White Pond Dr.
(234) 678-3612
dagneseswhitepondakron.com

Dante Boccuzzi Akron
21 Furnace St.
(330) 375-5050
danteakron.com

Diamond Grille
77 W. Market St.
(330) 253-0041
diamondgrille.com

Fred's Diner
930 Home Ave.
(330) 535-3733
fredsdiner.net/menu/

Ken Stewart's Lodge
1911 N. Cleveland Massillon Rd.
(330) 666-8881
kenstewartslodge.com

Marques
1201 E. Market St.
(330) 475-8355
marqueseastend.com

The Merchant Tavern
1824 Merriman Rd.
(330) 865-9510
themerchanttavern.com

Vaccaro's Trattoria
1000 Ghent Rd.
(330) 666-6158
vactrat.com

BURTON

JC's Restaurant
13816 W. Center St.
(440) 834-1900
jcs.restaurant

Warren's Spirited Kitchen
14614 E. Park St.
(440) 273-8100
warrensspiritedkitchen.com

Welshfield Inn
14001 Main Market Rd.
(440) 834-0190
thedriftwoodgroup.com/restaurants/welshfield-inn

CLEVELAND

Astoria Café & Market
5417 Detroit Ave.
(216) 266-0834
astoriacafemarket.com

Cleveland Chop
824 W. St. Clair Ave.
(216) 696-2467
clevelandchop.com

Fahrenheit
2417 Professor Ave.
(216) 781-8858
chefroccowhalen.com/fahrenheit-cleveland

Il Venetian
100 St. Clair Ave. NE
(216) 241-4800
ilvenetian.com

Marble Room Steaks & Raw Bar
623 Euclid Ave.
(216) 523-7000
marbleroomcle.com

Table 45
9801 Carnegie Ave.
(216) 707-4045
iccleveland.com

ELYRIA

Black River Tavern
1100 Gulf Rd.
(440) 365-1400
theblackrivertavern.com

Uncle Bo's Slow-N-Low BBQ
2000 Midway Mall
(440) 387-6614
unclebosbbq.com

KENT

Henry Wahner's
1609 E. Main St.
(330) 678-4055
kentmenus.com

Mike's Place
1700 S. Water St.
(330) 673-6501
mikesplacerestaurant.com

Ray's Place
135 Franklin Ave.
(330) 673-2233
raysplacekent.com

The Battleground Taproom & Mexican Kitchen
425 Cherry St.
(330) 548-9019
battlegroundbar.com

The River Merchant
911 N. Mantua St.
(330) 968-6376
therivermerchantkent.com

LAKE AT CHIPPEWA

Contessa's On the Lake
7364 Lake Rd.
(330) 441-0449
contessasonthelake.com

Oaks Lakeside
5878 Longacre Lane
(330) 769-2601 or
(800) 922-5736
theoakslakeside.com

LORAIN

Erie Steak & Seafood Co.
301 Lakeside Ave.
(440) 288-2501

MADISON

Cebar's Madison Tavern
6884 N. Ridge Rd.
(440) 428-9926
cebarsmadison.com

528 Tavern
111 N. Lake St.
(440) 428-6678

Joey's Italian Grille
2731 Hubbard Rd.
(440) 428-5191
joeysitaliangrille.com

Wild Burrito
125 N. Lake St.
(440) 307-9140
wild-burrito.com

YOUNGSTOWN

Prima Cucina Italiana
103 W. Federal St.
(330) 743-3000

V2 Wine Bar & Trattoria by Vernon
100 W. Federal St.
(330) 742-5595
v2byvernon.com

West 34
34 W. Federal St.
(330) 623-6540
westthirtyfour.com

East Central Ohio

Legacy Trail

Stunning natural beauty and re-created pioneer history blend in a state park in the foothills of the Appalachians, ***Beaver Creek State Park***. Wide, swift Little Beaver Creek rushes through deep gorges and past pine and fir forests, the locks of the old Sandy and Beaver Canal, and a restored pioneer village.

Private entrepreneurs constructed the canal between 1834 and 1848, connecting the Ohio River with the Ohio and Erie Canal. Though they spent $3 million on the project by its completion, the canal carried paying traffic only until 1852, when competition from the railroad doomed the canal era in this part of the state. Ironically, the directors of the Sandy and Beaver kept the Pennsylvania Railroad out of the county to avoid competition between the railroad and their canal—a move that had dire consequences for the canal towns in Columbiana County after the Sandy and Beaver failed.

Fifteen miles of hiking trails and numerous bridle trails follow Little Beaver Creek and wind through the woods up the steep foothills. Primitive camping areas are scattered

EAST CENTRAL OHIO

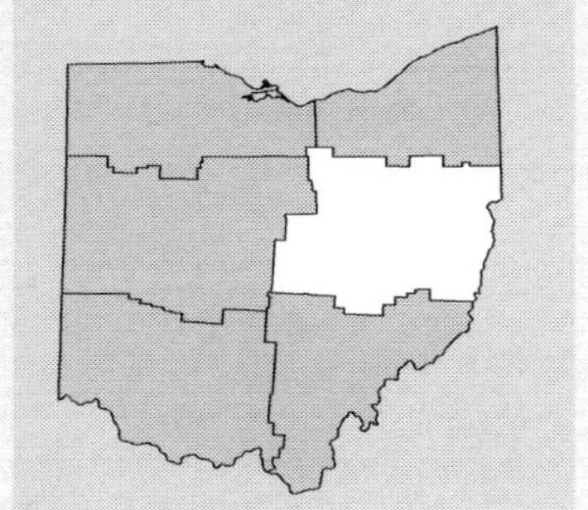

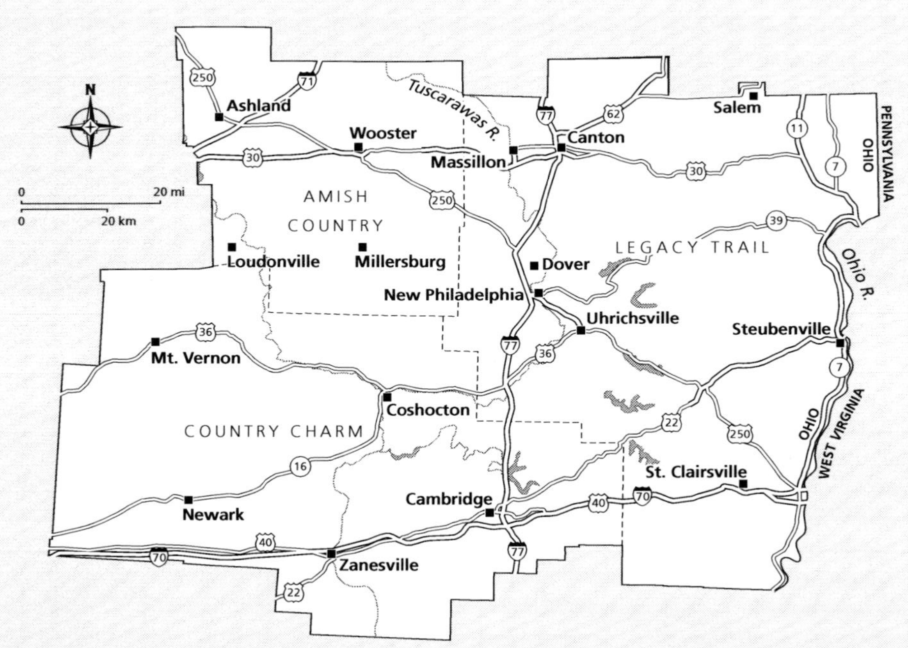

BEST ATTRACTIONS

- Beaver Creek State Park
- Cibo's Restaurant
- The McKinley Museum
- Pro Football Hall of Fame
- Canton Classic Car Museum
- Hoover Historical Center
- Canal Fulton
- Amish Door Restaurant & Village
- Warther Museum
- J.E. Reeves Victorian Home and Museum
- Zoar Village
- Fort Laurens State Memorial
- Schoenbrunn Village
- Quaker Meeting House
- Lehman's/Kidron Town and Country Store
- Pine Tree Barn
- Quailcrest Farm
- Mohican State Park

throughout the 3,000-acre park. The creek offers anglers a variety of fish, including smallmouth and rock bass.

Gaston's Mill, built by Samuel Conkle in 1830, dominates the park's reconstructed pioneer village. Originally powered by a large waterwheel, the mill operated until 1920, though in later years it used steam and gas engines to drive the massive grinding stones. When restored, it was converted back to waterwheel power, and on summer weekends visitors can observe the mill at work and may purchase stone-ground corn, wheat, and buckwheat flour. A pioneer church, schoolhouse, cabin, and blacksmith shop, all filled with antiques from Ohio's early settlement era, surround the historic mill.

Beaver Creek State Park is off OH 7 at 12021 Echo Dell Rd., 15 miles east of Lisbon; (330) 385-3091, (866) 644-6727 for camping and rental reservations; ohiodnr.gov/go-and-do/plan-a-visit/find-a-property/beaver-creek-wildlife-area. Open year-round.

The family known as the Fighting McCooks did not earn that moniker in barroom brawls. Rather, the Ohio McCooks earned that distinction because of their incredible family commitment to the U.S. military before and during the Civil War. In fact, Daniel McCook and his eight sons and the five sons of Daniel's brother John all served in the Union army. The Daniel McCook family included three major generals, two brigadier generals, one colonel, two majors, and one private. John McCook's sons served as a major general, two lieutenants, a commander, and a brigadier general.

About 1837 Daniel McCook erected the large brick home on the southwest corner of the public square in Carrollton. ***The McCook House*** was in the family until 1853, and it was acquired by the State of Ohio more than a century later. It is furnished with period pieces and relics from the McCook family.

The McCook House is on the square in Carrollton at 15 S. Lisbon St.; (330) 627-3345, (800) 600-7172. Open Memorial Day to Labor Day, Fri and Sat, 10 a.m. to 5 p.m.; Labor Day to mid-Oct, Sat, 10 a.m. to 5 p.m.; Sun, 1 to 5 p.m. Admission: adults $3; children (ages 6 to 12) $1.

It's not usual to see cows and bulls in farm fields in Ohio, so you might do a double take when heading down Muskrat Road toward the ***Dickinson Cattle Ranch***. During summer months, visitors can take bus tours through this working cattle ranch to see not only prize-winning cattle, but breeds that are not common in the Midwest. Perhaps the most striking of those is the Texas

Beaver Creek Ghost

Visitors to Beaver Creek State Park will want to bring a camera to get some pictures of the restored mill and locks, but be prepared to miss at least one of those shots if one of the park's ghosts is in residence. At Beaver Creek one of the men who was a lock keeper is said to continue to work shifts along the water's edge. If you visit "Jake's Lock," you may become part of his legend. In life, he sometimes worked the day shift; sometimes at night. At night he would light a lantern and keep watch for boats needing his services to traverse the lock. But one night, it is said, a bolt of lightning shot from the sky and hit poor Jake, killing him and propelling his body into the lock.

Visitors say that to this day they occasionally see the light from Jake's lantern bobbing along the side of the canal or even under the water where Jake fell that night. If you try to take a picture near the lock, the legend says that your camera may malfunction if Jake is working his shift. Be careful that your flash doesn't remind Jake of the fateful flash of lightning!

One of the 1830s locks is nicknamed "Gretchen's Lock." Tales say that Gretchen was the daughter of Gill Hans, an engineer who came from Holland to build the lock. His daughter never adjusted to the move to America and eventually grew sick and died in 1838.

Her family made plans to return to Holland to bury their daughter. Until they could, the coffin was temporarily placed in the stone sides of the lock. The arrangements were made and the family set sail with the coffin containing the remains of their homesick daughter.

But as fate would have it, their ship was sunk in a storm in the Atlantic. Legend says the girl, named Gretchen, has not found her rest, and instead she walks the lock that was her last, unhappy home.

longhorn. These magnificent creatures have horns that are about 5 or 6 feet from tip to tip. Longhorns can be many colors: speckled, brown, black, blue, even an orange color. Rivaling the Texas longhorns for, well, long horns is the ranch's herd of Watusi cattle. The horns of Watusi bulls measure 6 feet or more from tip to tip, while the base of the horns can be more than 2 feet around. These cattle are tall, too. Looking out the bus window will put you right about at horn-level with these huge animals.

Another interesting breed at the ranch is the Blue Lingo. Unlike the multicolored and speckled longhorn, Blue Lingos look like dark cows wearing a white cummerbund. They are more docile animals, but the big white stripe around their middles certainly make them striking.

This is not a tourist attraction, but a working cattle ranch. The owners breed animals for sale internationally. The ranch features the Longhorn Head to Tail Store, where you can purchase souvenirs and beef products. An example is the Barrel O' Beef, featuring longhorn jerky, longhorn beef sticks, and longhorn pepper stick summer sausage.

The Dickinson Cattle Ranch is at 35000 Muskrat Rd., Barnesville; (740) 758-5050. Open April through Oct, Mon through Sat, 10 a.m. to 5 p.m. Bus tour ticket: adults $12; children (ages 4 to 12) $5.

barnesville's "gay '90s mansion"

Founded in 1808 by James Barnes, a Quaker from Maryland, Barnesville prospered as a producer of tobacco and strawberries during the nineteenth century. As the town flourished, so did its banks. It was the Bradfields, the owners of the First National Bank, who built the town's most dramatic residence, what's known as the "Gay '90s Mansion."

This elegant 26-room, 11,000-square-foot structure, complete with dramatic turret, took five years to construct, and cost $60,000 when completed in 1893. In its prime, the mansion hosted Barnesville's most important dinners and parties, guests climbing the massive oak staircase to the third-floor ballroom. Today the mansion is a museum and the restored home of the local historical society. Located at 432 N. Chestnut St., the mansion offers guided tours Fri, Sat, and Sun May 1 through October 1 from 1 to 4 p.m. Other tours by appointment. Tours are $8 for adults and $2 for students under age 18. Call (740) 425-2926; belmontcountymuseum.com

Cibo's Restaurant serves authentic Italian cooking in a very unusual setting—an old movie theater. The Mohawk Theater, built in the early 1940s, presented feature films for the people of Waynesburg for decades. But since 1971 it has been spaghetti the pasta, not spaghetti the western, which attracts crowds at 134 W. Lisbon St.

At first, dining was limited to the Mohawk's old lobby, but now the entire theater has been remodeled and converted to a multilevel eating area, complete with ceiling fans and oak dividers. Italian favorites such as antipasto, pasta e fagioli (beans), spezzato (wedding) soup, and homemade chicken noodle soup constitute the list of appetizers. The reasonably priced entrees include spaghetti, rigatoni, cavatelli, lasagna, ravioli, and cannelloni, and for those who have trouble choosing from that list, a combination plate offers a sample of all the above. Cibo's offers American dishes as well—baked steak and chicken, plus family-style combinations of spaghetti, ravioli, chicken, lasagna, and baked steak. Pizza and sandwiches are also served. On Friday, a popular choice is gnocchi or rigatoni with one meatball for $10.29.

Cibo's is at 134 W. Lisbon St., Waynesburg; (330) 866-3838; cibosrestaurant.com. Open Thurs and Sun 11 a.m. to 8 p.m.; Fri and Sat, 11 a.m. to 9 p.m.

William McKinley was elected the 25th U.S. president in 1896. Five years later he was assassinated at the Pan-American Exposition in Buffalo, New York. He died in office on September 14, 1901. The story of this Ohio native's life and public career is preserved at ***The McKinley Museum***, a multifaceted complex that also includes the McKinley National Memorial, a hands-on science center for kids of all ages, a history museum, and a 65-seat planetarium.

Perhaps the most dramatic section of this vast museum is the Street of Shops. Visitors stroll down a nineteenth-century boulevard that is complete with a pioneer home; a general store; an early print shop; dentist's, physician's, and lawyer's offices; a photography studio; a hotel; a fire station; and a toy company and shop. There is also an 84-foot model train layout, including a Pennsylvania Railroad train station.

Included in this impressive complex is Discover World, an interactive scientific program geared for children and the young at heart. At the entrance to Discover World, you're greeted by the spine-tingling roar of a life-size allosaurus, with jaws that open and legs that move thanks to the magic of robotics. Ingenious inverted periscopes let you check out the plant and animal life in a series of ponds. Once aboard Space Station Earth, you find yourself in a scientific laboratory, where you can activate demonstrations on lasers and light waves, water in motion, and air under pressure.

The McKinley Presidential Library & Museum is at 800 McKinley Monument Dr. NW, Canton; (330) 455-7043; mckinleymuseum.org. Open Tues through Sat, 9 a.m. to 4 p.m. Admission: adults $10; senior citizens $9; children (ages 3 to 18) $8.

You might think that the likely home for the ***First Ladies National Historic Site*** would be somewhere in Washington, DC. You might think that, but you would be incorrect. It is actually in downtown Canton. The mission of the

First Ladies National Historic Site is to create a central location where people can explore the lives of our nation's first ladies and their contributions to our nation's history. The site is both a primary research facility and an educational center that includes three major components: the National First Ladies' Library online bibliographic database, the library in the historically documented Saxton McKinley home, and an educational center adjacent to the Saxton McKinley home in the former City National Bank Building.

The Saxton McKinley house is a two- and three-story brick building of irregular massing. It was constructed in two segments in 1841 and ca. 1865. It is significant as the only remaining residence with direct historical ties to President William McKinley in his hometown of Canton. It was the family home of McKinley's wife, Ida, and he and his wife lived in the house between 1878 and 1891.

kilnsaplenty

As early as 1806, small kilns were fired in East Liverpool to take advantage of the area's unique clay and produce the popular "yellow ware" pottery. James Bennett, a potter from England, walked into town in 1839 determined to build a pottery empire. Profits from his effort the first year were $250, a huge sum in those days and just the beginning of a dramatic expansion for East Liverpool's pottery industry. By the end of the century, more than one-third of all the kilns operating in the United States were in East Liverpool—239 of them.

The Saxton McKinley House in Canton celebrated its national debut as the home of the National First Ladies' Library with a dedication ceremony and Victorian Gala in June 1998, with former First Lady Rosalynn Carter. The public rooms of the house have been restored to their original splendor, complete with ornate historical wallpapers and period furniture. Great care has been taken to ensure that all design elements, including patterns of wallpaper, carpets, and area rugs, are authentic.

The renovated ballroom is, and always has been, located on the third floor of the house. Many parties were held in this ballroom, since the Saxtons were among the most prominent families in Canton. In President McKinley's study, all the wallpapers were custom-made by historic merchants to replicate wallpaper depicted in an early photograph of the study taken during his official residence. The photo revealed wallpaper that resembles an intricate quilt of Oriental scenes.

The library and parlor are decorated in the more opulent Italianate style that became popular after the Civil War. In this area there are twenty-three different wallpaper patterns in subtle shades of tan, grayish green, rose, and warm beige. The flow of the color and pattern creates an ambience that is feminine, but understated and elegant. Lace curtains, authentically reproduced from an 1876 pattern, are thrown over rods and pinned in place—just as the Victorians did it. The chrysanthemum-patterned Wilton carpet was loomed in the same mill that provided carpet for the White House at First Lady Dolly Madison's request.

The building housing the educational and research center was constructed in 1895 and has seven floors with approximately 20,000 square feet of usable space. It had a large skylight over the main banking room on the first floor that has been fully restored, as well as an extensive glass block floor under the skylight. There is extensive use of marble on the first-floor foyer/lobby and main banking room, as well as in the lobbies on the upper floors of the building.

stateflower timestwo

President William McKinley wore a red carnation in his lapel every day for 29 years. After McKinley's assassination in 1901, Ohio legislators searched for a fitting tribute to the fallen president. In his honor, they made the red carnation Ohio's state flower in 1904. Their resolution read: "for its beauty, its fragrance and its fitness, let it be adopted as the state flower of Ohio; and let the action of its adoption be to the memory of William McKinley."

Not contented with a single state flower, Ohio lawmakers declared the Trillium grandiflorum the state wildflower in 1987. They noted that the large-flowered or white trillium is found in all 88 Ohio counties and is easy to identify.

There is a 91-seat Victorian theater on the lower level, where films and documentaries on first ladies are shown, and author presentations and live lectures take place. The center also houses a collection of books that replicates the first White House library created by First Lady Abigail Fillmore.

The First Ladies National Historic Site is at 205 Market Ave. South, Canton; (330) 452-0876; firstladies.org. The site is open Tues through Sat from 9 a.m. to 4 p.m.; Sun in June, July, and Aug from noon to 4 p.m.; (Sun tours are offered in the summer); reservations recommended. Admission: adults $7; senior citizens $6; children (under age 18), $5.

Canton was once home to the Canton Bulldogs, an early-day powerhouse in professional football. Today Canton, where the National Football League began in 1920, is the home of the national shrine of professional football, the ***Pro Football Hall of Fame***. This five-building complex delights every pigskin addict, with action films, displays, and gridiron history. Why wait to celebrate the Super Bowl just once a year? Football fans have been flocking to the Lamar Hunt Super Bowl Gallery since it opened in 2009 to relive every Super Bowl and watch their favorite gridiron heroes again. Game highlights can be enjoyed via interactive video kiosks. The Super Bowl Theater brings the magic of a Super Bowl to life with all the hoopla and thrilling moments that make the annual pageant of professional football an eagerly awaited event. Discover how football started and how the merger of the American Football League and National Football League helped make professional football into the successful passion of today.

A 7-foot bronze rendition of Jim Thorpe greets visitors to this comprehensive museum. A 1912 Olympic gold medal winner in the pentathlon and decathlon, Thorpe is considered one of the most versatile athletes of modern sports, playing professional football, basketball and baseball. Exhibits trace the history of the sport from the first game in 1892 to the latest teams. In the Pro Football Photo Art Gallery, you'll find the best of professional sports photography. The African-American Pioneers display tells the story of African Americans in the NFL. A favorite here are the twin Enshrinee Galleries, where the best of the best are honored. Each year a new class is enshrined, to join the ranks of pro football legends. After your tour, stop by the museum store for those can't-be-passed-up football souvenirs.

The Pro Football Hall of Fame is at 2121 George Halas Dr. NW, Canton; (330) 456-8207; profootballhof.com. Open daily, 9 a.m. to 5 p.m. (until 8 p.m. during the summer). Admission: adults $33; senior citizens $29; children (ages 6 to 12) $26.

For those who appreciate the rumble seats, wooden-spoke wheels, and V-16 engines of antique automobiles, a stop at the ***Canton Classic Car Museum*** is a must. The museum, housed in one of Ohio's earliest Ford-Lincoln dealerships (1914–1929), comprises dozens of meticulously restored vehicles, from a blue 1906 Reo to a 1938 Cadillac convertible with a 452-cubic-inch, 185-horsepower engine.

Six Packard automobiles, from model years between 1920 and 1937, trace the evolution of that distinctive make. For elegant driving, the museum contains a Rolls-Royce—a red and white 1929 Phantom I convertible. The museum also has a rare Marmon Sixteen, which, according to an advertisement used at a 1931 automobile show, "looks and performs like no other car—16 cylinders, 200 horsepower and under $5,000."

The two-seat 1929 Kissel White Eagle Speedster (available with rumble seat) conjures up images of goggles, blowing scarves, and deserted country roads. The very rare 1914 Benham is the only survivor of the 19 cars produced by the short-lived automaker, which folded after only one year in business. Celebrity cars include Amelia Earhart's 1916 Pierce Arrow, Queen Elizabeth's 1939 Canadian tour car, and a movie car from *Those Daring Young Men in Their Jaunty Jalopies*. The museum also has an armor-plated, bulletproof 1937 Studebaker from the Canton Police Department.

In addition to the fine old cars, vintage gas and steam engines and other automotive paraphernalia are on display. In the restoration shop, future classics await rejuvenation.

The Canton Classic Car Museum is at 123 6th St. SW, Canton; (330) 455-3603. Open daily, 10 a.m. to 5 p.m. Admission: adults $7.50; senior citizens $6; students $5; children 4 and under, $3.

Daniel and Mary Hoover arrived in 1852 on their 82-acre farm, where Daniel's father had established a leather tannery. At the turn of the twentieth century, Daniel's son, W. H. Hoover, realized that the coming age of automobiles would drastically reduce the demand for leather goods such as harnesses and saddles. So W. H. Hoover searched for a new product for the Hoover Company, and bought the rights to inventor Murray Spangler's upright vacuum cleaner. In 1908 Hoover offered the public the first commercially viable upright vacuum cleaner, the Hoover Suction Sweeper Model O.

In less than a decade, the Hoover Company blossomed into an international concern. With its world headquarters in North Canton, the company has established the ***Hoover Historical Center*** on the family's original Stark County farmstead. Hoover history unfolds in the Italianate-style farmhouse accented with elegant Victorian decor.

A six-minute video presentation details the history of the company, and guided tours begin in the tannery, which was the original family home, where many leather-working tools and artifacts from the late 1800s are displayed. The two-story white farmhouse contains what has to be the world's most complete collection of antique vacuums, ranging from the 1869 Whirlwind Cleaner, which was the first manual vacuum cleaner offered for sale that picked up dust with suction, to modern Hoover units.

The Kotten Suction Cleaner, built in 1910, required the operator to stand and rock on the bellows to create suction—it sold for $25. The 1905 Skinner electric vacuum was advertised as a portable but weighed more than 100 pounds. Murray Spangler's original 1907 upright stands next to the Hoover Model O, which launched this multinational corporation. Other Hoover exhibits include old photos of W. H. Hoover and various Hoover factories around the world, early advertisements for Hoover products, World War II memorabilia, and some furnishings used by the family. Herb and flower gardens surround the museum, which hosts changing exhibits throughout the year.

The Hoover Historical Center is located at 1875 E. Maple St. NW, North Canton; (330) 499-0287; walsh.edu/hoover-historical-center.html. It's open Mar through mid-Dec, Thurs through Sat, with tours conducted hourly from noon to 3 p.m. No admission charge.

As the mules clip-clop down the towpath, for a moment you can imagine yourself back in the days of Ohio's canal era—people waving, men tossing horseshoes, barefoot boys fishing. The captain points out the sights, such as a dry dock where canal boats were built and repaired. In less than 30 minutes, you reach the Lock 4 turning basin. The captain describes how the lock works as the skillful crew poles the boat around for the scenic trip home. You float along in the *St. Helena III*, a 60-foot replica of the freight barges that slipped through the canal network crisscrossing the state more than 100 years ago.

Canal Fulton is a living canal town of 5,323 residents, where tourism and historical appreciation have replaced the commerce that once thrived on this section of the Ohio and Erie Canal. In addition to the authentic canal boat rides, Canal Fulton features an inviting nineteenth-century business district, listed on the National Register of Historic Places, with everything from antiques and gifts to candy and ice cream.

Other attractions include the Canal Days Museum and tours of a saltbox-style residence built in 1847. Biking along a section of the Cardinal Trail and canoeing on the Tuscarawas River are popular.

Canal Fulton is between Barberton and Massillon on OH 93; (330) 854-6835; discovercanalfulton.com. Canal boat rides are given daily except Mon at 1 and 2:30 p.m. in the summer, plus weekends in May, Sept, and early Oct. Adults, $10; senior citizens $8; children (ages 6 to 17) $5.

If cooking is the way to your heart, you will find just what you're looking for at the ***Amish Door Restaurant & Village***. The restaurant features family-style meals as well as a standard menu. This is Amish country, so fresh-baked breads and real mashed potatoes have got to be part of your meal, along with a country-fresh salad from the salad bar. Inside the restaurant is a bakery, so you can take some of those fresh baked goodies with you.

If you're spending some time in the area, the Amish Door Village offers fifty-two Victorian-style rooms in the modern Inn at Amish Door. Your stay includes a continental breakfast, and the inn offers such amenities as a heated indoor pool and a fitness room.

The Amish Door Restaurant & Village is located at 1210 Winesburg St., Wilmot; (330) 359-7996; amishdoor.com. Rates: $135 to $300 per night.

Europe's foremost woodcarvers proclaimed Ernest Warther "the world's master carver," and the intricately crafted carvings displayed at the ***Warther Museum*** give credence to that proclamation. Born near Dover, Ohio, in 1885, Ernest started carving at age 5 when he found an old pocketknife while tending the family's cow. His formal education ended in the second grade, and at the age of 14 he went to work in the American Sheet and Tin Plate Company's mill. During his 20 years at the plant, he used his spare time to perfect his craft.

That steel-rolling mill is preserved today in a 3-by-5-foot working model carved by Warther—a model built with thousands of small, handmade walnut parts. Warther mechanized not only the model's steel-rolling equipment, but also many of the workers, including the foreman raising a sandwich to his mouth, a second worker nodding off on the job, and a third "drinking" his lunch by raising a tiny bottle to his lips. An intricate belt-drive system designed by Warther and a sewing machine motor powered the model's many moving parts.

Warther's most widely acclaimed carvings, however, are the series he created tracing the history of steampower, particularly his many steam locomotives and trains. Starting with working models of the simplest steam devices dating from 250 BC, Warther produced models of the various developmental stages of the steam era. By far the most impressive of these are the dozens of steam railroad locomotives on display at the museum, many with hundreds of moving parts.

Warther used walnut for the dark pieces of his models and, in the early part of his career, pieces of bone for the white pieces. In later years, he could afford ivory and carved entire trains, some with as many as 10,000 parts, from pure white ivory. Warther used arguto, an oil-bearing wood, for the moving parts of his carvings, some of which have run for eighty years without repair.

Of the steam locomotives displayed at the Warther Museum, perhaps the most intriguing is the 8-foot replica of Abraham Lincoln's funeral train. An avid admirer of Lincoln, Warther spent a year at age 80 carving the ebony and ivory locomotive, coal car, funeral car, and passenger cars. Thousands of miniature parts make up the magnificent carving. As an example of the extraordinary detail work done by Warther, outside the restroom in one of the passenger cars there is even a tiny ivory key hanging on a hook on the wall.

Warther's exacting craft demanded fine precision knives and blades, and, not satisfied with those commercially available, he created his own custom cutlery. In fact, he supplemented his income by selling this cutlery, a business still operated by his family today. Ernest Warther died at the age of 87 in 1973, leaving his 64th carving incomplete. Footage of Warther working at his craft is shown in the Warther theater.

The small original museum behind the present one houses Mrs. Warther's button collection—more than 70,000 buttons, no two alike. Beautiful Swiss-style gardens surround the museums and the Warther home.

The Ernest Warther Museum & Gardens is at 331 Karl Ave., Dover; (330) 505-6003; thewarthermuseum.com. Open daily, 9 a.m. to 5 p.m. (last tour starts 1 hour before closing), Jan and Feb, 10 a.m. to 4 p.m. Closed major holidays.

TOP ANNUAL EVENTS

Maple Syrup Madness
Newark, Feb, Mar
(740) 323-2355, (800) 443-2937
dawesarb.org

Sertoma Ice Cream Festival
Utica, May
sertomaicecreamfestival.com

Dennison Railroad Festival
Dennison, May

Dulcimer Days
Coshocton, June
(740) 545-6265

Trumpet in the Land
New Philadelphia, June to Aug
(330) 339-1132
trumpetintheland.com

The Living Word Outdoor Drama
Cambridge, July through Sept
(740) 439-2761
livingworddrama.org

First Town Days Festival
New Philadelphia, 4th of July weekend
firsttowndays.com

Pro Football Hall of Fame Festival
Canton, late July to Aug
(330) 456-7253, (800) 533-4302
profootballhoffestival.com

Fredericktown Tomato Show
Fredericktown, Sept
tomatoshow.com

Ohio Swiss Festival
Sugarcreek, late Sept, early Oct
(330) 852-4113, (888) 609-7592
ohioswissfestival.com

Barnesville Pumpkin Festival
Barnesville, Sept
(740) 425-2593
barnesvillepumpkinfestival.com

Holmes County Antique Festival
Millersburg, Oct
(330) 674-6781
holmescountyantiquefestival.org

Algonquin Mill Fall Festival
Carrollton, Oct
(877) 727-0103
carrollcountyhistoricalsociety.com

Buckeye Book Fair
Wooster, Nov
(330) 262-2103
buckeyebookfair.org

Dalton Holidays Festival
Dalton, Dec
(330) 828-2323

Admission: adults $18; seniors $17; children (ages 12 to 17) $8; children (ages 4 to 11) $6.

A new century was just beginning when Jeremiah E. Reeves moved his family into a newly remodeled home in 1901. Originally built as a stately eight-room farmhouse around 1870, the house was expanded into a magnificent 17-room mansion by Reeves, Dover's wealthiest citizen. Its gleaming white exterior is enhanced by dormers, bays, turrets, classical columns, and a porte cochere. To the rear of this Victorian mansion is a large turreted carriage house.

Today the Dover Historical Society invites you to tour the ***J.E. Reeves Victorian Home and Museum*** for a magnificent look at turn-of-the-twentieth-century elegance.

Lush drawing-room draperies, gleaming windows of stained and leaded glass, luxurious parquet floors, and artistic mementos of the Reeves family all greet the eye. Nearly all the furnishings on display belonged to the Reeves family and are placed where they were when the family lived here. Other special features include a distinctive hand-carved oak grand stairway and a delightful third-floor ballroom.

Out in the carriage house, built in 1902, the first floor houses a marvelous 1892 two-horse carriage that belonged to the Reeves family, a one-horse sleigh, and a 1922 automobile. Upstairs, visitors find remnants of the old Dover post office, along with displays of early household tools and sports memorabilia, plus historic maps, photographs, and documents. Following the crooked stairs to the Tower Rooms rewards the visitor with collections of old-fashioned cameras and radios.

The J.E. Reeves Victorian Home and Museum is at 325 E. Iron Ave., Dover; (330) 343-7040, (800) 815-2794; doverhistory.org. Open June through Oct, Wed through Sun, noon to 4 p.m., plus special holiday tours in Nov and Dec. Admission: adults $10; senior citizens $9; children (ages 6 to 18) $5.

Seeking freedom from the new religious tenets in their native Kingdom of Wurttemburg in Germany, 300 men, women, and children known as Separatists, led by Joseph Baumeler, came to 5,500 acres they had purchased along the Tuscarawas River and established ***Zoar Village*** in 1817. Two years later, frustrated by their progress, the Zoarites abandoned personal property ownership to establish a communal system. Under the new system, all property in the village was owned by the Society of Separatists at Zoar, with men and women each given a vote in the election of a board of trustees. The board governed the day-to-day operations of the community, and under this system, with Baumeler remaining as leader of the group, Zoar flourished.

The community established its own farms for food products, a tin shop, a blacksmith shop, two blast furnaces, a bakery, a garden with greenhouse, and a wagon shop. Many of these enterprises produced more goods than needed by the village, with the surplus sold for profit at a store established by the villagers. The Zoarites even landed the contract to build a section of the Ohio and Erie Canal, which passed through their land.

In 1852, the assets of the society were more than $1 million, and the future appeared bright for this hardworking community. But a year later, Joseph Baumeler was dead, leaving a serious leadership void at Zoar. Baumeler had served as the inspiration of the village, as well as its financial administrator. After his death, Zoar began a gradual decline, which persisted for 40 years. Finally, in 1898, having lost its competitive edge both in agriculture and in industry, the community disbanded.

Many of the original Zoar buildings have been restored or reconstructed, allowing visitors to better understand the unique experiment that took place here. Inside the Number One House, an audiovisual presentation provides the history of the village. The rooms in this rambling two-story brick building, which once housed the aged and infirm, contain many original furnishings. In the music room, for example, is Peter Bimeler's magnificent hand-built pipe organ. Bimeler was the village miller, and he powered the organ with the mill's water turbine.

The second-floor windows provide a splendid view of the adjacent gardens and greenhouse. A guide at the greenhouse explains the religious significance of the formal gardens, with the large Norway spruce symbolizing Christ and the twelve slip junipers representing the apostles. The greenhouse, constructed in 1835, utilized a unique heating system—charcoal fires burned under the floor; vents funneled the warm air into the greenhouse—allowing the Zoarites to cultivate a wide variety of fruits and vegetables, including tropical fruits. In the Zoar bakery, huge wooden bins stored flour and meal, and the brick oven baked 80 loaves of bread per day.

Other buildings in the village include a tin shop, which has the tools, patterns, and products used and produced by the tinsmith, and the Bimeler House, with its outstanding collection of wool coverlets woven at the community's woolen mill. Knowledgeable guides provide information and answer questions in each building of the village. New in 2018 were eight white bicycles for adult visitors to ride to areas not typically included on Zoar's walking tour. Price is $6 for the first hour and $5 for each additional hour. Bikes can be rented via smartphone or in the Zoar store where bike helmets are available. It is the first freestanding bike rental station in Tuscarawas County.

Zoar Village is on OH 212, Zoar; (330) 874-3011, (800) 262-6195; historiczoarvillage.com. Open Apr through Oct, Fri and Sun, 11 a.m. to 4 p.m.; Sat, noon to 4 p.m. Admission: adults $10; children (ages 5 to 17) $5 for combo ticket to Historic Zoar Village and Fort Laurens Museum.

Named for Henry Laurens, then president of the Continental Congress, Fort Laurens, Ohio's only Revolutionary War fort, was constructed in 1778 as part of an ill-fated campaign to attack the British at Detroit. The 1,200 troops under the command of General Lachlan McIntosh, who built the fort, dubbed it "Fort Nonsense," since no attack on Detroit was ever executed. Supplying this wilderness outpost proved impossible, forcing the starving troops to survive on boiled moccasins while under siege from British-led Indians for a month. The fort was abandoned one year after it was built.

Today visitors to ***Fort Laurens State Memorial*** find the outline of the old fort, and a small museum that commemorates the conflict with both video and artifacts from the fort's excavation. The remains of soldiers who died defending Fort Laurens are buried in a crypt in the museum wall and at the Tomb of the Unknown Patriot of the American Revolution.

Fort Laurens State Memorial is at 11067 Fort Laurens Rd. NW, Bolivar; (330) 874-2059, (800) 283-8914; fortlaurensmuseum.org. Open May, Sat, 11 a.m. to 4 p.m.; Sun, noon to 4 p.m.; June through Aug, Wed through Sat, 11 a.m. to 4 p.m., Sun noon to 4 p.m.; Sept and Oct, Fri and Sat, 11 a.m. to 4 p.m., Sun, noon to 4 p.m. Admission: adults $5; children (ages 5 to 17) $3.

Missionary David Zeisberger migrated to the United States in 1737 to work with the American Moravian Church in Bethlehem, Pennsylvania. In 1772, accompanied by a band of Delaware Indians, Zeisberger traveled to the wilderness in Ohio to convert other Indians to Christianity, founding ***Schoenbrunn Village***.

The efforts at Schoenbrunn were interrupted by the coming of the Revolutionary War. The village was on the trail between the American outpost at Fort Pitt and the British at Fort Detroit, and neither side trusted the Moravians or their Christian Indians. Harassment eventually forced Zeisberger to abandon Schoenbrunn Village in 1777 and to relocate to a new settlement at nearby Gnadenhutten. Even there, they were not safe. The British arrested Zeisberger and other village leaders and transported them to Detroit for trial on charges of treason. While the leaders were away, American troops, seeking revenge for the death of a settler's wife and children, massacred the Christian Indians at Gnadenhutten by striking them with heavy coopers' mallets.

Mingo Junction

George Washington slept here—actually he camped here in the fall of 1770. He came via canoe to scout the land in the Ohio Valley, and he found rugged country and plenty of Indians. He was here to secure land for the officers and soldiers of the Virginia Regiment before the British tried to claim it.

Upon his arrival in poor weather, Washington and his party heard of a killing down river, the direction they were heading. It was unclear whether it was an Indian dispute or a simple homicide. After one night's rest, they left the spot that is known today as Mingo Junction and paddled downstream.

They arrived at Powhatan Point, from which Washington dispatched several in his party to uncover the truth about the alleged murder. They returned and told Washington that the rumors were untrue; the death had been an accidental drowning. On October 25, 1770, they departed, continuing their journey down the Ohio River.

Schoenbrunn Village today contains 18 reconstructed rustic log buildings, the original village cemetery, and 2.5 acres of planted fields. Log cots with stretched animal skins and a firepit in the center of the floor (with a hole in the roof for smoke to escape) are the only conveniences in some of these cabins. Others feature modest pioneer furnishings such as rough rope-spring beds, wooden baby cradles, spinning and flax wheels, and butter churns. Schoenbrunn's settlers constructed Ohio's first schoolhouse, a one-room building completed in 1773. In addition to the log structures, a museum displays Schoenbrunn artifacts excavated from the site, including nails, knives, horseshoes, and chips of cups, jars, and a kettle used at the village more than 200 years ago.

famous people from little cadiz

The little town of Cadiz boasts an impressive roster of native sons. Clark Gable was from this town, as was Edward Stanton, President Lincoln's secretary of war during the Civil War, and John Bingham, who also has a Lincoln connection. Bingham, an attorney, worked in William Henry Harrison's presidential campaign and was elected to Congress in 1854.

During his tenure in Washington, he served as special-judge advocate in the trial of Lincoln's assassins. He also was minister to Japan from 1873 to 1885.

Schoenbrunn Village is on OH 259 on the southeast edge of New Philadelphia; (330) 339-3636. ohiohistory.org/visit/browse-historical-sites/schoenbrunn-village/ Open Memorial Day to Labor Day, Tues through Sat, 9:30 a.m. to 5 p.m.; Sun, noon to 5 p.m. Admission: adults $8; senior citizens $6; children (ages 7 to 17) $4.

For a dramatic presentation of the story of David Zeisberger and the settlement of Schoenbrunn and Gnadenhutten, attend a performance of Paul Green's ***Trumpet in the Land***. Staged in a lovely hilltop outdoor amphitheater, this spirited drama uses a mix of song and dance, humor, adventure, and ultimately tragedy to tell of Zeisberger's missionary work in frontier Ohio.

Trumpet in the Land is presented at the Schoenbrunn Amphitheatre on University Drive, just off US 250, at 1600 Trumpet Dr. NE New Philadelphia; (330) 339-1132; trumpetintheland.com. Performances from June through Aug, Mon through Sat at 8:30 p.m. Wed performances of other musicals are at 6 p.m. Admission: adults $20; seniors and students (ages 13 to 17) $18; children (ages 12 and under) $10. Reserved tickets available. Tickets are cheaper on Mon and Tues bargain nights. A "behind the scenes" tour is offered at 6:30 every night that Trumpet in the Land is presented for $5 per person.

The ***Dennison Railroad Depot Museum*** has been drawing people from all across the United States since it opened in 1989. This fully restored railroad station gives the visitor a glimpse into the role that railroads played in America's past. At the turn of the twentieth century this depot was a busy crossroads, hosting twenty-two arrivals daily. In the 1940s the station became an oasis of homegrown comfort for many World War II service men and women passing through on the National Defense Railroad Route. The depot grew famous as more and more military men and women were welcomed by scores of volunteers at the Salvation Army Servicemen's Canteen. This canteen was the third largest in the country and served free food and provided a little hometown warmth to thousands passing through on their way to and from the fronts.

Visitors can relive the early eras of railroad travel by visiting the museum and the various restored areas, including the women's lounge and the ticket booth. The large model N-scale train display will fascinate children, even the adult kind. You can also experience the flavor of the 1940s in the Pennsy Dining Company, which is filled with photos, hosts a documentary video, and serves pasta, seafood, and steaks.

For a fun night of dreams, stay at the ***Historic Times Square Coach***. Guests can book the full Pullman car or a single compartment or double compartment suite. The whole car offers five bedrooms with 16 beds plus 2 ½ shared baths. Prices range from $800 a night for the whole car to $125 a night for a one-bedroom compartment with two beds and shared bath. In early December, the Polar Express pulls out for a magical journey to the North Pole. Storytellers read the popular tale, elves entertain with songs and games, and hot chocolate and chocolate chip cookies made by Mrs. Claus are served. At the North Pole, passengers do not get off, but Santa gets on the train to visit with children on the way back. Of course, passengers get a special jingle bell. Polar Express price: $42 for balcony seating, $55 for coach seating, and $75 for first-class seating.

The Dennison Railroad Depot Museum is at 400 Center St., Dennison; (740) 922-6776, (877) 278-8020; dennisondepot.org. Open Tues through Fri, 10 a.m. to 5 p.m.; Sat, 11 a.m. to 4 p.m.;

thehousethat jackbuilt

You might know that Bellaire is the site of the original "house that Jack built." But did you know that "Jack" was a mule? Englishman Jacob Heatherington immigrated to this area and worked his way up from a laborer hauling coal to an industrialist. His faithful mule, Jack, helped him move coal in those early years, and Jacob never forgot this. So, when he erected a mansion in 1870, he referred to it as the "house that Jack built" and even took the old mule on a tour of the home's interior, describing the features as they clip-clopped through the magnificent residence. Jack died shortly afterward, and Jacob, grief-stricken, buried him nearby under an apple tree.

Sun, 11 a.m. to 3 p.m. Admission: adults $8; senior citizens $6; children (ages 7 to 17) $4.

The ***Quaker Meeting House***, set in a field in a hilly section of Jefferson County, housed the annual August meeting of 2,000 Ohio and Pennsylvania Quakers for nearly a century. Constructed in 1814, this impressive three-story brick structure measures 92 feet by 60 feet and has walls 2 feet thick.

The Society of Friends relocated an entire meeting from North Carolina to Jefferson County in 1813 and built the meetinghouse of brick fired right on the site. The interior of the building is one large room, with the original floors, poplar benches, and a large balcony. A massive wooden center divider splits the room—four men in the attic raised and lowered this divider as needed. Men sat on one side of the room during the meetings, women on the other side, and young men and women sat in their respective balconies. The elders and overseers used the facing benches—benches resting on a small platform and facing the congregation. "Strict services" took place here until 1909, with no formal ceremony or music; the group simply meditated in silence until a member felt moved to speak out. The interior of the meetinghouse is exactly as it was 170 years ago, though it has been more than 70 years since the Quakers last gathered in Jefferson County.

The Quaker Meeting House is just off OH 150 in Mount Pleasant at 298 Market St. Open by appointment Apr through Oct; call (740) 769-2893 or (800) 752-2631; ohiohistory.org. Admission for a tour of six buildings: adults $15; children (ages 6 to 12) $7. Tours of Meeting House only: adults $6.

Amish Country

Ohio's largest Amish and Swiss Mennonite communities are in four east central Ohio counties: Holmes, Wayne, Tuscarawas, and Stark. The Amish espouse a simple agrarian lifestyle and reject the use of automobiles and electricity as potentially disruptive to that lifestyle. Living in the twentieth century without electricity creates a demand for unusual products, such as kerosene-powered refrigerators, and one Wayne County business, ***Lehman's***, has established itself as the nonelectric appliance and equipment supplier for the area's substantial Amish population.

Although Lehman's stocks the nails, wire, and garden tools found in every hardware store, the bulk of the floor space is dedicated to merchandise such as gas-powered washing machines, and gas and kerosene lamps. Wood- and coal-burning cooking and heating stoves fill one large showroom, with many of the cooking stoves ornately trimmed in chrome and costing from $700 to $3,000.

Other items in Lehman's inventory include hardwood fruit presses, an apple parer, a cherry stoner, and a bottle capper. How many other stores carry a variety of hand-crank butter churns and a hand-powered cream separator that produces 85 liters of milk per hour?

The store's crowded hitching posts, used by the Amish to secure their horse-drawn buggies, indicate the popularity of Lehman's with the local Amish population, but in recent years Lehman's has attracted another type of customer—people drawn to wood- and coal-burning appliances because of the increasing cost of utilities. Lehman's sells a 156 -page catalog for $6. It's full of major appliances, small gristmills, copper wash boilers, sausage stuffers, noodle makers, and carbide lamps. And city people have been known to purchase unique nonelectric devices, particularly the fancy chrome cooking stoves, simply for use as decorative pieces.

Lehman's Outlet Store is located on the square across the parking lot from Lehman's at 13110 Emerson Rd., Apple Creek. The store offers great deals on closeout, overstock, and clearance items. The inventory changes daily, so you never know what you might find.

Lehman's is located at 4779 Kidron Rd., Kidron; (888) 438-5346; lehmans .com. Open Jan through May, Mon through Thur, 9 a.m. to 5 p.m.; Fri and Sat, 9 a.m. to 6 p.m.; June and July, Mon through Sat, 9 a.m. to 6 p.m.; Aug through Dec, Mon through Thurs, 9 a.m. to 5:30 p.m.; Fri and Sat, 9 a.m. to 6 p.m.

Just down the street is the ***Kidron Town and Country Store***, where you can purchase an array of Amish clothing—men's broadfall barn-door pants, black felt church hats, and wide-rimmed flat or mushroom-top straw hats.

Upstairs you'll find quilting supplies, and the store also offers fresh-cut meats, fresh fruits and vegetables, and other bulk food items. It has long been the custom of the Amish to come in from the fields at noon and enjoy *es midaugh*. They continue that tradition at the store, serving a hearty midday meal prepared by local Amish women in their restaurant. The restaurant opens at 7 a.m. for breakfast and serves lunch until 2:30 p.m.

The Kidron Town and Country Store is at 4959 Kidron Rd., Kidron; (330) 857-2131; kidrontownandcountry.com. Open Mon through Sat, 8 a.m. to 7 p.m. Shoe department open Mon through Sat, 7 a.m. to 7 p.m.

After establishing their Christmas tree farm, Robert Dush and his son Roger's next challenge was to convert a barn built in the 1860s into a Christmas shop and country store, the ***Pine Tree Barn***. This massive old barn has been designated a Wayne County Historic Landmark, and its original rough-hewn beams and floors create a rustic atmosphere.

What started as a gift shop in 1980 has evolved into a complete home furnishing and accessories center, featuring indoor and outdoor lighting, carpeting, floor coverings, and window treatments, plus gifts and accessories, all displayed on three floors in this marvelous historic structure. In fact, Roger Dush and his wife, Rita, offered a complete interior decorating and design service. The family business is now under the direction of daughter Julie Kilbourne and her husband Matt Kilbourne.

The gift shops at Pine Tree include a Colonial Williamsburg shop; a floral shop featuring silk and dried flowers, wreaths, and garlands; and a year-round Christmas shop. Christmas is a special time of year at Pine Tree; you'll find thirty or more fully decorated trees throughout the structure, along with hundreds of unique ornaments and baubles.

A similar transformation took place at The Granary, the Pine Tree's dining facility. In the early '80s, this former dairy barn's old grain bins were converted into a small kitchen, serving simple refreshments. Today The Granary presents gourmet lunches of crepes, quiches, soups, salads, pastas, pizza, fresh breads and muffins, and sandwiches. Top off your meal with a slice of one of the sour cream fruit pies, a Pine Tree Barn tradition for more than 20 years. The Granary also offers beer and wine.

Large windows along the back wall of the barn provide those eating lunch with a view down the hill to the private 40-acre lake and rows of young Christmas trees. Diners also see antique farm implements on the walls of the barn and the block and tackle that once hauled bales of hay up from the ground level to the second-floor loft. The Granary Restaurant at Pine Tree serves lunch only daily from 11 a.m. to 2:30 p.m. Reservations are strongly advised.

The Pine Tree Barn is on OH 226, 4374 Shreve Rd., 4 miles south of Wooster; (330) 264-1014; pinetreebarn.com. Open Mon through Sat, 9 a.m. to 5 p.m.; Sun, 10 a.m. to 5 p.m.

Before Deanna and Andy Troutman converted their property into a vineyard, the previous owner used it to raise chickens and sell produce. The winery building formerly served as one of the chicken coops. In 1997, the Troutmans moved in and began planting their vineyard the next year. By the fall of 2000, the first crop was harvested, and ***Troutman Vineyards*** unveiled their first three wines the following summer.

Deanna and Andy, who also serves as vineyard manager at Wolf Creek Vineyards, currently have sixteen wines ready to pour. During the holidays, try their Chambourcin Ice Wine, aged in French oak barrels with a hint of raisin and walnut. Another favorite is their White Menagerie Seyval blanc, an award-winning fruity yet dry German-style white. Free live music is offered the second and fourth Saturdays of the month from 6 to 8 p.m.

Troutman Vineyards is at 4243 Columbus Rd., Wooster; (330) 263-4345; troutmanvineyards.com. Open daily Mon through Thurs, 11 a.m. to 6 p.m.; Fri and Sat, 11 a.m. to 9 p.m.; Sun, noon to 5 p.m. Winter hours are Fri, noon to 6 p.m.; Sat, noon to 8 p.m.; and Sun, noon to 5 p.m.

Out-of-state antiques dealers have frequented Jeromesville, Ohio, for years, but most native Ohioans are unaware of the town's reputation as an antiques stop.

The natural beauty of the Mohican area, with its steep and rolling hills, swift rivers, and deep forests, once prompted author Louis Bromfield to remark, "I live on the edge of paradise." Visitors to the area quickly realize that statement was no exaggeration.

White pines flourish along the ridges of the ***Mohican State Park***, while hemlock abounds in the hollows and gorges.

Cabins in Ohio's state parks typically are located in scenic surroundings, but the 25 two-bedroom Mohican State Park cabins, isolated from the rest of the park in woodlands along the bank of Clear Fork Creek, may just be in the most picturesque setting of any cabins in Ohio.

They come furnished with all linens, blankets, and kitchen equipment, and may be rented in the summer for full weeks only. (There are no restrictions on the length of stay the rest of the year.) Canoeing and rafting are favorite summertime activities on Clear Fork Creek, and hiking, fishing, and camping are also popular in the park.

Mohican State Park cabins are just north of OH 97 at 3116 OH 3, Loudonville; (866) 644-6727, (419) 994-5125; ohiodnr.gov/go-and-do/plan-a-visit/find-a-property/mohican-state-park. Open year-round. Rates range from $150 to $160 per night; early reservations are a must.

stateflag/ pennant

Visitors may be surprised to see what appears to be a pennant flying overhead at public buildings and parks in Ohio, where they would expect a state flag to fly. That is Ohio's state flag. No other state flag has a pennant shape.

Cleveland designer John Eisenmann created this unusual design in the 1880s. At the wide end of the pennant is a blue triangle with a large circle and seventeen stars. The thirteen stars clustered closest to the circle represent the thirteen colonies. The four stars at the apex of the triangle represent the next four states admitted to the union, since Ohio was the 17th state to join. The circle represents the Northwest Territory, but with a smaller red circle at its center; it also forms an O for "Ohio."

Another lodging option in the lush Mohican State Park is the impressive stone-and-timber ***Mohican Lodge and Conference Center***, perched on a bluff overlooking Pleasant Hill Lake. Each of the 96 rooms in the lodge has a private balcony or patio, many with views of either the lake or the woods surrounding the lodge. Facilities include indoor and outdoor pools, two tennis courts, shuffleboard, a sauna, an exercise room, and a game room. In addition to the meals served in the dining room, poolside barbecues are offered occasionally during summer months.

The Mohican Resort is on OH 97, 6 miles west of Loudonville; (800) 282-7275, (419) 938-5411; mohicanlodge.com. Open year-round. Rates: $125 to $200 per night, double occupancy.

The confluence of Black Fork River and Clear Fork Creek forms the scenic Mohican River, probably Ohio's most popular stream for canoeing, kayaking, and rafting. Canoe liveries rent hundreds of canoes and kayaks in the Loudonville area, from as early as April to as late as November. With prices of $25 and up per canoe and trips lasting from 2 hours to several days, the liveries provide access to these scenic waterways. One of the liveries, on OH 3 south of Loudonville and north of Route 97, is the ***Mohican Adventures Camping, Canoe, and Fun Center***, which also has cabins, go-karts, horseback rides, waterslides, and miniature golf; (800) 662-2663, (888) 909-7400; mohicanadventures.com. Many other liveries operate in the area, and a complete list is available from the Loudonville Chamber of Commerce, 131 W. Main St., Loudonville 44842, (419) 994-4789; loudonvillechamber.com; or by calling (800) BUCKEYE or visiting the website for Ohio's tourism information center, ohio.org.

The fertile, rolling farmland of Holmes County is the center of Ohio's largest Amish community, with 20,000 of the 145,000 Amish nationwide living in the area. Amish men and women can be seen in the markets, restaurants, and shops, or driving their black horse-drawn buggies through the pastoral countryside.

Amish restaurants in Holmes and surrounding counties serve simple country cooking at reasonable prices, and shops sell Amish goods, such as quilts.

This section of east central Ohio also contains a sizable Swiss Mennonite population, and there are many cheese houses producing Swiss cheese from the milk brought in by Amish dairy farmers.

The Amish were the largest group of the 1694 Swiss Brethren split, following the leadership of Jacob Ammann, from whom the sect gets its name. Facing religious persecution in their native Germany and Switzerland, they began a migration to the United States in the 1730s, settling in Pennsylvania. The move to Ohio took place in 1808, and Holmes County, Ohio, now is the world's largest community of Amish. The Amish continue the agricultural traditions of the past 200 years.

Artist Heinz Gaugel painted the history of the Amish-Mennonite-Hutterite people in a spectacular 10-foot-by-265-foot cyclorama called ***Behalt***, which means "to remember." Completed in 1992 after four years' labor, Behalt spans the centuries from the time of Christ to the Amish migration to the New World to the present day. Behalt is permanently displayed at the Mennonite Information Center, where guides use the cyclorama to educate visitors about Amish history, culture, and lifestyle.

Behalt and the Mennonite Information Center are at 5798 CR 77, Berlin; (330) 893-3192, (877) 858-4634; behalt.com. Open Apr through Oct, Mon through Sat, 9 a.m. to 5 p.m. Open Nov through Mar, Mon through Sat, 9:30 a.m. to 4:30 p.m. Admission: adults $12; children (ages 6 to 12) $6.

Gloria and Eli ***Yoder's Amish Home*** is a 116-acre working farm that can be explored by visitors to Amish country. Children will enjoy the horses, rabbits, chickens, sheep, cows, pigs, and goats that fill the barn. Adults will probably be more interested in the two farmhouses, both built more than a century ago. The first home on your tour contains furnishings typical of an Amish farmhouse in the late 1800s. Built in 1866, this home last served as a residence more than 40 years ago. Its wood floors, simple heavy furniture, wood-burning stove, and people-powered appliances (such as a pump sewing machine) give a glimpse of the lifestyle of Amish farm families.

The larger home, constructed in 1885 and occupied for more than a century, is similarly furnished but contains some unusual items such as gas floorlamps.

Religious services have been held here many times, as in most Amish homes and barns. These services take three full hours to complete.

The Amish bakery offers a large selection of jams, jellies, bread, cinnamon rolls, and cookies, made fresh daily at the bakery.

Walk down by the brook to visit the one-room schoolhouse and learn how the Amish parochial school system works. Be sure to open one of the textbooks, written mostly in English with a few German words scattered here and there. How can the Amish use a modern copy machine if they don't have electricity? An Amish teacher explains how it is done, for an interesting lesson in ingenuity.

Many who visit here enjoy buggy tours of the property, which even has a hilltop family cemetery. Inside the craft shop, you'll discover quilts, dolls, pottery, woodwork, and many other country favorites.

Yoder's Amish Home between Trail and Walnut Creek at 6050 OH 515 in Millersburg; (330) 893-2541; yodersamishhome.com. Open May through Oct, Mon through Sat, 10 a.m. to 5 p.m. Tours: adults $8.25; children (ages 2 to 12) $4.75. Buggy rides: adults $4.75; children $3.75.

If you admire fine handmade quilts, stop by the ***Helping Hands Quilt Shop***. A nonprofit enterprise with all proceeds donated to charities and missions, the shop stocks hundreds of marvelous quilts in every conceivable pattern and color combination. Many of these are sewn in the large, sunlit quilting room in the back of the shop, where Helping Hands serves a social function in addition to its contributions to charity.

Helping Hands will quilt your quilt top, custom design a quilt for you, or even finish a quilt you have already started. The shop also sells quilted pillow covers, quilting books, embroidery kits and floss, quilting needles, thread, fabrics, stencils, and patterns—in short, everything a quilter could need. Also visit the Quilt Museum, with its many antique quilts.

The Helping Hands Quilt Shop is at 4818 OH 39, Berlin; (330) 893-2233; helpinghandsquilts.com. Open Mon through Sat, 10 a.m. to 4 p.m.

A variety of romantic options await guests of ***Donna's Premier Lodging*** in the heart of Amish country. Along with rooms in the main building, Donna's offers a variety of upscale log cabins, chalets, villas, and bridal suites. Honeymoon and anniversary chalets are two-level, brick, freestanding guest cottages located on a wooded hillside. Designed as luxurious retreats, they feature a main level with a king-size bed, a brick fireplace, and a heart-shaped Jacuzzi for two. The lower level is a recreation room with another fireplace and a billiard table. Throughout the chalets you will find elegant touches such as leaded glass windows, chandeliers, and homemade cookies for your late-night snack. Chalets are equipped with two televisions, stereo, CD player, microwave, coffeemaker, and a refrigerator. The log cabin is similarly equipped but has a queen-size bed tucked in a loft.

Whether summer or winter, the cabin, cottages, and chalets offer guests natural views and a good opportunity to wander just outside the door to visit with the birds or enjoy the woodland displays.

Donna's Premier Lodging is located ½ block off Main St. at 5523 East St., just behind the Helping Hands Quilt Shop, Berlin; (330) 893-3068, (800) 320-3338; donnasofberlin.com. Rates: $149 to $399 per night.

Opened for guests in 1996, ***Garden Gate Get-A-Way*** has a surprisingly long history. Many elements in the home are from a dismantled one-room schoolhouse. The original bell tower is now perched on the roof's south peak, and the original foundation stones now form many of the retaining walls and line the flowerbeds. Inside, lumber, oak flooring, tongue-and-groove ceiling, and wainscoting have found new uses in this modern facility.

Innkeepers Carol and Doug Gardner offer five very different guest rooms. The Potting Shed Room features a picket fence headboard, a cane chair, and a hickory rocker. The Briar Patch Room features engraved headboards and individual furnishings. The Magnolia Garden Room has a cherry finish electric fireplace with a 32-inch flat-screen TV above it. The Summer Breeze Suite offers a king bed and the only two-room suite. The Garden Gate Suite has a corner

ALSO WORTH SEEING

Salt Fork State Park, Cambridge

Steubenville Murals, Steubenville

Fort Steuben, Steubenville

two-person jetted tub and a large oak fireplace. All rooms have private baths and coffeemakers, plus private entrances

Added in 2009, two cottages are popular lodging options. The Falls Kiss Cottage has a peninsula fireplace and an Amish-made bed. The Spring Desire Cottage features an Amish-made sleigh bed and a Roman-style jetted tub.

The beautiful gardens include a grape arbor, birdhouses, and porch swings. Previous owner Roger Steiner's design talent is on display with the fieldstone landscaping and winding brick paths through the lush gardens.

Garden Gate Get-A-Way is located just outside Berlin at 6041 Township Rd. 310; (330) 674-7608; garden-gate.com. Room rates: $125 to $145 per night; cottages are $185 to $195 per night. Low season rates are $75 for rooms and $145 for cottages per night.

I first heard about a "modern" inn that opened outside Millersburg, right in the heart of Amish country, I must admit I was skeptical. I envisioned a motel-like structure on a bulldozed and paved chunk of earth, and I wasn't thrilled by the prospect. ***The Inn and Spa at Honey Run*** does not fit that description in the least. As you motor up a winding county road, through dense vegetation, your curiosity can't help but be aroused. And when you reach the tasteful contemporary structure that is the Inn and Spa at Honey Run, it's difficult not to let out a sigh of approval. Carefully blended into the surrounding trees—trees so close that I'm not sure how they managed to get the inn up without disturbing them—is a truly unique getaway. Lots of exposed wood, inside and out, creates a harmony between the inn and the peaceful forest. The adults-only inn's twenty-five guest rooms combine a potpourri of styles—everything from Shaker and Early American to very contemporary. Cherry, pine, oak, and walnut furnishings complete these rooms; some feature bi-level floor plans with skylights. All have living areas and tabletop space for work (if absolutely necessary), writing, card playing, or whatever.

Up a hill from the main inn are twelve additional guest rooms in a most unusual setting—dug into the hillside. Called the Honeycomb, this earth-sheltered building looks down onto a peaceful landscape.

Each room has a stone patio and gas log fireplace. Additional accommodations are two cottages nestled in the woods. The Trillium and the Cardinal feature two bedrooms with hot tubs on the deck.

If you can't stay the night, then come by and enjoy an excellent meal in the Tarragon dining room, which has a wall of glass for viewing the trees and wildflowers. The inn prides itself on its from-scratch recipes, including some spectacular pastries and desserts, and regional specialties. The dining room is open daily to all for breakfast, lunch, and dinner, by reservation.

The Inn and Spa at Honey Run is 3 miles northeast of Millersburg off OH 241 at 6920 CR 203; (330) 674-0011, (800) 468-6639; innathoneyrun.com. Lodging rates: $249 to $949 per night for two people.

Charm is the state's only predominantly Amish town, and evidence of that fact includes the popularity of the local icehouse (since the Amish don't use electric refrigerators), the town's harness shop (for the horse-drawn buggies and field horses' leather needs), and the hitching posts.

Just up the road is the "home of Ohio Baby Swiss Cheese," the ***Guggisberg Cheese Company***, founded by Alfred and Margaret Guggisberg. Born in Switzerland, Alfred began work in a cheese factory more than 40 years ago at the age of 16. Alfred passed away in 1985, and his son, Richard Guggisberg, is now company president. Today their plant produces 1,000 five-pound wheels of baby Swiss Mon through Fri between 8 a.m. and noon, cheese that is then shipped worldwide. Local Amish dairy farmers supply the milk, which arrives daily in horse-pulled wagons. Visitors to the plant can see the cheese forming in large stainless-steel vats by looking through the windows that connect the plant with the retail store. Guggisberg stocks a wide variety of cheeses in addition to Ohio baby Swiss, and cuckoo clocks, books, gift items, and ice cream are also sold.

Guggisberg Cheese Company is at 5060 OH 557, north of Charm; (330) 893-2500, (800) 262-2505; babyswiss.com. The store is open year-round Mon through Sat from 9 a.m. to 5 p.m. Closed Sun.

statebird/fish/insect

The designation of the cardinal as Ohio's state bird was uncontroversial; the Ohio General Assembly unanimously made it official in 1933. Lawmakers deemed the choice appropriate because the cardinal is a permanent resident of the state, its song is pleasing to hear, and its coloring is impressive. But other species have not had it so easy. A debate in the 1980s between fans of the walleye and boosters of the smallmouth bass resulted in a legislative standoff; neither side could muster the votes to be declared Ohio's state fish. One species did make the cut: the ladybug. Legislators declared it the state insect in 1975.

If you want to unwind after a day of touring Amish country, the ***Guggisberg Swiss Inn*** is waiting to welcome you with a comfortable room and a country-style breakfast. The inn is a modern structure set in Amish farming country. You can hike or picnic nearby or just take a walk around the inn pond to watch the swans. In the winter months sleigh rides take guests into the rolling countryside.

Rooms are air-conditioned and all have private baths and in-room coffee. The Inn also offers a new cabin overlooking a pond with a full kitchen, whirlpool tub, fireplace, and king-size bed in the loft. Two-night minimum for $479.90. Breakfast is included in the room rate and takes advantage of the wonderful, fresh goodies available in farm country. Dinner is also served. Reservations required.

The Guggisberg Swiss Inn is at 5025 OH 557, Millersburg, just north of Charm; (330) 893-3600, (877) 467-9477; guggisbergswissinn.com. Rates: $129.95 to $209.95 per night.

Opened in the fall of 2013, the ***Doughty Glen Winery*** has become an exciting addition to Guggisberg Swiss Inn. Along with a selection of wine, Doughty Glen also offers horseback riding on premises at Amish Country Riding Stables. Wine tastings are available in the lobby at Guggisberg Swiss Inn. Wines range from sweet Concord to a pleasant Pinot Noir. The winery is open Mon through Sat from 11 a.m. to 6 p.m. guggisbergswissinn.com/doughty-glen-winery; 5025 OH 557, Millersburg; (330) 893-3600.

Country Charm

The nearly 10,000 acres that constitute ***The Wilds*** have made a dramatic transformation—from an open strip mine to North America's largest preserve for endangered species. American Electric Power reclaimed the land and then gave it as a gift to the public to spur the creation of this unique facility. Animals from around the world are free to roam the rolling hills; visitors observe them from open-air safari buses, which take them past every species imaginable.

The preserve is divided in large sections where African, Asian, and North American wildlife live and thrive. During your visit, you might encounter camel, exotic deer, wild horses, or rhinos. Zebras and giraffes mingle with gazelles and antelopes in the preserve's African environment. During your visit, you'll learn the issues affecting the survival of each species.

The Wilds offers many adventures, including mountain biking, birding, fishing safari, horseback safari, zipline safari, and exploration of the butterfly habitat. The Wilds has a snack shop, grill, and Overlook Cafe and Restaurant. The restaurant menu includes specialty sandwiches and wraps, burgers, chicken, salads, bottled beer and wine, desserts, and daily meals made fresh from the Wilds' organic garden and local farmers' market.

Enjoy an exclusive, overnight stay in a private yurt at Nomad Ridge or at The Lodge, a private luxury cabin, or The Wilds' Cabins at Straker Lake.

The Wilds is at 14000 International Rd., Cumberland; (740) 638-5030; thewilds.org. Open daily May through Oct. 10 a.m. to 4 p.m. Select tours available by reservation from Nov to Apr. Open-Air Safaris cost $35 per person. Other tours are also available.

Eastern Ohio, western Pennsylvania, and northern West Virginia were once the center of the U.S. glassware industry, and Cambridge, Ohio, was an important city for the glass business. The large Cambridge Glass Company dominated glass production in Guernsey County, opening in the spring of 1902 and shutting down half a century later. Although the boom in glassmaking has since passed, ***Mosser Glass*** preserves the heritage of the industry and offers free tours of its factory to the public. Mosser manufactures glass pitchers, goblets, candleholders, lamps, and animal figures such as frogs, owls, cats, and rabbits.

During the tour, guides explain glassmaking, from heating glass powder to 2,000 degrees in the furnace to forming molten glass in a cast-iron mold. After being pressed in a mold, the shaped glass goes under a flame "glazer," which smooths the surface by reheating the exterior. From there, the molded hot glass cools in a special oven called a Lehr, which uniformly reduces the temperature to prevent shattering. Mosser Glass cranks out 150 pieces of glass per hour.

Mosser Glass is ½ mile west of I-77 on US 22 at 9279 Cadiz Rd., Cambridge; (740) 439-1827; mosserglass.com. The retail store is open Mon through Fri, 8 a.m. to 5 p.m. Tours are given Mon through Fri from 8 a.m. to 9:45 a.m. and 11 a.m. to 2 p.m. No tours will be given from Dec 22 to Jan 6. No admission charge.

You will find ***Georgetown Tavern on the Hill*** surrounded by 5 acres of planted grapes, sitting on top of a ridge overlooking the city of Cambridge. The family-owned business produces a variety of wines. The list includes familiar whites, reds, and blushes. However, in addition to that more familiar Chardonnay or Merlot, those looking for something a little different will find sweet fruit wines such as apple, cherry, or blackberry as well. The wines, along with selected Ohio-made and -grown products, are available in the retail shop.

Free live music is offered Thurs, Fri, and Sat from 6 p.m. to 9 p.m. Founded in 2015, Southside Brewing Co. is a micro-brewery offering craft beer. Georgetown Vineyards is located at 62920 Georgetown Rd., Cambridge; (740) 435-3222; georgetownvineyards.com. The restaurant menu features choices such as pizza, nachos, fish and chips, and spaghetti and meatballs along with wine and craft beer. Open Mon through Thurs from 11 a.m. to 9 p.m.; Fri and Sat from 11 a.m. to 10 p.m.

Roscoe Village served as an important canal port during the Ohio and Erie Canal's boom years in the 1840s and 1850s, with wheat and wool exports traded for coffee and calico. The 308-mile canal extended from Cleveland to Portsmouth, contained 146 locks, and cost more than $7 million to build. Construction of the canal took seven years, ending in 1832 when the canal completed the link between Lake Erie and the Ohio River.

Located near the confluence of the Muskingum, Walhonding, and Tuscarawas Rivers, the 23 brick and frame buildings in the village have been restored to their appearance during the canal's heyday, making Roscoe Village (originally called Caldersburgh) Ohio's only complete canal town restoration. Seven new buildings have been added to this historic village.

Seven exhibit buildings, shops, restaurants, and horse-drawn canal boat rides on the replica Monticello III all contribute to the appeal of this unique village. You can purchase tickets to the exhibit buildings and craft demonstrations at the Edward E. and Frances B. Montgomery Visitor Center, which is open year-round. This three-story structure offers a wide-screen film presentation of the history of the canal and the village, and displays a large, detailed map of the locks and elevation changes along the canal's more than 300-mile span.

Costumed interpreters and craftspeople welcome visitors to the nineteenth-century buildings, including the blacksmith's shop, the print shop, the one-room schoolhouse, and the 1840s-period home of Dr. Maro Johnson. You'll see rugs and wall hangings being woven on two antique looms, and the village potter throwing pots, bowls, and vases on an old-fashioned kick wheel.

In one of the exhibit buildings, the Toll House, Roscoe's first toll collector, Jacob Welsh, registered incoming canal boats and collected passage fees. Also on display is the compass used in the construction of the canal in the 1820s and 1830s, a canal boat model that travels through a set of double locks, and a working model of a gristmill.

Roscoe Village is on OH 16 and OH 83 near OH 36 at 600 N. Whitewoman St., Coshocton; (740) 622-7644, (800) 877-1830; roscoevillage.com. Open daily from 10 a.m. to 4 p.m. Living History guided tours are available daily Apr through Dec at 11 a.m. and 2 p.m. Self-guided tours are available on Fri, Sat, and Sun from June 14 to Labor Day. Canal boat rides daily except Mon in the summer, weekends in Sept and Oct. Festivals and special events are held throughout the year. Admission to exhibit buildings: adults $13; senior citizens $12; students (ages 6 to 18) $10.

The ***Johnson-Humrickhouse Museum***, located in Roscoe Village, contains five major galleries, each with its own theme. American Indian artifacts including baskets, pottery, beadwork, blankets, and weapons are represented and range from prehistoric to more recent times. Of particular note are the Inuit totem poles, scrimshaw, and carved argilite, ivory, and bone artifacts.

The Historic Ohio Gallery celebrates yesterday in Ohio with a re-created pioneer home and furnishings, plus antique tools, farm implements, rare firearms, dolls, clocks, pottery, and glassware. An extensive treasury of Asian artifacts features Chinese and Japanese porcelains, lacquerware, embroidery, metals, wood sculptures, and splendid carvings in jade, bone, ivory, soapstone, and horn. A Japanese samurai warrior, fully armored, stands guard beside a case filled with Japanese swords.

One gallery is devoted to fine European and American decorative arts and includes cut and pressed glassware, delicate china, precious metals, wood carvings, and an unusual collection of knife rests.

For a mystery that has never been solved, see the Newark Holy Stones, a set of controversial stone artifacts discovered in the 1860s in the Newark earthworks. The four objects are said to suggest a link between the "Lost Tribes of Israel" and the mound builders.

The Johnson-Humrickhouse Museum is located at 300 N. Whitewoman St., Roscoe Village, Coshocton; (740) 622-8710; jhmuseum.org. Open daily, Memorial Day through Labor Day, noon to 4 p.m.; Jan and Feb, Fri and Sun, noon to 4 p.m.; Mar through May, Tues through Sun, noon to 4 p.m.; Sept through Dec, Tues through Sun, noon to 4 p.m. Admission: adults $5; children (ages 7 to 18) $4.

Farmer and engineer George Crise took three years, from 1915 to 1918, to build the fine old structure that is today the ***White Oak Inn***. He used white oak from his land for the soul of his home and red oak to produce intricate flooring.

Some of the antiques that complete the ten guest rooms at the White Oak Inn are Crise family originals, and each room in the main building is named for the type of wood that predominates in it. All rooms have private baths; the queen-size first-floor suite features a wood-burning fireplace and whirlpool tub. The former chicken house has become a spacious guesthouse with three rooms, all with fireplaces. The latest additions to the inn are two luxury cottages of log cabin construction, each with fireplace, two-person whirlpool tub, and private deck.

Guests congregate in the light and spacious living room, mingling, reading, or just rocking in front of the fire. Innkeepers Ian and Yvonne Martin offer full breakfasts for their guests, and dinners can be arranged by advance reservation. The inn is located in a dry township and cannot sell alcoholic beverages. However, guests are welcome to bring their own beverages. The inn's remote location invites walks or bicycle rides down country roads, far

a yankee pens "dixie"

I wonder how Confederate soldiers and sympathizers would have reacted if they had known that a Yankee from Mount Vernon, Ohio, had written their beloved anthem, "Dixie?" Probably would have spit out their grits.

Daniel Decatur Emmett was a minstrel performer who had moved to New York City when he penned "Dixie" in 1859. It was later played in the South and was quickly adopted as the battle cry for secession. Emmett returned to his hometown of Mount Vernon in 1888 where he died on June 28, 1904, at the age of 88.

away from city noise and hassle. On clear nights, the sky dazzles with brilliant star displays.

The White Oak Inn is 4 miles east of the junction of OH 36 and OH 62 at 29683 Walhonding Rd. (OH 715), near Millwood; (740) 599-6107, (877) 908-5923; whiteoakinn.com. Rates: $145 to $325 per night, double occupancy, with full breakfast. Reservations and a deposit are required; there is a two-night minimum stay most weekends.

Approximately 200 million years ago, a layer of hard flint pushed toward the earth's surface in an area now known as Flint Ridge. Erosion exposed some of the flint, attracting Native Americans to the area 8,000 to 10,000 years ago.

Although the weathered flint on the surface was too brittle to be of much value, the Native Americans discovered a vein of high-quality flint 1 to 10 feet below and established crude quarries to extract the material. Using tremendous physical effort and large hammer stones, they pounded bone and wooden wedges into the flint, breaking it into removable chunks.

They used the flint to form arrowheads and spear points, scrapers, and other tools, and to start fires. Because of the demand for flint in prehistoric times, Flint Ridge was considered neutral ground, with members of any tribe allowed to quarry there. White settlers later rediscovered Flint Ridge, using the mineral for buhrstones in gristmills and as roadbed on a nearby section of the National Road.

Today the ***Flint Ridge Ancient Quarries and Nature Preserve*** is built around one of the prehistoric Native American quarries. The museum features an impressive collection of scrapers, drills, hoes, knives, and projectile points. One flint sample contains an excellent impression of a coral animal, created during one of the times when this part of Ohio was under the sea.

A large topographical map illustrates the extent of the ridge in eastern Licking and western Muskingum Counties. Other displays include an explanation of the calendar of geological time and descriptions of the various layers of rock in the region, from the surface to 468 feet underground.

State Gemstone and Fossil

The Columbus Rock and Mineral Society led the charge to honor flint as Ohio's official state gemstone. They pointed to its importance to Native Americans in Ohio for making knives, arrowheads, and spear points, its use for flintlock guns and millstones by early white settlers, and its value as a semiprecious stone when cut and polished. In 1965, the Ohio General Assembly concurred, designating flint as Ohio's state stone.

Twenty years later, lawmakers were at it again, this time to recognize a state fossil. Despite numerous jokes suggesting that some of the older members of the General Assembly were in the running for this honor, the actual winner was the trilobite, an extinct marine crustacean found in the limestone and shale beds of southwestern Ohio, among other places.

A thick forest of beech, maple, and oak surrounds the museum, and hiking trails pass by old quarries and exposed outcroppings of red, yellow, brown, and creamy flint. One trail takes hikers by two small streams, and abundant wildlife, including deer, squirrels, chipmunks, and birds, can be observed in the park. The park is open year-round.

Flint Ridge Ancient Quarries and Nature Preserve is at 15300 Flint Ridge Road, Glenford; (740) 763-4127; flintridgeohio.org. The museum is open May through Oct, Sat and Sun, 10 a.m. to 4 p.m.; June through Aug, Fri, Sat, and Sun, 10 a.m. to 4 p.m. Admission: adults $3; senior citizens $2; children (ages 6 to 18) $1.

August Heisey was born in Hanover, Germany, in 1842 and came to America with his family a year later. His career in the glass industry began in Pittsburgh in 1861 but was interrupted by his service with the Union army during the Civil War.

After the war and several sales positions in the glass business, in 1893 Heisey began formulating plans for his own glass company. He chose Newark as the site for this new enterprise because of its abundance of natural gas and low-cost labor. The factory opened in 1896 and grew to employ several hundred workers.

In 1900 the famous "H within a diamond" trademark was designed by Heisey's son, George Duncan Heisey. Two other sons ran the company, which produced the colored glass and glass animals so popular with collectors today. The company closed for Christmas vacation in 1957 and never reopened; it was no longer competitive in world markets.

Today the best of Heisey Glass is on display at the ***National Heisey Glass Museum***. The museum is housed in what was once the home of Samuel

Dennis King, a prominent Newark attorney. It was built in 1831 and was moved to Veterans Park in 1973. The museum is run by the Heisey Collectors of America. In 1993 the collectors constructed a new wing at the museum, adding two large galleries and a media center where a 26-minute video is shown. Inside, you browse through room after room of Heisey glass; hundreds of patterns are displayed, including pieces in all production colors. Examples of experimental pieces, photographs, molds, and tools complete the collection.

The National Heisey Glass Museum is at 169 W. Church St., Newark; (740) 345-2932; heiseymuseum.org. Open Wed through Sat, 10 a.m. to 4 p.m. Admission: adults $5; free for children under age 18.

ohio'sstate tree/juice

There was a time when being called a "buckeye" was an insult, the equivalent of being labeled a "hick." Its origin as a put-down comes from the fact that rural Ohio pioneers used wood from buckeye trees to build their cabins and carve their furniture.

Attitudes about the term gradually changed, and the tree's fruit—a brown nut—was described as resembling the eye of the noble buck deer. In 1953, the buckeye was officially designated Ohio's state tree, and Ohio has been the Buckeye State ever since.

The recognition of Ohio's state beverage has been less successful. In 1963 Governor James Rhodes took office and launched a campaign to promote the consumption of Ohio products.

Since tomatoes are a significant crop, he encouraged the drinking of tomato juice. What started as a joke—the naming of tomato juice as Ohio's state beverage—became law in 1965. Cheers.

Housed in a block-long complex of historic buildings, ***The Works: The Ohio Center of History, Art, and Technology*** is a unique center dedicated to lifelong learning. Through its four primary subject areas—Digital Works, Glass Works, Art Works, and Museum Works—students of all ages experience technology and the arts in provocative settings. The state-of-the-art digital lab enables students to create multimedia presentations using Photoshop, Freehand, Illustrator, Flash, InDesign, and other software. Design students from area colleges work on real projects for real clients in the community. Art Works classes include everything from watercolors to papier-mâché sculpture, from beadwork to painting with dyes on silk.

In the Glass Works, the furnace melts the batch at 2,300 degrees Fahrenheit and keeps it at a 2,100-degree working temperature. The studio has one glory hole, which heats the glass as it is being formed, and a bench equipped with basic glass tools—blowpipes, jacks, shears, etc. Students learn time-honored glassblowing techniques, and some of the work is available for purchase in the gift shop. The Museum Works occupies the Scheidler Machine Works building, which was constructed in 1861. Built by Reinhard Scheidler, the factory was used to manufacture steam engines and line shaft sawmills. On display are a renovated interurban car, an operating factory, historical landmarks of Licking County and Ohio, Shops of Yesterday, plus many other exhibits.

The Works is at 55 S. First St., Newark; (740) 349-9277; attheworks.org. Open Tues through Sat, 9 a.m. to 4 p.m. Admission: adults $12; senior citizens $10; children (ages 3 to 17) $8.

The 1,650-acre ***Dawes Arboretum***, established by Bertie Burr Dawes and Beman Gates Dawes in 1929, blends rolling meadows, deep woods, and cultivated gardens. Perhaps the most beautiful area is the Japanese garden designed by noted landscape architect Makoto Nakamura. In Nakamura's design, a small lake with islands connected by arched bridges and plantings of pine, flowering cherries, Japanese yew, and Japanese maple creates a tranquil environment. Another popular area is the cypress swamp, where southern native bald cypress trees grow and produce "knees."

The holly collection contains more than 100 distinct types of holly, and the sugar maples at Dawes provide the sap for the annual production of maple syrup. One section of the arboretum consists of the deciduous climax forest that once blanketed central Ohio. In a climax forest, tree seedlings are able to grow in the shade of parent trees, thus reproducing the forest indefinitely in a cycle of growth and regeneration.

One feature of the arboretum can be fully appreciated only from the air—a 2,100-foot-long series of hedges that spells out "Dawes Arboretum." Other collections at Dawes include oaks, crab apples, flowering shrubs, and conifers. In addition to the forests, meadows, and gardens, there are three ponds and a lake. The visitor center offers nature exhibits, a bird-watching area, an indoor beehive, which the bees enter from the outside through a clear plastic tube, and a fine bonsai display.

Beman and Bertie Dawes moved into the Daweswood House in 1916. Built in 1867, this two-story brick home contains antique furnishings and other of the Daweses' possessions, including portraits of famous family members William Dawes, who rode with Paul Revere, and Charles Gates Dawes, who served as vice president in the Coolidge administration. Guides conduct tours of the home on Sat and Sun at 3:15 p.m.

The Dawes Arboretum is on OH 13, 5 miles south of Newark at 7770 Jacksontown Rd., SE; (740) 323-2355, (800) 443-2937; dawesarb.org. The visitor center is open Mon through Sat, 8 a.m. to 5 p.m.; Sun and holidays, noon to 5 p.m. Grounds are open daily Mar through Sept, Sun through Thurs, 9 a.m. to 7 p.m.; Fri and Sat, 9 a.m. to 8 p.m. Oct daily 9 a.m. to 7 p.m. Nov through

Feb daily 8 a.m. to 5 p.m. Admission is $10 for adults and $5 for children (ages 5 to 15).

Perhaps Ohio's prettiest small town, Granville dates its founding to 1805, by settlers from Granville, Massachusetts, and Granby, Connecticut. The nineteenth-century shops and homes in the picture-postcard community are painstakingly maintained. Up on a hill is Denison University, and a more perfect setting for spending college years is difficult to imagine.

In addition to the crafts and antiques shops, Granville boasts historic inns providing overnight accommodations. Orrin Granger built the ***Buxton Inn*** (known as The Tavern in Granger's day) in 1812, and the inn has operated continuously since then. The inn housed Granville's first post office and served as a stagecoach stop on the Columbus-Newark line. An addition in 1851 formed the U-shaped structure with center courtyard that exists today. The Buxton is named for one of its more colorful proprietors, Major Buxton, who owned the inn from the close of the Civil War until his death in 1905. Mr. and Mrs. Orville Orr purchased the inn in 1972 and spent two years researching and completely restoring this outstanding structure, which is now listed on the National Register of Historic Places. Urban Restorations owner Bob Schilling bought the historic inn in 2016 and gave it a major makeover.

The Buxton serves fine cuisine in tasteful period dining rooms, each unique in mood and ambience. Antiques are proudly displayed throughout the inn, and the brick-floored center courtyard provides a delightful outdoor dining area. Blooming plants in hanging baskets and small potted trees combine with the splash of a nearby fountain and candlelit tables to make the courtyard a most pleasing place.

For dinner, choose from seafood such as fresh Atlantic salmon and, one of my favorites, seafood Chesapeake (shrimp, scallops, and whitefish in a rich pecan cheese sauce over Buxton rice en casserole). Other dinner menu options include filet mignon, pork chops, salmon, crab cakes, shrimp skewers, meatloaf, chicken piccatta, and cioppino (a mixture of shrimp, scallops, crab, mussels, and clams in a tasty tomato broth served with garlic crusted bread). Dessert options include gingerbread with hot lemon sauce or five-layer white chocolate raspberry torte.

Luncheon selections such as salads, soups, and sandwiches like the cheesesteak (prime rib, mushrooms and onions) join entrees that include quiche, crepes, eggs Florentine, and seafood Chesapeake.

The Tavern, once part of the Underground Railroad and sleeping quarters for stagecoach drivers, is located in the original 1812 Main House of the Inn. The space has original stone walls and brick floor and is a popular spot for a bar drink. Stagecoach drivers once cooked their meals on an open fire in the stone-walled basement of the inn and slept on straw beds around that fire. With its rough beams and imposing stone fireplace, the basement tavern retains the flavor of those early years. The tavern serves a casual menu of sandwiches and appetizers.

The latest addition is the 1812 Lounge & Garden Room. The 1812 Lounge offers casual dining plus a cozy bar and 1800s mirrored chandelier. The Garden Room is an atrium-style space with brick floors and decorated with plants and flowers. The Lincoln Room, formerly the Main Dining Room, is located in the original part of the inn. Guests can look through the same wavy glass windows that Abraham Lincoln once viewed. Enjoy the original fireplace and woodwork.

The Buxton Inn also offers overnight accommodations in guest rooms furnished with antiques. The Buxton offers twenty-five guest rooms in the inn, the Main House, and four other historical homes. Lodging ranges in price from $109 to $205 per night. A continental breakfast is included with lodging.

Buxton Inn's Bonnie Ghost

If an inn has a ghost or two in residence, it is best if they are happy lodgers. Such is the case at the Buxton Inn. According to legend, and those who have had the pleasure of a meeting, the resident spirits of the Buxton Inn are just continuing to play the role of host and hostess.

If the feminine fragrance of gardenia perfume wafts heavily across the air on the stairway, the Lady in Blue is nearby. This spirit is supposed to be that of Ethel Bounell, better known as "Bonnie." The former actress turned innkeeper was the owner and operator of the inn from 1934 to 1960. She died in room 9. She is reported to have had a theatrical streak and was known for both her gardenia perfume and her love of blue dresses.

In life and death she apparently loves the inn. According to staff and guests, she often is heard walking up and down the stairs or opening and closing doors. Guests have reported being awakened by a woman, who generally expresses concern over their comfort.

While Bonnie may be tending guests, the tales of the inn say that she doesn't have to handle that duty alone. The first innkeeper, Major Buxton, has also appeared to both staff and guests. The nattily attired gentleman, sporting a mustache, is apt to show up in the bar or come up behind staff, perhaps just to check that all is running smoothly.

While the occasional ghostly footsteps, door banging, or mysteriously rearranged objects sometimes have given visitors a start, the ghosts also give the Buxton a unique character. Since the inn traditionally receives high ratings for service, who can blame the former innkeepers for hanging around just to make sure that your stay is something special?

The Buxton Inn is at 313 E. Broadway St., Granville; (740) 587-0001; buxtoninn.com. The inn serves a continental breakfast daily, full breakfast Sat and Sun mornings. Lunch is served Tues through Sat, 11:30 a.m. to 3 p.m.; Sun brunch, 10 a.m. to 2 p.m. Dinner hours are Tues through Sat, 5 to 9 p.m.

Across the street from the Buxton sits the Tudor-style ***Granville Inn***, built in 1924 by the president of the Sunday Creek Coal Company, John Sutphin Jones. Offering the elegance of an English manor house, the lobby is furnished with splendid antiques and lush Oriental rugs. The dining room features high ceilings, ornate brass chandeliers, and sandstone fireplaces. In warm weather, meals are also served outside the tall French doors on the flagstone terrace, which is surrounded by a manicured lawn, gardens, and towering trees. The Granville Inn offers three dining spaces—The Oak Room, The Tavern, and The Patio. The evening menu at the Granville Inn features a variety of steaks, chops, seafood, chicken, and house specialties such as steak Diane and crab and cauliflower risotto. Another favorite is the scallops Lavallee, pan-seared day-boat sea scallops served over mushroom, bacon, and asparagus hash. For a tasty appetizer, try the Heartland cheeseplate, a changing presentation featuring fine Ohio handcrafted cheese, seasonal fruits, and crisps. (Yes, crackers, but they call them crisps.)

Luncheon selections include soups, salads, and sandwiches. With any meal at the Granville Inn, the house specialty desserts are chocolate hazelnut praline terrine with salty caramel sauce, Ohio apple tarte tatin with Velvet vanilla ice cream, and creamy cheesecake.

The Granville Inn specializes in creative cocktails such as the Sunset in Granville with Hendricks gin, fresh lime juice, muddled blood orange and agave with a cayenne and salt rim. Or try the Big Red Margarita with freshly muddled strawberries, espolon tequila, orange liquor, and a salt rim. The Big Red is a tribute to the nearby Denison Big Red student-athletes, a winning school in the NCAA.

The Granville Inn's thirty-nine guest rooms are individually decorated and have an understated charm and dignity. Prices range from $125 to $425 per night, including a continental breakfast.

The Granville Inn is at 314 E. Broadway St., Granville; (740) 587-3333, (888) 472-6855; granvilleinn.com. Lunch is served Mon through Fri, 11 a.m. to 2 p.m. Dinner is served Mon through Thurs, 5 to 9 p.m.; Fri and Sat, 5 to 10 p.m.; and Sun, 4 to 7 p.m. Brunch is offered on Sun from 11 a.m. to 4 p.m.

A focal point of Granville life, the ***Robbins Hunter Museum*** (at 221 E. Broadway St.) is one of the most prominent residential examples of American Greek revival architecture. Built in 1842 by successful businessman Alfred Avery, the home was a private residence until 1903, when it served as the home of Denison University's Phi Gamma Delta fraternity, and from 1930 to 1956 it was home to the Kappa Sigma fraternity.

Robbins Hunter Jr. was a collector with a vision for the future. The Avery Downer House that visitors see today is a result of Hunter's foresight and hard work. Hunter lived in the house from 1956 to 1979; even then his goal was to see it become a museum. To make that possible, Hunter gathered antiques he believed would be lovely additions to the Grecian building. Hunter also left provisions in his will that would ensure the Avery Downer House would survive long after his death. Opened as a museum in August 1981, the house has been restored to its former grandeur and seems a fitting legacy for the man who loved this beautiful landmark.

The Robbins Hunter Museum (740-587-0430; robbinshunter.org), is open seasonally Wed through Sat from 1 to 4 p.m. No admission charge. Call for seasonal opening.

The growing season in Ohio welcomes a variety of fruits and flowers to ***Lynd Fruit Farm***, and Lynd Fruit Farm welcomes visitors to pick the best from the fields. Home of Ohio's largest apple orchard, Lynd has 80,000 trees, and during September and October, you can pick your own apples. Fall also brings pumpkins and squash to pick or cornstalks to use for autumn decorating. A "show" apple orchard tells the history of the fruit. Apples from colonial times hang on trees next to the latest test varieties. You may also want to hop on a hayride, and let one of the farm's ten antique John Deere tractors give you a ride around the farm. In addition to these seasonal activities, the farm hosts other events, such as cooking and plant propagation demonstrations. Call ahead for dates and times. Lynd Fruit Farm is located at 9399 Morse Rd. SW, Pataskala; (740) 927-1333; lyndfruitfarm.com.

The Lynd Fruit Farm Market is open daily from 9 a.m. to 7 p.m. from July through Oct; Nov through mid-Dec, from 10 a.m. to 5 p.m. until the end of the growing season. U-pick hours are Fri, Sat, and Sun in Sept and Oct from 9 a.m. to 6 p.m. The family is known mostly for their apples but they also grow peaches, plums, pears, nectarines, berries, sweet corn, pumpkins, and more. Also sold at the market are produce and products from local farmers, many of whom are Amish. Local items featured at the market include baked goods, salsa, granola, honey, candy, maple syrup, spices, popcorn, and frozen custard.

Lynd's Blue Frog Farm at 5499 Sportsmanclub Rd. in Johnstown; lyndfruitfarm.com/blue-frog-farm/, offers blackberries, peaches, raspberries, cherries and more. U-pick in the berry patches usually runs from mid-June through August. The farm is named after a brilliant blue bullfrog that resided in the pond during the spring of 2012.

A devastating fire at ***Ye Olde Mill*** near Utica in April 1986 completely destroyed the hundred-year-old structure. Only the 18-foot, 2,000-pound waterwheel and the quarry stone survived the blaze.

But the Velvet Ice Cream Company, which operates the mill and has its headquarters next door, set about building a new Ye Olde Mill of rough-sawed oak and poplar. This new building now sells country crafts and other gift items, and, not surprisingly, Velvet Ice Cream, a Dager family tradition since 1914.

The 1870-vintage building destroyed by fire was not the first mill on this site—a sawmill was erected here in 1817, and a larger one went up in 1827. You can find out about this and more at the museum of milling history and ice cream that is part of Ye Olde Mill. In fact, the ice-cream museum, Ohio's first and only, traces the history of ice cream from Roman times to the present.

Once you've picked up a cone full of your favorite ice-cream flavor, step outside to the 20-acre parklike picnic area. Relax at the picnic tables while watching the ducks frolic in a picturesque pond. The mill also houses a down-home restaurant, complete with deli sandwiches, soups and salads, and finger food. A petting zoo, nature trail, historic 1817 gristmill with waterwheel, and tours of the ice-cream factory round out your visit. The free 30-minute public walking tours are offered May through Oct, weekdays from 11 a.m. to 3 p.m.

Ye Olde Mill is located 10 miles north of Newark on OH 13 at 11324 Mt. Vernon Rd., Utica, (800) 589-5000, (740) 892-3921; velveticecream.com. Open daily, May through Oct, 11 a.m. to 7 p.m. (to 8 p.m. during the summer, 5 p.m. in Oct).

Imports dominate the basket industry in the United States today, but one Ohio family spotlighted four generations of handcrafted basket making. Before the turn of the twentieth century, John Longaberger began weaving baskets for his neighbors and local potteries, which used them for storing and shipping fragile products. John's son, J.W. Longaberger, expanded the business after World War I and taught his twelve children the art of basket making in the evening, after he worked a full day at a nearby paper mill. But over the years, inexpensive cardboard, plastic, and metal containers drastically reduced the industrial demand for Longaberger's baskets, and production slowed to a trickle.

In the 1970s, however, J.W.'s son, Dave, revived the business after becoming convinced a new market existed for good quality, handmade baskets.

The baskets were constructed of hard maple from Ohio, Michigan, Pennsylvania, Wisconsin, New York, and Maine. As a testament to the emphasis on quality at Longaberger, each weaver initialed and dated each basket. Independent Longaberger home consultants sold the baskets, along with pottery, wrought-iron products, and fabric accessories in home shows throughout the country. However, Longaberger went out of business in 2018 and sold its seven-story, basket-shaped building in July 2018.

In November 2019, Xcel Brands acquired the Longaberger brand. A New York-based design and consumer products company led by Robert D'Loren as CEO, Xcel Brands intends to continue working with the skilled Longaberger artisans in Dresden to manufacture Longaberger Heirloom quality baskets. The company is also working on other product categories including food, pottery, and other home decor products, many of them made in local communities around the United States and abroad.

As the name indicates, the ***National Road–Zane Grey Museum*** actually houses two museums—one presenting the story of the building of the National Road connecting the western territories with the original eastern states, and the other commemorating author Zane Grey, the Zanesville, Ohio, native known through his travels and writing as the High Priest of the Outdoors.

Built in stages from 1811 to 1838, the National Road stretched from Cumberland, Maryland, to Vandalia, Illinois. George Washington originally conceived the idea of constructing a road into the new nation's western lands, and the ninth U.S. Congress approved funds for this first federally supported road in 1806.

Workers earned $1 per day to clear a 66-foot-wide path and to build a 30-foot-wide roadbed of broken stone using hand tools, mules, oxen, and horses. The National Road was vital to the development of the frontier—as each section of the road opened, settlers loaded their Conestoga wagons and headed west.

The museum displays horse-drawn carts, buggies, and wagons (including a Conestoga wagon), plus antique bicycles and automobiles—all methods of transportation utilized on the National Road (which eventually became US 40 and reached all the way to California). A 136-foot diorama depicts the chronology of the road, from its construction and use by early settlers moving west to farmers herding their livestock on the road and the road's revival after the invention of the bicycle and automobile. Other exhibits include photographs of sections of the road under construction and fully equipped interiors of blacksmith and wheelwright shops.

Author Zane Grey, born in 1875, acquired his passion for hunting and fishing around Dillon Falls, near his home in Zanesville. Grey attended dental school at the University of Pennsylvania, where he also played on the college baseball team. But he abandoned his dental career to write, achieving national prominence with his sixty western novels, many of which were later filmed as motion pictures. He used the money from his books and movies to finance his worldwide fishing trips and big-game hunting expeditions.

The museum displays many of Zane Grey's books, magazine articles, and posters from his motion pictures, plus the lures and hunting rifles used on his travels. There is also a complete replica of the study he added to his Altadena, California, home, where he penned many of his works.

The National Road–Zane Grey Museum is at the Norwich exit of I-70, 10 miles east of Zanesville at 8850 East Pike; (740) 872-3143, (800) 752-2602; ohiohistory.org/visit/browse-historical-sites/national-road-zane-grey-museum/. Open from the last Sat in May through Oct 31, Wed through Sun, 10 a.m. to 4 p.m. Admission: adults $7; senior citizens $6; students $3.

A fairly unremarkable brick building in downtown Zanesville houses a unique enterprise. The ***Alan Cottrill Sculpture Studio and Gallery*** is where the Zanesville artist both creates and displays his art. Cottrill and a cadre of artists and artisans bring his work from idea to bronze.

The second-floor gallery shows off numerous bronze sculptures created by Cottrill, as well as photographs of larger Cottrill pieces and installations. But visitors can also get a unique look behind the scenes by visiting areas of the studio to see how the process of creating a bronze sculpture begins, from drawing to preparing molds for casting. While the actual pouring of the bronze is done at a foundry, most other steps are undertaken at the studio.

The Alan Cottrill Sculpture Studio and Gallery is located at 110 S. Sixth St., Zanesville; (740) 453-9822; alancottrill.com. Open Mon through Sat, 9 a.m. to 5 p.m. Call for an appointment at other times.

Spend a peaceful respite in a fragrant apple orchard at ***Cabin in the Orchard Bed and Breakfast***, located 10 miles south of Zanesville off OH 555 at 2230 Irish Ridge Rd. The two-bedroom, two-bath, fully furnished luxury log cabin is in the Thomas Family Orchard. Amenities include a hot tub, fireplace, gas grill on the patio, large porch overlooking a pond, orchard, and vineyard. The refrigerator is stocked with breakfast food for guests to prepare at their

HELPFUL WEBSITES

Ohio Division of Travel and Tourism
ohio.org

Canton/Stark County Visitors Bureau
visitcanton.com

Holmes County Chamber of Commerce
holmescountychamber.com

Tuscarawas County Visitors Bureau
traveltusc.com

Wayne County Visitors Bureau
wccvb.com

leisure. Rates are $195 to $225 for one to four guests. Call (740) 674-6814 or (800) 915-9903 or check the website at cabinintheorchard.com.

Learn about famed astronaut John Glenn in New Concord. Across the street from the entrance to Muskingum College (alma mater of the senator, astronaut, and former resident) is Glenn's boyhood home. The home was donated to Muskingum College in 1999. The college leased the building to the John and Annie Glenn Foundation, which moved the house to its current site and restored it to its late 1930s condition. The building is now home to the ***John and Annie Glenn Historic Site***.

Senator Glenn's father built the home in 1923. The modest-looking frame house was opened as the John and Annie Glenn Historic Site in 2002. Visitors to the site will see a 20-minute video presentation on the lives of John and Annie Glenn and can tour the first-floor rooms. Glenn's bedroom looks much like it did in his boyhood, complete with model airplanes and a crystal radio set. Exhibits showcasing the Glenns' hometown of Concord are also part of the site's displays of Ohio living history.

The John and Annie Glenn Historic Site is located at 72 W. Main St., New Concord; (740) 826-3305, (800) 752-2602; johnglennhome.org. Open May through Oct, Wed through Sat, 10 a.m. to 4 p.m.; Sun, 1 to 4 p.m.; Closed Nov through Apr but open for groups by appointment. Admission: adults $7; senior citizens $6; students $3; children younger than age 6 free.

Places to Stay in East Central Ohio

ASHLAND

College House Bed & Breakfast
134 College Ave.
(419) 289-2093
collegehousebb.com

Surrey Inn Hotel Ashland
1065 Claremont Ave.
(419) 289-7700
surreyinnashlandoh.com

BERLIN

Berlin Carriage House
5453 East St.
(330) 893-6600
berlincarriagehouse.com

Berlin Encore Hotel & Suites
4365 State Rd. 39
(888) 988-2414
berlinencorehotel.com

Berlin Grande Hotel
4787 Township Rd. 366
(330) 403-3050
berlingrandehotel.com

Berlin Heritage Inn
4703 State Rd. 39
(330) 893-6600
berlinheritageinn.com

Berlin Village Inn
5135 State Rd. 39
(330) 893-2861
berlinvillageinn.com

Blessings Lodge
5174 Township Rd. 359
(800) 293-8301
amishcabinsohio.com

Coblentz Country Cabins
5130 Township Hwy. 359
(330) 893-8007
amishcountrylodging.com

Donna's Premier Lodging
½ block off Main St.
at 5523 East St.
(330) 893-3068
(800) 320-3338
donnasofberlin.com

Garden Gate Get-A-Way
6041 Township Rd.
(330) 893-3999
(330) 674-7608
garden-gate.com

Lodging on the Square
4877 W. Main St.
(330) 893-1060
lodgingonthesquare.com

CANAL FULTON

Bertram Inn at Glenmoor
4191 Glenmoor Rd. NW
(330) 966-3600
glenmoorcc.com/Hotel

CANTON

Hambleton House B&B
2716 Market Ave. N.
(740) 632-8775
hambletonbb.com

Villas at Gervasi Vineyard
1700 55th St. NE
(330) 497-1000
gervasivineyard.com

CHARM

The Guggisberg Swiss Inn
5025 OH 557
(330) 893-3600
guggisbergswissinn.com

DRESDEN

Inn at Dresden
209 Ames Dr.
(740) 754-1122
theinnatdresden.com

Pines of Dresden Bed &Breakfast
42 W. Dave Longaberger Ave.
(740) 754-4422
thepinesofdresden.com

GRANVILLE

Broadway Guest House
644 W. Broadway
(740) 877-3186
thebroadwayguesthouse.com

Granville Inn
314 E. Broadway
(740) 587-3333
granvilleinn.com

Welsh Hills Inn
2133 Cambria Mill Rd.
(740) 321-1493
welshhillsinn.com

Orchard House Bed & Breakfast
4058 Columbus Rd.
(740) 651-1850
orchardhousegranville.com

LORE CITY

Salt Fork Park Lodge & Conference Center
14755 Cadiz Road
(800) 282-7275
saltforkparklodge.com

LOUDONVILLE

Landoll's Mohican Castle
561 Township Rd. 3352
(419) 994-3427
landollsmohicancastle.com

Mohican State Park Lodge and Cabins
OH 3, just north of Loudonville
(419) 938-5411
(800) 282-7275
mohicanlodge.com

MILLERSBURG

Barn Inn B&B
6838 County Rd. 203
(330) 674-7600
thebarninn.com

Berlin Woods Treehouses
5331 County Rd. 626
(330) 893-2100
amishcountrylodging.com

Hillside Inn
5676 Township Rd. 362
(330) 893-1122
hillsidevillaohio.com

Hotel Millersburg
35 W. Jackson St.
(330) 674-1457
hotelmillersburg.com

Inn and Spa at Honey Run
off OH 214 at 6920 CR 203
(330) 674-0011
innathoneyrun.com

Main Street Lodge
4792 E. Main St.
(330) 777-0555
mainstreetlodgeberlin.com

Whispering Pines Tree House
5492 County Rd. 201
(877) 997-5337
amishcountrylodging.com

MILLWOOD

White Oak Inn
29683 Walhonding Rd.
(740) 599-6107
whiteoakinn.com

MOUNT VERNON

Mount Vernon Grand Hotel
12 Public Square
(844) 700-1717
mountvernongrand.com

Mount Vernon Inn
601 W. High St.
(740) 392-9881
themountvernoninnohio.com

NEWARK

Cherry Valley Hotel
2299 Cherry Valley Rd. SE
(740) 788-1200
cherryvalleyhotel.com

Trout Club
2250 Horns Hill Rd.
(740) 366-2770
thetroutclub.com

STEUBENVILLE

Bayberry House Bed & Breakfast
741 North Fourth St.
(740) 632-2899
bayberryproperties.com

WAYNESVILLE

Hammel House Inn
121 S. Main St.
(513) 855-4044
hammelhouse.com

WOOSTER

Market Street Inn
356 N. Market St.
(330) 262-4085
marketstreetinnwooster.com

St. Paul Hotel
203 S. Market St.
(330) 601-1900
stpaulhotelwooster.com

ZANESVILLE

Cabin in the Orchard
2230 Irish Ridge Rd.
(740) 674-6814
(800) 915-9903
cabinintheorchard.com

Headley Inn Winery & Vineyard
5345 W Pike
(740) 487-1446
headleyinn.com

Places to Eat in East Central Ohio

ASHLAND

O'Bryan's Pub
1065 Claremont Ave.
(419) 207-8400
obryansashland.com

South Street Grille
121 South St.
(419) 496-0735
thesouthstreetgrille.com

BERLIN

Boyd & Wurthmann Restaurant
4819 E. Main St.
(330) 893-4000
boydandwurthmann.com

Plain & Simple Diner
4774 State Rd. 62
(330) 473-1005
plainandsimplediner.com

CANAL FULTON

Bocca Grande Italian Restaurant
4490 Erie Ave. NW
(330) 832-2162
boccagrande.com

Dragonfly Winery
215 Market St. W.
(330) 854-4832
dragonflyontheriver.com

Sisters Century House Restaurant
123 S. Canal St.
(330) 854-9914
canalfultoncenturyhouse.com
(breakfast and lunch only)

CANTON

Bombay Sitar
5111 Fulton Dr. NW
(330) 305-0671
bombaysitar.com

Mint & Lime Asian Bistro
7180 Fulton Dr.
(330) 280-3868
mintandlimeasianbistro.com

Thai Lanna Sushi Bar
7257 Fulton Dr. NW
(330) 818-1789
thailannasushi.com

That Little Italian Kitchen
5730 Fulton Rd. NW
(330) 499-2248
thatlittleitaliankitchen.com

GRANVILLE

Aladdin Diner
122 E. Broadway
(740) 920-4144
aladdindiner.com

Broadway Pub
126 E. Broadway St.
(740) 587-0252
broadwaypuboh.com

Buxton Inn
313 E. Broadway
(740) 587-0001
buxtoninn.com
Lodging is also available.

Granville Inn
314 E. Broadway
(740) 587-3333
granvilleinn.com
Lodging is also available.

Mai Chau Restaurant
133 N. Prospect St.
(740) 920-4680

MILLERSBURG

Berlin Farmstead
4757 Township Rd. 366
(330) 893-4600
dhgroup.com

Tarragon at the Inn at Honey Run
6920 CR 203
(330) 674-0011
innathoneyrun.com
Lodging is also available

MOUNT VERNON

Alcove Restaurant & Lounge
116. S. Main St.
(740) 392-3076
restaurantmountvernonoh.com

Burrata Woodfired
668 N. Sandusky St.
(740) 393-2003
burratawoodfired.com

Fiesta Mexicana
308 W. High St.
(740) 397-6325
fiestamexicanamv.com

Ichiban Sushi & Hibachi
1558 Coshocton Ave.
(740) 830-6323

WAYNESBURG

Cibo's Restaurant
134 W. Lisbon St.
(330) 866-3838
cibosrestaurant.com

Hammel House Inn & Restaurant
121 S. Main St.
(513) 855-4044
hammelhouse.com
Lodging is also available.

Remember When Tea Room
370 Old Stage Rd.
(513) 855-1135
rememberwhentea.com

WILMOT

The Amish Door Restaurant & Village
1210 Winesburg St.
(330) 359-5464
(888) 246-7436
amishdoor.com
Lodging is also available.

ZANESVILLE

Adornetto's
2224 Maple Ave.
(740) 43-0789
adornettos.com

Giacomo's
2236 Maple Ave.
(740) 452-7323
adornettos.com/giacomos

Old Market House Inn
424 Market St.
(740) 454-2555
adornettos.com/the-old-market-house-inn

Southeast Ohio

River Region

At the conclusion of the Revolutionary War, Congress passed the Ordinance of 1787, which opened up new land west and north of the Ohio River for settlement. A group of soldiers and officers from the Revolutionary conflict, along with other New Englanders, formed the Ohio Company of Associates to settle in this frontier territory. On April 7, 1788, a party of 48 men on a crude barge followed the Ohio River to the Muskingum River, arriving at today's location of Marietta, Ohio. By July of that year, Governor Arthur St. Clair had established the first civil government west of the Allegheny Mountains in Marietta, with the settlement destined to be Ohio's first city and gateway to the Northwest Territory (Ohio, Michigan, Indiana, Illinois, Wisconsin, and part of Minnesota). The city was named for Queen Marie Antoinette, in gratitude for the support France had provided the colonies during the war with the British.

Rufus Putnam, a general under George Washington during the Revolution, led that 48-man party in April 1788 and supervised the construction of a walled fortification with four

SOUTHEAST OHIO

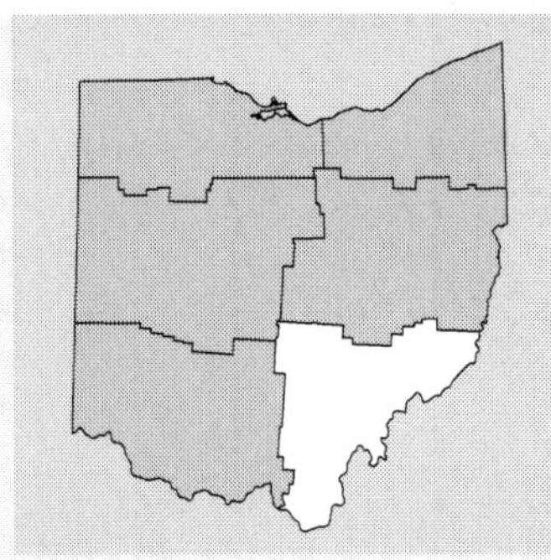

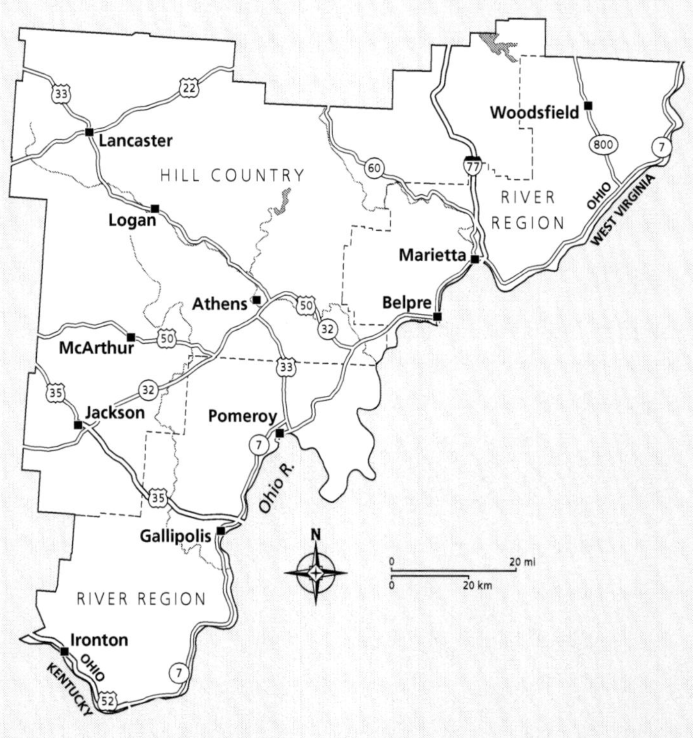

blockhouses to discourage Indian attacks. Putnam's home was part of that fortification and still exists today, completely enclosed in the ***Campus Martius Museum***. Putnam coined the name Campus Martius, which means "field of wars," but the Treaty of Greenville in 1795 virtually ended hostilities in the region.

Putnam's 1788 home rests on its original foundation and contains furnishings from the Putnam family. Guides describe the hardships of early pioneer life and explain the use of the various kitchen and household implements on display.

The museum also exhibits hundreds of items from Marietta's early days, such as the compasses and surveyors' chains used to plat the city. Other collections include Dr. John Cotton's surgical equipment (he practiced medicine in Marietta from 1815 to 1847), antique musical instruments, and a very unusual studio portrait camera from the early 1900s.

A lower level exhibit highlights "Paradise Found and Lost: Migration in the Ohio Valley, 1850-1970." The exhibit explores two important eras of migration that helped shape Ohio's future. The first wave between 1850 and 1910 was when many rural Ohioans moved to cities from farms to find work. The second wave between 1910 and 1970 brought people from Kentucky and West Virginia to industrial centers like Dayton and Akron in search of employment.

The exhibit includes interactive computer programs tracing migration patterns. It also features artifacts and accounts from emigrants' diaries and journals. Among the items is a jacket worn by country music singer Dwight Yoakam who was the son of Appalachian emigrants.

An outdoor patio features an outstanding assortment of Franklin stoves, a water pumper (ca. 1853) used to fight fires, and the enormous pilot wheel from the sternwheel towboat *J.C. Risher*, which worked the Ohio River from 1873 until it sank in 1919. A military display includes the sword used by General Putnam during the Revolutionary War (he later gave this sword to George Washington), old rifles and muskets used by early settlers in the area, uniforms

BEST ATTRACTIONS

Campus Martius Museum	Our House Tavern
Ohio River Museum	Bob Evans Farm
Valley Gem	Buckeye Furnace State Memorial
Lafayette Hotel	Lake Katharine State Nature Preserve

and dress swords from the War of 1812, and a Confederate flag captured at the Civil War battle of Chancellorsville, plus uniforms, saddlebags, and a fife and drum used by Civil War soldiers.

The Campus Martius Museum is at the corner of Washington (OH 7) and Second Streets at 601 Second St., Marietta; (740) 373-3750, (800) 860-0145; mariettamuseums.org. The museum is open year-round Mon and Wed through Sat, 9:30 a.m. to 5 p.m.; Sun noon to 5 p.m. Admission: adults $10; students (kindergarten through college) $5; children (ages 5 and under) free.

With their tall smokestacks puffing black ash and their paddleboards splashing the waters of the Ohio and Muskingum Rivers, the great stern-wheelers plied these waterways carrying freight and passengers during the nineteenth century. Marietta was once a thriving port; its history is interwoven with that of the rivers and the steamboat era.

The ***Ohio River Museum*** stands on the bank of the Muskingum River, just down the street from Campus Martius. The museum actually consists of three separate buildings connected with covered outdoor walkways. One building's maps, models, and illustrations trace the origins of the Ohio River—the role of glaciers in its development and the natural history of the region. A half-hour multimedia presentation describes the river's more recent past, from its early exploration to modern-day commercial and recreational usage.

The most popular building features dozens of detailed models of stern-wheeled paddleboats, with the statistics and a narrative of each vessel provided, plus other riverboat memorabilia such as newspaper clippings, passenger tickets, bills of lading, and stern-wheeler travel brochures. The museum also houses a fine collection of steam whistles and a complete set of woodworking tools used for shipbuilding.

The major outdoor attraction at the Ohio River Museum—the 175-foot, 342-ton *W. P. Snyder, Jr.*—was the last steam-powered stern-wheeled towboat to operate in America. It is now permanently docked on the Muskingum River right behind the museum; visitors walk the gangplank to explore this proud vessel from engine room to pilothouse. Built in 1918, the *W. P. Snyder, Jr.* plied America's rivers until 1955.

Other outdoor exhibits include a skiff built in 1885, believed to be the oldest such boat in the inland lakes region, which was used during one of the many floods that rampaged in Marietta prior to the installation of flood-control dams. The museum also has a replica of an early flatboat, the flat-bottomed, square-cornered boat used to float heavy cargo downstream. Propelled only by the river's current, flatboats were dismantled (their wood sold for construction projects) upon arriving at their destination.

The Ohio River Museum is at the corner of Front and Saint Clair Streets at 601 Front St., Marietta; (740) 373-3750, (800) 860-0145; mariettamuseums.org. Open Apr through Labor Day, Mon through Sat, 9:30 a.m. to 5 p.m.; Sun, noon to 5 p.m.; open Sept and Oct, Sat, 9:30 a.m. to 5 p.m.; Sun, noon to 5 p.m. Admission: adults $10; students (kindergarten to college) $5, free for children ages 5 and under. At press time for this book, the Ohio River Museum was closed for construction of a new Ohio River Museum. The original museum opened at its current location in 1973. Check the website for updates on reopening.

Given the importance of stern-wheelers to Marietta's past, it seems only proper to survey the city and surrounding area from aboard one—the **Valley Gem**, which docks adjacent to the Ohio River Museum. The ship's captain pilots this 300-passenger excursion vessel down the Muskingum and Ohio Rivers on 90-minute cruises.

During the trips, he points out the historic places of interest along the shoreline, including the location of Fort Harmar (built in 1785). Large stone blocks spelling "Marietta" mark the landing once used by arriving steamboats, and this landing is now the site of the annual stern-wheeler festival. Graceful stern-wheelers come from all parts of the inland waterway system to compete in races, and generally show off during this annual weekend of activities.

The *Valley Gem* departs from the landing under the Washington Street Bridge at 601 Front Street, Marietta; (740) 373-7862; valleygemsternwheeler.com. Check the schedule for dinner cruise dates and times, as well as for murder mystery cruises. Narrated sightseeing cruise rates: adults $16; senior citizens $15; children (ages 3 to 12) $8. Dinner cruise rates: adults $49, senior citizens $47, children (ages 3 to 12) $39.

ohio's state song

Ohio's state song, "Beautiful Ohio," was written in 1918 by Ballard McDonald and Mary Earl. But the song is not about the state of Ohio; rather, its focus is the Ohio River. That did not stop the General Assembly from designating it as Ohio's official state song on October 24, 1969.

Even more curious was the selection of "Hang On Sloopy" as Ohio's state rock song in 1985. Made popular by the McCoys, a Dayton rock band, "Sloopy" is a favorite of the Ohio State University Marching Band.

A delightful dining option is ***Benny & Babe***, formerly the Buckley House Restaurant, located in the heart of downtown Marietta near the confluence of the Ohio River and Muskingum River. Built in 1879 as a private residence, the Victorian-style home with double porches is listed on the Ohio Historic Register. Opened in 2008, the restaurant is on the first floor of the house. Guest seating includes the exterior front porch and back deck overlooking landscaped gardens.

Two months after the former Buckley House Restaurant closed in October 2021, the building was purchased by Benny & Babe food truck owners Ben and Amy Postlethwait. Formerly, the upstairs level was used as a private residence, but the new owners have added an entire floor of dining and gathering options. Ben, who has been a chef for two decades, describes the menu as Southern-inspired small plates with an emphasis on farm-to-table cuisine.

Popular menu items include oysters with Calabrian citrus hot sauce, pickled onions, charred corn, and Alabama sauce; beets with whipped goat cheese, walnuts, fig jam, and balsamic reduction; shrimp cakes with chochow and tarragon lime aioli; fried green tomatoes with bacon jam, smoked blue pimento, and Aleppo aioli; Sugar Butte hot fried chicken with smoked gouda mac and cheese, brussel sprouts, and Alabama white sauce; smoked trout with Texas-style creamed corn, jicama-apple slaw, and smoked tomato buerre blanc; scallops with pimento grits, broccolini, cauliflower, and harissa; and prime filet with porcini rub, smashed fingerling potatoes, asparagus, carrots, wild mushrooms, and bordelaize. A wine menu features sparkling cider, red, white, and rose wine plus wine-based cocktails. Beer and cocktails are also available.

Johnny Appleseed Apparition

As you travel throughout Ohio, you may want to conjure up a mental image of the famous Johnny Appleseed. Many of the state's apple orchards, as well as countless lone apple trees, stand as a monument to the man who brought seeds to the farmers of Ohio. A more formal monument at the Washington and Noble County line was dedicated to his memory on September 25, 1942, the 168th anniversary of his birth.

Some say that this is not the only reminder of the famous wanderer that a visitor can experience in this area of Ohio. Just after the monument was dedicated, people began reporting that the man himself was coming back to visit. Some folks were pretty amazed to look up into one of Johnny's apple trees and see a smiling man with a long gray beard swinging his legs and calling out a greeting.

Because Johnny adhered to a religious sect that believed in communication with the departed, local tale tellers say it seems natural that he would try to make an appearance in some of his former haunts.

If you travel through Appleseed country, you may catch a glimpse of a shadow of a man in baggy pants held up with one suspender. You may wonder at the appearance of a man who reaches up to adjust the cooking pot he wears for a hat. But whether or not you see Johnny's spirit as an apparition, you certainly will see his spirit in the strong limbs and the glistening fruits of Johnny's apple trees.

Save room for dessert choices like Peach Blueberry Galette with honey bourbon whipped cream and pecan crumble in a flaky pastry crust or matcha strawberry eclair dipped in white chocolate matcha and filled with strawberry pastry cream. Benny & Babe is at 332 Front St., Marietta; (740) 885-2023; bennyandbabemov.com. Open Thurs, Fri, and Sat from 5 to 9 p.m. Reservations recommended.

One of the finest examples of Gothic revival architecture in Ohio can be found in a mansion in Marietta known as ***The Castle***. The Castle was built in 1855 and was home to Ohio senator Theodore Davis. The house, listed on the National Historic Register, had fallen into disrepair, but was rescued by the Bosley family, who began renovations in the 1970s. Some restoration projects continued past the year 2000. The home's distinctive features make it easy to see why it's called the "castle." It has a wonderful octagonal tower and stone-capped spires. The attic has a trefoil window and the master bedroom and other rooms have stained-glass windows, which have been salvaged and returned to their former glory. Mosaics and intricate woodwork have also been restored or replaced. The fireplace has a scagliola fireplace surround, which is plaster carefully colored and polished to resemble marble. The papier-mâché moldings are another unusual feature. They follow a fashion begun in the mid-eighteenth century when papier-mâché was used to craft delicate and detailed molding and painted to resemble wood or precious metals.

On the grounds, a lovely gazebo, once the covering for the well, has been returned to the mansion grounds to grace the gardens. The cast-iron fence and herb garden have been restored as well. Decorations and furnishings reflect the period in which Senator Davis would have occupied the home.

Start your tour in the restored carriage house, where a videotape presentation and introductory exhibits will set the scene. Check the website for

capital of the territory

During the days of the Northwest Territory, the capital of the territory was wherever the territorial governor and judges convened. In July 1788, Arthur St. Clair, the first territorial governor, arrived in Marietta and instituted the first government under the Ordinance of 1787. By 1790, Governor St. Clair had moved his headquarters to Cincinnati, making it the capital of the territory.

By 1798, the territory had 5,000 white male inhabitants, and Congress gave it permission to elect a legislature. In 1799, twenty-two representatives and Governor St. Clair met in Yeatmen's Tavern in Cincinnati. By the September session, when William Henry Harrison was elected the first territorial delegate to Congress, a new two-story frame building on Main Street was the home of the new legislature.

seasonal and special programs at the Castle. Holidays such as Christmas and Easter mean special decorations, and exhibits and musical programs are often held during the winter months. Tours are offered every half hour and take about 50 minutes.

The Castle is at 418 Fourth St., Marietta; (740) 373-4180; mariettacastle.org. Open April through December, spring and fall hours are Mon, Thurs, and Fri, 10 a.m. to 4 p.m.; Sat and Sun, 1 to 4 p.m.; June 1 through August 31, Mon, Tues, and Thurs through Sat, 10 a.m. to 4 p.m.; Sun, 1 to 4 p.m.; Sept 1 through Dec 31, Mon and Thurs through Sun 1 to 4 p.m. Admission: adults $10; senior citizens $9.50; children ages 5 to 17, $7; ages 5 and under, free.

During your visit be sure to take a walking or driving tour of Marietta's stately residential neighborhoods. The city contains hundreds of nineteenth-century homes, many on charming brick streets.

For overnight accommodations, the ***Lafayette Hotel*** is at the landing where steamboats once unloaded their passengers and cargoes on cruises between Pittsburgh and Cincinnati. Nautical memorabilia decorate the lobby, restaurants, and lounge in this building, including brass pilot instruments, a pilot wheel, and paintings and photographs of the stern-wheelers that once traveled the nation's rivers.

The hotel's seventy-seven guest rooms have been renovated and feature classy Victorian-style furnishings. Four even offer private balconies facing the river. Special Marietta lodging and entertainment packages are also available at the historic Lafayette.

The first liquor license in Marietta was issued to the Lafayette Hotel on January 19, 1934. Toast that special day with a drink in the Riverview Lounge, where the large hardwood bar was handcrafted by Amish workers. Overlooking the Ohio River, the lounge celebrates its river ambience with original riverboat paintings and model stern-wheelers.

The Café Lafayette offers Starbucks coffee along with pastries and cookies. Even if you are not dining there, peek into the Gun Room Dining Room. Adorning the Gun Room are reminders of the hotel's river heritage, including a boat's telegraph, steering arms, steamboat instruments, a bell, a compass, and bell pulls.

The Gun Room is known most for its famous collection of long rifles, handcrafted and dating from 1795 to 1880. Each rifle is numbered and a description with a brief history hangs just inside the entrance to the room. One of the most unusual weapons is a percussion rifle made by J.J. Henry and sons, who accompanied Benedict Arnold to Quebec in 1775. The company later went on to make muskets for the U.S. Army.

The Lafayette Hotel is at the corner of Front and Greene Streets at 101 Front St., Marietta; (740) 373-5522, (800) 331-9336; lafayettehotel.com. Rates: $109 to $310 per night. Check the website for special rates and packages.

How many people can say they had a massage in a grain bin? You can as a guest at the ***Stockport Mill Inn***. The inn is housed in an impressive mill built in 1906, the last surviving mill building on the Muskingum River. After its long career as, primarily, a flour mill, the building now houses an inn with fourteen guest rooms and the Restaurant on the Dam. In the basement of the mill, safely located behind glass, guests can view the historic double turbines that generate hydroelectric power. Too corroded to restore and use, the mill's original turbines have been replaced by these twins from the same era, which now produce about 800,000 kilowatt hours of electricity each year—enough to supply the electrical needs of the mill, with some extra to sell to the local utility company.

A restaurant, gift shop, and a wheelchair-accessible guest room are housed on the first floor. The original grain bin that is now home to the massage therapy room is on the second floor. Unique guest rooms are on the second floor too, as well as the third and fourth, and even the cupola. The riverboat rooms are named for Ohio riverboats and have private baths with claw-foot tubs, all with private terraces with views of the river. One suite, the Captain Hook, which sleeps eight, has a large sitting area, and a stairway up to the Mill's cupola. No, it was not named for the famous fictional pirate. It was named for Isaac Newton Hook, a riverboat captain in the 1800s. A couple of notes for the traveler: Stockport is a dry town, so do not plan to order wine or a drink with dinner. However, diners are welcome to bring their own wine or drink to the restaurant. Also, this inn is in a historic building, so don't expect the uniformity in heating and ventilation systems that you would find in a more modern building.

The Stockport Mill Inn is at 1995 Broadway Ave., Stockport; (740) 559-2822; stockportmill.com. Rates: $99 to $299 per night.

The settlement of Gallipolis resulted directly from what had to be one of the first land speculation schemes in U.S. history. A congressman and his business associates received a congressional grant for 3.5 million acres in southern Ohio. These investors planned to secure the funds to pay for this land by reselling large tracts to Europeans. They formed the Scioto Company and dispatched a sales representative to France, who easily sold tracts to 500 upper-class French citizens ready to leave the turmoil in their country. These 500 men, women, and children set sail for America in 1790, but by the time they arrived in the New World, the Scioto Company had failed, leaving the immigrants without their property.

After negotiations with Congress, the French were given frontier land on the Ohio River. Since these immigrants were largely noblemen, professionals, and artisans, pioneer life quickly took its toll. Half of the party deserted the frontier during the first two years for "more civilized" areas.

But those remaining in what is today Gallipolis endured, and the town's strategic location on the river spurred its growth. In 1819, Henry Cushing constructed a tavern and inn, and that two-story building still exists, now a museum known as ***Our House Tavern***.

The doors, floors, and even the lock on the front door at Our House Tavern are all original. A grandfather clock built in 1780 still keeps time, and the museum contains Chippendale and Hepplewhite furnishings that belonged to early Gallipolis settlers. In the dining room, for example, is a magnificent cherry dining room table set with delicate French plates and serving trays. The second-floor ballroom still has the original carved wooden chandeliers.

The name Our House comes from the sales pitch its owner, Henry Cushing, would give when he met boats arriving at the docks. To keep the newcomers from going to the other inn in town, he would tell them, "Come to our house." The inn's most famous guest was the French general and statesman Marquis de Lafayette. After his first trip to the colonies in 1777 to fight with the Americans against the British, Lafayette returned to France and convinced his countrymen to enter the war against England. America never forgot Lafayette's aid during the Revolution, and in 1825 he made a triumphant return to the United States, which included a 2½-hour visit to Gallipolis and Our House on May 22. The coat he wore and one of the violins used to entertain him are displayed at the museum.

Another important Frenchman planned to come to Gallipolis with the original 500 settlers but at the last minute he let his fiancée go without him. Had he made the trip to America, history would have been dramatically altered. His name was Napoleon Bonaparte; his fiancée's portrait hangs above a fireplace at Our House Tavern.

Our House Tavern Museum is at 434 First Ave., Gallipolis; (740) 446-0586, (800) 752-2618; ohiohistory.org. The museum is open Memorial Day through Labor Day by appointment. Site staff can usually respond within 30 minutes for a tour. Admission: adults $5; senior citizens $4; children $1.

Bob Evans has made his mark in two related businesses—as a manufacturer and distributor of his country sausage and as the proprietor of the Bob Evans Restaurants. After World War II, Evans opened a 12-stool restaurant near Gallipolis. Not satisfied with the sausage available commercially, he started making his own. This blossomed into a sausage business, and he devoted more and more of his time and energy to it. Once Bob Evans Farms Sausage was firmly established in the marketplace, he once again concentrated on the restaurant business, opening a second location in 1962 and coordinating a major expansion in the late 1960s. Today, Bob Evans operates more than 600 restaurants in twenty-four states and is a leading producer of pork sausage under the Bob Evans and Owens brand names.

The ***Bob Evans Farm*** is home to the Homestead Museum, the Craft Barn, the original Bob Evans restaurant, and many unique events. The museum reflects the history of the company, and guests sit at the reconstructed counter for the first restaurant owned by Bob Evans. Visitors also browse the thousands of homemade arts and crafts in the Craft Barn. Now on the National Register of Historic Places, the Farm also has an old cistern where stagecoach travelers watered their horses, several reconstructed historic cabins, a schoolhouse, ancient Indian burial mound, and Revolutionary War cemetery where original area settlers are buried. Special events throughout the year include a bluegrass festival, an antique car and power equipment show, and a gospel sing. The most popular event is the Farm Festival in October, which celebrates the harvest season as it was in rural America of yesteryear.

Bob Evans Farm is on OH 588, 1 mile east of Rio Grande at 791 Farmview Rd. in Bidwell; (740) 245-5304, (800) 944-3276; bobevans.com. The farm is open daily April through December 23, 10:30 a.m. to 5:30 p.m. The Bob Evans Restaurant, located on Farm property, is open year-round.

Hill Country

The 100-mile-long, 30-mile-wide belt of southern Ohio and northern Kentucky known as the Hanging Rock Iron Region once produced the iron demanded by the booming Industrial Revolution. Eighty charcoal furnaces operated in this region from 1818 to 1916, furnishing iron ingots used to manufacture railroad and farm equipment, heavy machinery, and even the cannons and gunboats used in the Civil War. Abundant quantities of the iron ore, limestone, and timber needed for iron production caused the proliferation of furnaces in the region, and furnace communities sprang up near these facilities.

While many of the region's sandstone stacks today stand in silent memory of this once vital industry, at ***Buckeye Furnace State Memorial***, Ohio's only restored charcoal furnace, all buildings have been reconstructed. Visitors learn the history of the Hanging Rock region and the basics of iron making by reading the many signs along Buckeye's self-guided tour.

The furnace was built into a hillside, and the raw materials (iron ore, limestone, and charcoal) were brought by wagon to the top of the hill, where the charcoal was stored under a stock shed to keep it dry, and the limestone and ore were graded and sorted. (The charcoal was produced at a separate location by slowly burning timber under mounds of earth.) Laborers mixed and poured enormous quantities of these materials into the top of the furnace: In a 12-hour shift, they would measure and load 57,000 pounds of ore, 1,900 pounds of limestone, and 800 bushels of charcoal. As the charcoal burned, temperatures in the furnace reached 600 degrees, causing the impurities in the iron ore to mix with the limestone, forming a waste product called slag. Since molten iron is heavier than slag, the iron could be removed from the bottom of the furnace by opening a stone dam at its base. The liquid iron flowed into sand molds known as pigs. The process of loading raw materials (the "burden") and drawing off the slag and molten iron was continuous—the furnaces operated twenty-four hours a day.

Down the hill from the stock shed and loading area, the Buckeye Furnace general store contains merchandise typical of the nineteenth century. The companies often paid the laborers in scrip, rather than currency, which could only be used at the company store or to pay for company lodging. As a result, some workers were continually in debt to their employers.

The discovery of richer and more easily transported Lake Superior iron ore caused the decline of the Hanging Rock Iron Region. Buckeye Furnace shut down for the last time in 1894, closing a chapter in the state's industrial history.

Buckeye Furnace State Memorial is off OH 124, 10 miles east of Jackson, at 123 Buckeye Park Rd., Wellston; (740) 384-3537, (800) 860-1144; ohiohistory.org/visit/browse-historical-sites/buckeye-furnace/. Open daylight hours year-round. Museum and gift shop open Memorial Day weekend through October 31 on Fri through Sun, noon to 4 p.m. No admission fee.

Northwest of Jackson, the ***Lake Katharine State Nature Preserve*** contains 2,019 breathtaking acres of rolling wooded hills, dense vegetation, and a cool, clear lake. Stop by the manager's office for maps of the main hiking trails (which are located across the lake from the office) and walk down the path near the office for your first view of tranquil Lake Katharine.

moresaltplease

Long before white settlers explored what is today Jackson County, Native Americans came to Salt Creek for its salt. The first whites to take advantage of the creek did so in 1798. They drew water from 30-foot wells and boiled it away in huge kettles. Due to the low salinity of the water, up to fifteen gallons of water were required to produce each pound of salt. Because of the importance of salt in preserving meats, both Congress and the Ohio Legislature passed laws regulating the Jackson saltworks. The discovery of other saltworks both more accessible and with higher salinity led to the decline of Salt Creek's commercial value.

It's a scenic drive to the parking area adjacent to the start of the three main trails on the east side of the lake. The Calico Bush Trail, a favorite in late April and May with wildflower lovers, leads hikers past abundant calico bush (mountain laurel) in full bloom on and between the exposed sandstone formations.

The Pine Ridge Trail crosses Rock Run, a gurgling stream that supplies Lake Katharine's sparkling water, and follows the lakeshore. This 2-mile trail then rises through a ridge of pines to a spectacular overlook.

Ohio's Youth Conservation Corps completed the preserve's most demanding trail in 1979—Salt Creek Trail. Traveling 2 miles through steep hills, wooded ravines, cliffs, and creeks, hikers pass abandoned drift mines, early Native American worksites, and burial pits.

Visitors to this pristine preserve frequently spot varied wildlife, including wild turkey and deer, and occasionally a bobcat or king snake. Because this is a nature preserve, no bank fishing, swimming, or picnicking is allowed, and nonmotorized watercraft are permitted on the winding lake by written permit only, with a maximum of five boats allowed per day.

Lake Katharine State Nature Preserve is 3 miles northwest of Jackson off US 35 on CR 59 at 1703 Lake Katharine Rd.; (740) 286-2487; ohiodnr.gov/go-and-do/plan-a-visit/find-a-property/lake-katharine-state-nature-preserve. Open daylight hours; no admission charge.

Just north of Lake Katharine, under a protective roof, rests a large slab of black hand sandstone with some remarkable Native American carvings—the ***Leo Petroglyph***. Probably carved by the Fort Ancient Indians more than 700 years ago, the petroglyph has forty carved figures, with a fish, a bird, and three human feet plainly visible. The most intriguing carving shows an Indian wearing an elaborate headdress. Nature trails penetrate the deep woods and skirt the upper cliffs of the gorges and forests surrounding the petroglyph.

The Leo Petroglyph is on CR 28, off US 35, 4 miles northwest of Jackson; ohiohistory.org/visit/browse-historical-sites/leo-petroglyphs-nature-preserve/. Open daylight hours; no admission charge.

Sue and Jim Maxwell created a most unusual lodging experience in southeast Ohio: a replica of a twelfth-century Norman castle known as ***Ravenwood Castle***. Longtime Anglophiles, the Maxwells traveled extensively throughout England and Scotland and were attracted to castles and the medieval period. Surrounded by the Wayne National Forest and just 7 miles from the Hocking Hills, Ravenwood Castle sits atop a wooded hill. More than 100 acres of forest and large rock formations surround the castle.

Ravenwood's crenelated towers contain the guest rooms and suites. Although the building is new, the Maxwells collected architectural antiques for several years. Each guest room or suite has a stained-glass window, usually

TOP ANNUAL EVENTS

Vinton County Wild Turkey Festival
McArthur, May
(740) 596-7077
vintoncountytravel.com

Moonshine Festival
New Straitsville, May
(740) 334-2239
explorehockinghills.com

Oak Hill Festival of Flags
Oak Hill, May
oakhillfestivalofflags.org

Commercial Point Homecoming
Commercial Point, June
(740) 983-4836

Poston Lake Bluegrass Festival & Jam
Stewart, July
(740) 591-7113
athensohio.com

Gallipolis River Recreation Festival
Gallipolis, July 4th weekend
(740) 446-0596
gallipolisriverrec.com

Lawrence County Fair
Proctorville, July
(740) 532-4333
lawrencecountyohiofair.com

Fireman's Old Time Festival
Laurelville, July
(740) 332-4691
hockinghills.com

Lancaster Festival
Lancaster, July
(740) 687-4808
lancasterfestival.org

Jackson County Fair
Wellston, July
jacksoncoohfair.com

All-American Soap Box Derby
Akron, July
(330) 733-8723
soapboxderby.org

Civil War Encampment Days
Malta and McConnelsville, July
(740) 962-4909
visitmorgancountyohio.com

Pig Iron Day
Jackson, Aug
(740) 286-2707
jacksonohio.us

Parade of the Hills
Nelsonville, Aug
paradeofthehills.org

Baltimore Festival–Canal Lock Days
Baltimore, Aug
baltimorefestival.org

Sweet Corn Festival
Millersport, Sept
(740) 467-3639
sweetcornfest.com

Ohio River Sternwheel Festival
Marietta, Sept
(800) 288-2577
sternwheel.org

in the bathroom, a fireplace with Victorian mantel and gas logs, antique light fixtures, and many feature wonderful old doors. The wood moldings around the doors and windows and the castle's five stairways are inspired by centuries-old motifs from Great Britain's stately homes and castles. Each room also has a balcony or private deck overlooking the forest.

Common areas include the Great Hall, with three large stained-glass windows from an old church at one end and a huge arched stone fireplace at the other. Ornate and heavily carved museum-quality Gothic tables and chairs furnish the Great Hall, where guests dine in a convivial "old English" atmosphere. On the lower level is a library stocked with books on a wide variety of topics, a game room, and the charming Rose and Thistle Pub.

Jim and Pam Reed loved staying at Ravenwood Castle. It was one of their favorite getaway spots. When the Reeds heard that the Ravenwood was for sale in early 2012, they decided to write the next chapter in the magical tale of the lovely castle.

The fairytale castle has seven guest rooms—Rapunzel's Tower, the Duke's Dungeon, the Queen Elizabeth Suite, the Queen Victoria Suite, the Empress Matilda Suite, the Shakespeare Suite, and the King Arthur Suite. Rates are $149 to $249 per night, double occupancy, including full breakfast.

A small village of medieval-style cottages, each with a whirlpool bath, fireplace, and kitchenette, provides another unique lodging option. Surrounding the Castle, the village cottages offer themes in keeping with their names—the Candlemaker's Cottage, the Merchant's Cottage, the Spinster's Cottage, the Woodcutter's Cottage, the Clock Tower, the Silversmith's House, Baker's Cottage, Brewer's Cottage, and Cinderella's Coach House. Rates are $159 to $309 per night, double occupancy.

A short drive or walk from the castle is Huntman's Hollow—Fletcher's Cabin, Fisher's Cabin, Forester's Cabin, Tanner's Cabin, and Trapper's Cabin. The cabins are $149 to $159 per night, double occupancy.

Ravenwood Castle serves breakfast to all regular room guests, dinner in the Great Hall on most Fridays and Saturdays at 7 p.m. Reservations are required. The Raven's Roost Pub is open most Fridays and Saturdays from 5 to 10 p.m., offering beer, wine, and mixed drinks as well as pub food. Raven's Roost Pub is also open for on-site guests daily but cannot serve alcoholic beverages on Sundays.

Ravenwood Castle is near the intersection of OH 56 and OH 93 at 65666 Bethel Rd., New Plymouth; (740) 596-2606, (800) 477-1541; ravenwoodcastle.com.

Ohio's state parks offer hundreds of cabins throughout the state, most of them modern, two-bedroom deluxe models. For those seeking more rustic and less expensive lodging, ***Lake Hope State Park*** provides the widest selection of types of cabins in the state park system. In addition to deluxe cabins, Lake Hope has twenty-one standard cabins with wood-burning fireplaces. These cabins, available April through October, accommodate up to six people in four rooms and contain complete kitchens. A third type, the sleeping cabins, has one to four bedrooms, fireplaces, and refrigerators, but no cooking facilities. As with the modern deluxe cabins, the sleeping cabins are available year-round.

The 3,000-acre park includes 120-acre Lake Hope, with its large beach and swimming area, in a heavily wooded section of Vinton County. The park has miles of hiking trails, as does the adjacent state forest. Lake Hope State Park also contains the remains of an old charcoal furnace—Hope Furnace.

Opened in December 2012, the $5 million ***Lake Hope Lodge*** has arisen like a phoenix from the ashes of the original 1950 structure, which burned to the ground in 2006. The new 14,645-square-foot lodge, built of local timber cut from the Zaleski State Forest, overlooks Lake Hope. The lodge includes a restaurant, cafe, park office and cottage check-in, and gift shop. A banquet hall and caterer's kitchen are located on the lower level.

The lodge restaurant offers home cooking with an emphasis on using Ohio products. A traditional barbecue pit is fired by pure hickory wood. The restaurant is open year-round Mon through Thurs, 11 a.m. to 8 p.m.; Fri and Sat, 11 a.m. to 9 p.m.; Sun, brunch 10 a.m. to 2 p.m., dinner 4 to 8 p.m. Call the Lodge at (740) 596-0601.

Pencil Sharpener Museum

When Paul Johnson retired in 1988, his wife Charlotte gave him two pencil sharpeners shaped like little metal cars. She didn't know what she was starting. Over more than two decades, the retired minister collected about 3,450 pencil sharpeners and no two are alike.

Visitors were welcome to tour Paul's collection which he displayed in a one-room building in his yard. When Paul died in 2010, his wife allowed the building and collection to be moved to the Hocking Hills Regional Welcome Center at 13178 State Route 664 S. Now people from around the world come to visit. Probably the farthest away was visitors from Australia. Some guests even donate a pencil sharpener. As long as the museum doesn't already have one like it, they welcome the donations.

The museum is an easy stop with free admission and friendly folks in the visitor center to share information and brochures about popular Hocking Hills. The layout in the museum is exactly the way Paul had it. Lighted shelves are organized by categories—food, animals, history, sports, holidays, transportation, and many others. Sharpeners are shaped like the Eiffel Tower, Cinderella's carriage, Santa Claus, a violin, U.S. presidents, Batman, Remington typewriter, and much more.

There is also a book in the museum that tells how to sharpen a pencil. That might come in handy for children today who seem to use computers and technology more than old-fashioned pencils and the creatively shaped sharpeners. Hocking Hills Tourism Association (740) 385-9706; explorehockinghills.com

Lake Hope State Park is at 27331 OH 278, 5 miles north of Zaleski in McArthur; (740) 596-5253, (866) 644-6727; ohiodnr.gov/go-and-do/plan-a-visit/find-a-property/lake-hope-state-park. Cabin rates range from $85 to $125 per night.

Southeast Ohio contains thousands of acres of rugged, hilly countryside covered with thick forests, but the most geologically intriguing area may be the 10,000-acre ***Hocking Hills State Park and Forest***. Steep hills, deciduous and evergreen forests, caves, rivers, waterfalls, and abundant plant and animal life provide outstanding recreational opportunities.

A warm, shallow ocean covered Ohio some 300 million years ago and deposited the bedrock of shale and black hand sandstone found in the area. Black hand sandstone is so named because of a large black hand drawn on a slab of the stone near Newark. Probably drawn by Native Americans, the hand may have served as a marker pointing the way to the outcroppings of flint found at Flint Ridge.

Though primitive man may have used the caves, recesses, and cliffs in the Hocking Hills as long as 7,000 years ago, pottery fragments confirm the Adena Indians lived here from the time of Christ to AD 800. White settlers did not discover the lush forests and flowing streams in these hills until the 1790s.

Old Man's Cave, one of the six major formations in the park, so awed Richard Rowe with its natural beauty in the early 1800s that he decided to live at the cave as a hermit for the rest of his days. Rowe was the "old man" for whom this cave is named. A deep gorge runs along the cave, which is actually a major recess in the sandstone cliff, and water flowing through the bottom of the gorge is hurled over two waterfalls and into the Devil's Bathtub, a large pothole formed in the sandstone by swirling rock and gravel in the stream water. Hiking trails follow the ridges on both sides of the gorge, and a third trail snakes through the hemlocks, beeches, and yews at the bottom of the gorge.

Decades of erosion have created another spectacular sandstone formation called Ash Cave, a 700-foot horseshoe-shaped rock ledge that forms a recess 100 feet deep. Mounds of ash found here by early settlers indicated that this

ALSO WORTH SEEING

Wayne National Forest, Athens

Slate Run Living Historical Farm, Canal Winchester

Burr Oak State Park, Glouster

large rock roof was a popular camping site for Native Americans. Hiking trails run along both ridges and the floor of the gorge, past a 90-foot waterfall.

The Rock House, a massive recess completely enclosed by rock except for the open "windows," is the most cavelike formation in the park—certainly more so than Ash Cave or Old Man's Cave—yet of the three it is the only one not named a cave. Another misnomer is nearby Cedar Falls, a waterfall named by pioneers who mistakenly identified the dense forest as cedar, when in fact it is hemlock.

In addition to the six major formations in the park, hiking trails explore thousands of acres in the thickly wooded state forest. The park has forty deluxe cabins in a secluded, peaceful setting. The cabins are available year-round but are rented for full weeks only during summer months, with rates of $155 per night. Other park features include campsites, a 17-acre fishing lake, and a summer naturalist program, plus picnic tables, barbecue grills, and shelters scattered throughout the area.

Hocking Hills State Park is 14 miles west of Logan, at 19852 OH 664 South; (740) 385-6165 (camp office), (740) 385-6841 (park office), (866) 644-6727 (reservations); thehockinghills.org.

The original innkeeper's ambitious goal when he conceived of ***Glenlaurel***, his Scottish country inn and cottages, was to build the premier romantic getaway of the Midwest. Situated on 140 wooded acres and backing up to the rocks of Camusfearna Gorge, Glenlaurel welcomed its first guests in 1994.

This full-service resort is a great country escape any time of the year. The eight stone fireplaces of the Manor House and its guest rooms take the chill out of a fall day. A double whirlpool tub in each private bath overlooks the hemlock and trillium. The Carriage House and the Manor House both offer rooms and suites—four rooms and three suites total. Tucked away in a dense woods, each of the seven features an open-air hot tub on a private deck and a kitchenette.

Then there are the crofts, a smaller version of a cottage. A croft is about 450 square feet, compared with a cottage, which is about 700 square feet. Glenlaurel offers four East Crofts on Thistle Ridge and three West Crofts overlooking Brannock Burn Ravine. Each croft has a kitchenette, living room, queen bedroom, gas log fireplace, screened porch, and hot tub on a private deck.

Glenlaurel is famed for its gourmet cuisine served with a Scottish flair. Dinner consists of three-, six-, and seven-course meals served by candlelight with bagpipe music and Scottish poetry. Gourmet dining includes legendary light-as-air Belgian buttermilk waffles topped with maple cream and strawberry-rhubarb sauce. A "typical" dinner: orange-tomato-basil soup, mixed greens with balsamic vinaigrette, soy-sesame-ginger-marinated salmon over basmati rice with roasted vegetables, finished with a slice of mixed-berry sour cream pie.

Glenlaurel is 5 miles west of US 33, just off OH 180, at 14940 Mt. Olive Rd., Rockbridge; (800) 809-7378; glenlaurel.com. Rates are $229 to $269 for rooms, $249 to $325 for suites, $295 to $379 for crofts, and $329 to $429 for cottages, per night, double occupancy, including full breakfast. The resort also has a spa, wellness center, and Scottish Links golf course.

It took more time and money than its creators ever imagined, but the ***Inn and Spa at Cedar Falls*** was worth the wait. Situated on a hillside meadow, surrounded on three sides by Hocking Hills State Park, the inn represents years of work and an investment of a half million dollars.

First, shingle and plaster were removed from the 1850s-vintage farmhouse, purchased from an 86-year-old woman who was born here, to reveal its original log-and-mud construction. A second log building was moved on site, and the union of these structures now houses a gourmet kitchen and two indoor dining areas in the Kindred Spirits restaurant. The plank flooring and period pieces give this room a pioneer ambience—it's a place where guests watch culinary artistry in progress. The inn is filled with the aromas of American country cooking—apple-smoked pork loin, bean soup, bread pudding with whiskey sauce, or chicken with morel sauce.

The inn's garden supplies herbs and edible flowers. Meals are prepared with the local growing season in mind. A new menu is presented each season. Entrees include pan-seared jumbo scallops, rabbit confit, chicory-coffee rubbed filet mignon, grilled pork medallions, truffle mac and cheese, and cornmeal-crusted trout. The menu also suggests wine and beer to complement each meal. Exceptional breakfasts, lunches, and dinners are served either in the log house or out on the patio. For an additional $25 delivery fee, guests can have breakfast delivered to their door between 8:30 and 9:15 a.m.

The Inn and Spa at Cedar Falls offers some unusual overnight accommodations. Housed in a modern, barn-shaped building are nine guest rooms. Though similar in design to contemporary motel rooms, with individual heating and air-conditioning units, they are furnished with antiques and wood floors. Each has an up-to-date private bath but no telephone or television. Rocking chairs and tables make the second-floor balcony a delightful spot for reading or just soaking up the hilly landscape. A dozen cozy cottages have been built, each with a gas log stove, a large whirlpool tub, and a private deck. Five log cabins are scattered throughout the inn's 75 acres, each with privacy, cooking facilities, and its own personality.

The Inn and Spa at Cedar Falls also has custom yurts–20-foot diameter circular shelters made of Douglas fir, wrapped in insulation and covered with architectural fabric. Wood rafters reach to the sky for an open atmosphere with a bounty of natural light. Yurts boast a king-size bed or two twin beds, full bathroom with tiled shower, gas log stove, microwave, refrigerator, wood deck, and more. The yurts are heated and air-conditioned for year-round use. The yurts, guest rooms, and cottages don't have TVs. The five log cabins have large flat-screen TVs for playing DVDs, but regular TV reception is not available. Free Wi-Fi is available throughout the property.

The newest overnight option at the Inn and Spa at Cedar Falls is a trio of Hocking Hills geodomes that offer out-of-this world stargazing. Constructed of wood and canvas with floor-to-ceiling plastic windows, the domes feature more than 706 square feet of interior space and ceilings that tower 14 feet at the highest point. The geodomes offer one king-size bed, a small dining table and chairs, a couch, coffee table, kitchenettes with retro-style appliances, and custom bathroom with a glass shower. The geodomes are the first in the United States to have indoor plumbing, air-conditioning, and electricity. Children under 12 and pets are not permitted in the geodomes because the structure can be easily damaged.

The Spa at Cedar Falls is a secluded retreat of luxurious simplicity tucked gently in these Hocking Hills. From traditional massages to body mud wraps, guests will feel the stress of everyday life ease beneath the hands of their therapist. The Spa at Cedar Falls is surrounded by the fresh air and natural environment of the Hocking Hills—a wilderness retreat inspired by the land it borders. A section of the prairie meadow that predominates here has been mowed, so guests can stroll down the hill to an outstanding lookout. Here you might encounter deer, fox, or raccoon, while birders view yellow finches, bluebirds, woodpeckers, ruffed grouse, and wild turkey.

Although the inn occupies a clearing right on OH 374, wooded hiking trails meander nearby. The Buckeye Trail, which connects Old Man's Cave with Ash Cave, is easily joined from here. Or hike to Rose Lake for some trout fishing. Cross-country skiing is a winter favorite.

Owners Zac and Lauren Loomis, who bought the property in 2019, want their guests to enjoy the natural wonder of this area as much as they do. And although the kitchen serves overnight guests, others are welcome for dinner if they call ahead and make reservations. Seasonal delights are prepared at mealtimes when visitors come together to share their day's adventures. Lunch is served daily from 11:30 a.m. to 1:30 p.m. Holidays are special times here—the inn provides a homey retreat full of holiday spirit.

The Inn and Spa at Cedar Falls is located at 21190 OH 374, 10 miles southwest of Logan; (800) 653-2557; innatcedarfalls.com. Rates: $249 to $389 per night, double occupancy, including full breakfast. Open year-round.

Wyandot Woods is a welcome retreat for those seeking to get off the beaten path, with six cabins nestled in the trees around a spring-fed lake.

The cabins are well separated from one another, and each has a private dock on the lake—a perfect spot to fish for largemouth bass, yellow perch, and bluegill, or to launch one of the canoes provided for each cabin. Lake swimming is a favorite summer pastime here, or you can loll and sunbathe out on the diving platform floating in the center of the lake. Whatever you choose to do here, the limited number of cabins ensures that you will never encounter a crowd.

Cabins here range from one-bedroom single stories to the bi-level Cedar House with two large decks, an indoor hot tub, and two-plus bedrooms. Each cabin at Wyandot Woods has a deck, porch swing, wood-burning stove with glass front for fire watchers (as well as electric heat), and an outdoor barbecue grill. All are comfortably furnished in pleasing earth tones, and they have plenty of windows looking out on the dense forest. Complete kitchens round out the facilities here.

Wyandot Woods is east of Laurelville, off OH 180 at 14352 Long Run Rd; (877) 365-8009, (740) 746-0243; wyandotwoods.com. Rates: $115 to $275 per night, depending on the size of the cabin, day of the week, and season. Open year-round. Reservations are required.

Another Hocking Hills lodging option, set on 100 wooded acres, is ***The Chalets***. These eighteen A-frames, sprinkled on a hillside, are three-room structures, complete with lofts. Each chalet sleeps four and has a deck with a private hot tub, a wood-burning fireplace (plus central heating and air-conditioning), and an efficiency kitchen. Rates for A-frames: $139 to $289.

In addition to the A-frames, The Chalets offers more than fifty cabins ranging in size and situated in more secluded locations throughout the hills. These deluxe log homes feature large stone fireplaces, private hot tubs, TVs and DVDs, central air, handmade furniture, and fully equipped kitchens. Four large lodges accommodate groups of up to sixteen guests.

The quiet, isolated location makes this an ideal year-round retreat. Facilities also include a large outdoor swimming pool and recreation area. More than 800 acres of state forest adjoin the property and are available for hiking and exploration.

The Chalets is at 18905 OH 664 South, south of Logan; (800) 762-9396, (740) 385-6517, (740) 385-8941; chaletshh.com. Rates: $125 to $1,379 (for a 7-bedroom, 3½-bath lodge) per night, double occupancy. Reservations required.

In addition to hiking and camping, canoeing and horseback riding are popular in the Hocking Hills. ***Hocking Hills Adventures*** provides rental

Washboard Museum

Since 2003, the Columbus Washboard Co. in Logan has sent more than 5,000 care packages to American soldiers in Iraq and Afghanistan. Inside the package is a present from the past to help make soldiers' lives more comfortable. Not only does the free kit contain a small washboard stamped with the words "Proud to be an American," it also has soap, clothesline, wooden clothes pin, a small tub, and directions on how to use the products.

The gift may be unusual but letters from recipients show that it is much appreciated. "We want to thank you from the bottom of our hearts," one handwritten letter reads. "It means so much to us to know that there are people back home who care."

A request from a young Ohio soldier is what started the whole project. In a note, the soldier said his family was from near Columbus and that they had used the washboards. He wanted to know what it would cost to send him a washboard to use where he was stationed.

The answer? The company sent it to him free.

The Columbus Washboard Co. started in 1895 when Frederic Martin Sr. began building washboards in his Columbus backyard to sell.

During World War II, sales skyrocketed to more than a million washboards sold in one year. But demand began to dwindle in the late 1960s with advances in automated washing machines. In 1999, the company announced it was closing its doors. That's when a group of investors stepped forward to save it. They couldn't see such an important part of history being lost. The group packed up the antique machinery and moved it to an old shoe factory 50 miles southeast in the small Ohio town of Logan. The site also contains the world's largest washboard—24 feet by 12 feet—attached to the exterior of the building.

Today, five employees make about 20,000 washboards each year by hand. Visitors are welcome to tour the factory, look at the small museum, and shop for washboards and other cleaning products. Many of the boards sold today are for other uses. Some are used for decoration, while others are turned into magazine racks and other items by woodcrafters. Some washboards are even used by musicians as percussion instruments.

A great place to see those instruments in use is the annual Washboard Music Festival, held annually on Father's Day weekend in downtown Logan. The free festival features authentic Appalachian bluegrass and folk music, along with arts and crafts vendors, regional food, and a children's area with rides and games. The Washboard Company offers free tours during the festival. Columbus Washboard Co. at 4 Main St. in downtown Logan: (740) 380-3828: columbuswashboard.com. Reservations are required for tours which cost $8 for adults; $6 for senior citizens and active military; $5 for children up to age 18.

equipment along the picturesque Hocking River, with trips ranging from two to six hours at rates from $38 to $95 per canoe. Kayak trips range from two to six hours at rates from $50 to $60. The livery is at 31251 Chieftain Dr., Logan; (800) 686-0386, (740) 385-8685, (740) 385-2503; hockinghillscanoeing.com. Canoe rentals are available Apr through Oct; daily between June and Aug, on weekends or by appointment in Apr, May, Sept, and Oct. Kayaks, rafts, inner tubes, go-karts, miniature golf, and a driving range also are available. A classic '80s game room features pinballs, video games, pool tables, and a 16-foot ball bowler. Campsites also are available with fees from $26 to $35. Eight cabins sleeping from 3 to 6 can be rented for $75 to $150 per night.

A unique way to experience the natural beauty of the Hocking Hills is riding the rails. The ***Hocking Valley Scenic Railway*** departs from its Nelsonville Depot for leisurely jaunts through the woods. The route between Nelsonville and Logan was once a part of the original Hocking Valley Railway's Athens Branch. The Hocking Valley was eventually merged into the Chesapeake & Ohio Railway in 1930.

The Hocking Valley Scenic Railway offers diesel-powered rides through the beautiful rolling hills of southeastern Ohio aboard vintage equipment. The primary locomotive was built for the Chesapeake & Ohio Railway in October 1952 by the Electro-motive Division of GM. In the 1970s, along with a few other C&O "Geeps," it was transferred to the Chicago, South Shore & South Bend Railroad for use in the C&O subsidiary's freight service. It has been restored and returned to its 1952 as-delivered paint scheme.

The coaches used were built in 1927 by the Standard Steel Car Company for the Chicago, Rock Island & Pacific Railroad. Each coach can seat 100 passengers and weighs 95,200 lbs. They were used for commuter runs between Chicago and Joliet, Illinois. The coaches are heated in the winter, so a comfortable and enjoyable ride is to be had with

ohio's bulgaria liberator

The man hailed as one of the greatest figures in the history of Bulgaria was born on a farm near New Lexington in 1844. Januarius MacGahan, the "Liberator of Bulgaria," hoped to be a teacher but was unable to land a job with the local school district. Instead, in the early 1870s, he traveled throughout Europe and eventually became a war correspondent in the Balkans, where he filed eyewitness accounts of Turkish atrocities. His reporting shifted British public opinion regarding their support for Turkey and encouraged Russian intervention. MacGahan crossed the Danube with 100,000 Russian soldiers and received a hero's welcome. MacGahan lived out his life in Constantinople and died there in 1878. His body was returned to the United States; he's buried at New Lexington's Maplewood Cemetery.

Santa Claus during the annual Santa trains. Other vintage rolling stock is under restoration and on display.

The Hocking Valley Scenic Railway departs from 33 E. Canal St. (US 33), Nelsonville; (740) 753-9531, (800) 967-7834; hvsry.com. Trains depart every Sat and Sun between Memorial Day and the last weekend in October. Special event trains operate throughout the year. Check the schedule for special holiday train trips. Santa specials run the last weekend in Nov and the first three weekends in Dec, Sat and Sun, at 11 a.m. and 2 p.m., plus 7 p.m. the first three Fri nights in Dec. Rates for the Nelsonville East Logan train ride which lasts two hours: adults $21; seniors $19; children (ages 3 to 12) $16. Other train rides are also available.

Nature herself has given this site its name, Wahkeena, which is a Native American word meaning "most beautiful." The 150-acre ***Wahkeena Nature Preserve***, at the edge of the Hocking Hills, is blessed with so many natural assets that it serves as a center for both outdoor education and nature study.

But the casual visitor won't have to study too hard to see how the preserve got its name. Much of the area is forested with lovely tulip trees as well as oaks. Mountain laurel, brilliant rhododendron, a host of wildflowers, and more than two dozen kinds of fern grace the landscape. While you may not think of Ohio as home to the exotic orchid, Wahkeena boasts eight native varieties of the flower, including the pink lady's slipper.

Visitors can hike two interpretive trails and a floating boardwalk into the preserve. Look closely and you may be able to catch glimpses of the preserve's permanent residents: white-tailed deer, woodpeckers, maybe even a hawk or an owl. The land itself is noteworthy, with sandstone cliffs part of the preserve's vista, the famous black hand sandstone.

Although you can do your own exploring, naturalists also offer guided hikes and walks focusing on wildlife, plantlife, or even the ways of the early pioneers in the area. Check in advance for topics, dates, and times.

The Wahkeena Nature Preserve is located at 2200 Pump Station Rd., Sugar Grove; (740) 746-8695, (800) 297-1883; wahkeenanaturepreserve.com. Open mid-March through mid-Nov, Wed through Sun, 8 a.m. to 4:30 p.m. No admission fee.

Square 13, a National Register Historic District, is one of the original blocks of Lancaster, a block noted by architectural historians as one of the finest collections of nineteenth-century architecture in a concentrated area in the nation. Within Square 13 on Lancaster's "Main Hill" is the ***Sherman House Museum***, the birthplace and early home of noted Civil War general William Tecumseh Sherman, and his brother, U.S. Senator John Sherman, author of the Sherman Antitrust Act, who also served in two presidents' cabinets. This museum is furnished as it would have been when the Sherman family lived there (the home was built between 1811 and 1816) and contains an extensive collection of General Sherman's Civil War memorabilia, mementos, and artifacts. One room is the study of William and John's father, Charles Sherman, who was a justice on the Ohio Supreme Court.

The Sherman House Museum is at 137 E. Main St., Lancaster; (740) 687-5891, (740) 654-9923; shermanhouse.org. Open Apr through mid-Dec, Tues through Sun, noon to 4 p.m. Admission: adults $6; students (ages 6 to 18) $2.

The ***Decorative Arts Center of Ohio*** is a statewide organization that promotes the appreciation of decorative arts and finds its impressive home in the Reese-Peters House. Within this venue there are permanent and special exhibitions, plenty of art classes and workshops for children and adults, and a gift shop where you can find a souvenir or a book to help you learn more and celebrate decorative arts.

The house itself is a grand piece of art. The Greek revival–style home was built around 1835 by William James Reese, the son of a wealthy merchant. After getting a degree in law, Reese came to settle in Lancaster and married into a famous family. His wife, Elisabeth Sherman, was the sister of Senator John Sherman and General William Tecumseh Sherman.

Reese ultimately lost the magnificent house in the financial panic of 1837. Luckily, after the house went through a series of owners, the final private owners donated it to Fairfield County. The house was renovated and became the home to the Decorative Arts Center, thanks to the authorization of more than $1 million in capital funds from the Ohio State Legislature.

The Decorative Arts Center is located at 145 E. Main St., Lancaster; (740) 681-1423; decartsohio.org. Open Wed through Fri, 11 a.m. to 4 p.m.; Sat and Sun, 1 to 4 p.m. No admission charge.

The Georgian Museum, an elegant two-story brick mansion, sits on a hill looking down on Lancaster's central business district, just as it has for almost two centuries. Constructed in 1831 for prominent businessman Samuel Maccracken, the Georgian mixes federal architecture with Regency features and Empire furnishings. The Federal influence can be seen in the symmetrical placement of doors, windows, and fireplaces, while the Regency features are exemplified by the curved bay windows along the west wall. Classic Ionic columns, each containing a complete tree trunk for structural support, form the west portico.

Maccracken came to Lancaster from Big Springs, Pennsylvania, in 1810. Later elected to the state legislature, he introduced the bill funding construction of Ohio's canal system. While serving as Ohio canal funds commissioner, Maccracken raised $6 million in Europe for the project.

This 13-room mansion is furnished with handsome pieces dating from the mid-1800s, including some of Maccracken's possessions. The original pine floors and woodwork remain intact, as do the original doors, doorframes, and ornate arches. The spiral staircase features a cherry spindle handrail, and a large skylight allows light to spill down the stairs.

Splendid blue marble fireplaces from the quarry in King of Prussia, Pennsylvania, grace the two large parlors, as do matching French chandeliers (ca. 1820). One of the upstairs bedrooms contains a fine Regency bed (ca. 1800)—the type of bed preferred by generals in the Civil War, since it could be assembled and disassembled easily by the troops. One unique item in the museum is a 1792 senility cradle. Similar in design and function to a baby's cradle, cradles such as this were used by old people who were no longer ambulatory.

Hanging on the wall in one of the stairways are original Fairfield County land grants signed by Presidents Jefferson and Madison. Also on display is an American flag with eighteen stars—the U.S. flag from 1816 to 1820. The basement houses the kitchen, equipped as it was in the 1830s, and a unique dry well, where groundwater from the surface drained by way of pipes and was dispersed into the ground beneath the basement.

The Georgian Museum is at 105 E. Wheeling St., on the corner of East Wheeling and North Broad Streets, Lancaster; (740) 654-9923; thegeorgianmuseum.org. Open Apr through mid-Dec, Tues through Sun, 1 to 4 p.m. Admission: adults $6; students (under age 18) $2.

After your tour of the Georgian, be sure to walk up East Wheeling Street for a view of the magnificent restored homes in a hilly, shaded section of Lancaster.

Abundant clay deposits in eastern Ohio, particularly in Perry and Muskingum Counties, encouraged the manufacture of pottery and ceramic wares in this section of the state. Pottery production in these counties dates to the early nineteenth century, and twenty-two major pottery companies once generated clay products in the area. Only eight of those firms remain in business, but the ***Clay Center of Ohio*** preserves

all'spotteryin crooksville

Given its name, you might suspect Crooksville is notable for the poor character of its citizenry. That is not the case. Instead, Crooksville made its reputation as a center of the pottery business.

The rich clays beneath its soil spawned pottery giants such as Crooksville Pottery Company, the Star Stoneware Company, and the Diamond Stoneware Company in the late nineteenth century. The arrival of rail service in 1890 established Crooksville as "Clay City," and launched a competition with another Ohio pottery town, East Liverpool.

the history of the industry and displays samples of the diverse output of those factories.

Set on a hilltop in a cluster of trees, the center consists of five open-air exhibit buildings. Guides provide the background and explain the processes used to produce the assortment of vases, jugs, pots, and pitchers, plus plates, saucers, and other dinnerware—each unique in shape, color, and clay mixture. Some of the older pieces include stoneware jugs and jars from the 1850s, and even older earthenware, which was made from very soft red clay.

The yellow ware, so named because of its yellow hue, came from the East Liverpool, Ohio, area, as did the most unusual brown Rockingham pottery. Rockingham (also manufactured in Vermont and Great Britain) can be easily identified by the pitcher handles, which are shaped like a dog—a dog that appears to be looking into the pitcher. The guides also explain the obvious similarity in style of pieces from different companies—the firms frequently hired employees away from one another, and these employees often brought to their new employer the techniques and processes used by competitors.

Modern pottery displays include samples of dinnerware and decorative pottery currently in production at the remaining local companies. The museum also exhibits pottery-making equipment such as molds and old potter's wheels, plus examples of industrial uses of ceramics—drain tubes, shingles, chimney liners, and even filters for air-pollution devices. A resident potter demonstrates the craft of hand-throwing vases, bowls, and jugs, and describes glazing and finishing procedures. Two large shelter houses have been added at the center, where antique pottery is sold on special occasions, the proceeds used to help support this facility.

moonshine festival

Legal moonshine? Yes, in New Straitsville in late May you can see demonstrations of moonshine brewing as part of the Moonshine Festival. The character of hill country culture of days past comes back to life in the streets as the music of fiddles and banjos fills the air. There are always plenty of games for the kids, as well as displays and sales of local crafts and plenty of local food specialties.

The Clay Center of Ohio is on OH 93 between Roseville and Crooksville at 7327 Ceramic Rd. NE (CR 96); (740) 319-0138; crooksville.com. The center is open Wed through Sat, 9:30 a.m. to 5 p.m.; Sun, noon to 5 p.m. Admission: adults $4; senior citizens $3.50; children $2.

Cattle ranch? Ohio? Yep. ***The Smoke Rise Ranch Resort*** is a working cattle ranch on 2,000 acres in the rolling hills of southeastern Ohio. Visitors can play cowboy or cowgirl, rounding up strays on horseback, doctoring sick calves, checking fences and water tanks, and driving the herd from pasture to pasture. Or you can just enjoy the scenery, exploring it on foot or in the saddle on the more than 100 miles of trails. Other activities include ranch rodeos, team penning, riding lessons, dinner dances, and music festivals.

A wildlife management area and the Wayne National Forest, totaling more than 30,000 acres, border the ranch. The terrain ranges from rock bluffs to lush green bottomland. The abundant ponds provide water for your trail horse and a great place to stop and fish away an afternoon.

Accommodations range from bunk-style cabins to picturesque campsites. Other amenities include a heated swimming pool, a hot tub, and a clubhouse with a full kitchen.

Smoke Rise Ranch Resort is at 6751 Hunterdon Rd., Glouster; (740) 767-2624, (800) 292-1732; smokeriseranch.com. Open for trail riding daily, 8 a.m. to 6:30 p.m. Lodging is $75 to $165 per night. Primitive camping is $25. RV hookup is $30. Office hours are Mon through Sat, 8 a.m. to 8 p.m.; Sun, 8 a.m. to 5 p.m. Hours vary during the off-season of Nov through Mar.

It was Harriet and Ora Anderson, she a well-known local artist and he a banker and philanthropist, who decided southeastern Ohio was in need of a cultural arts center. Their quest for a home for their vision led them to an unlikely structure: a historic dairy barn, built in 1914, once part of a large farm minutes from the heart of Athens.

By the time the Andersons discovered the ***Dairy Barn*** in 1977, it was scheduled for demolition in nine days. They rallied area residents and artists and saved it from the wrecking ball. In 1978 the facility was placed on the National Register of Historic Places, protecting it from future demolition.

After a loft renovation, this unique 11,000-square-foot exhibit space today hosts international exhibitions, festivals, performances, and activities for all ages, and all consistent with its mission: to offer exhibitions, events, and educational programs that nurture and promote area artists and artisans, and to draw attention and visitors to southeast Ohio. In the international arts community,

HELPFUL WEBSITES

TourismOhio
ohio.org

Hocking Hills Tourism
explorehockinghills.com

Athens County Visitors Bureau
athensohio.com

Marietta–Washington County Convention & Visitors Bureau
mariettaohio.org

the Dairy Barn is best known for its contemporary art quilt exhibition. In 2018, the Ora Anderson Trail was opened for the community to engage in healthy experiences outdoors.

The Dairy Barn Arts Center is at 8000 Dairy Lane, Athens; (740) 592-4981; dairybarn.org. Open year-round, Wed through Sun, noon to 5 p.m. General admission is $5, free for children under 12. Free admission on Wed.

Places to Stay in Southeast Ohio

ATHENS

Athens Central Hotel
88 E. State St.
(740) 595-0500
athenscentralhotel.com

Deer Ridge Bed & Breakfast
5090 Fisher Rd.
(937) 974-3215
deerridgebedandbreakfast.com

GLOUSTER

Burr Oak Lodge & Conference Center
10660 Burr Oak Lodge Rd.
(740) 767-2112
stayburroak.com

Smoke Rise Ranch Resort
6751 Hunterdon Rd.
(740) 767-2624
(800) 292-1732
smokeriseranch.com

LOGAN

Bear Run Inn Cabins & Cottages
8260 Bear Run Rd.
(800) 369-2937
bearrun.com

Bourbon Ridge Retreat
21174 Goat Run Honey Fork Rd.
(800) 836-9279
bourbonridgeretreat.com

Hocking Hills Inn & Coffee Emporium
13984 OH-664 Scenic
(740) 270-2697
hockinghillsinnandcoffeeemporium.com

Hocking Hills State Park Lodge & Conference Center
20020 OH-664
(800) 282-7275
hockinghillsparklodge.com

Inn and Spa at Cedar Falls
21190 OH 374
(740) 385-7489
(800) 653-2557
innatcedarfalls.com

Lotus Lake Lodge
10010 Stage Rd.
(614) 795-6887
lotuslakelodge.com

Old Man's Cave Chalets
18905 OH 664
(800) 762-9396
chaletshh.com

Tree Houses at River Ranch
11201 Highland Park
(740) 216-4717
treehousesatriverranch.com

Worthington of Logan
72 W. Second St.
(740) 385-1111
worthingtonoflogan.com

LANCASTER

Burtonwood Lodging Co.
148 W. Fair Ave.
(740) 654-0032
burtonwoodlodging.com

MARIETTA

Hackett Hotel
203 Second St.
(740) 374-8278
thehacketthotel.com

Lafayette Hotel
101 Front St.
(740) 373-5522
lafayettehotel.com

NELSONVILLE

Hyde House Bed & Breakfast
138 Fort St.
(740) 856-7848
1stchoicecabinrentals.com/hyde-house

Primrose Bed and Breakfast
167 Fort St.
(740) 753-3105
1stchoicelodging.com

NEW PLYMOUTH

Cherry Ridge Retreat
22097 Cherry Ridge Rd.
(740) 380-7777
cherryridgeretreat.com

Ravenwood Castle
65666 Bethel Rd.
(740) 596-2606
(800) 477-1541
ravenwoodcastle.com

POMEROY

Carpenter Inn & Conference Center
39655 Carpenter Dyesville Rd.
(740) 590-3202
carpenterinn.com

ROCKBRIDGE

Buckeye Cabins
15747 Rocky Fork Rd.
(800) 344-3456
buckeyecabins.com

Glenlaurel
14940 Mt. Olive Rd.
(800) 809-7398
glenlaurel.com

Harvest Moon Cottages
25873 Big Pine Rd.
(740) 279-5694
harvestmooncottages.com

ZALESKI

Lake Hope State Park Cabins
OH 278, 5 miles north of Zaleski
(740) 596-4938
(866) 644-6727
ohiodnr.gov/go-and-do/plan-a-visit/find-a-property/lake-hope-state-park

Places to Eat in Southeast Ohio

ATHENS

Ciro Italian Kitchen & Bar
120 W. Union St.
(740) 447-5121
ciroinathens.com

Dynasty Restaurant
498 Richland Ave.
(740) 249-4317
ezordernow.com

Purple Chopstix
371 Richland Ave.
(740) 592-4798
purplechopstix.com

Restaurant Salaam
21 W. Washington St.
(740) 594-3800
restaurantsalaam.com

Tavolino
9 N. Shafer St.
(740) 592-2004

Zoe
24½ E. State St.
(740) 592-4443
zoefinefood.com

GALLIPOLIS

El Toril
1510 Eastern Ave.
(740) 446-1375
eltorilmexican.com

Five Rivers Indian Cuisine
234 Third Ave.
(740) 441-5871
fiveriversoh.com

Zack & Scotty's
300 Second Ave.
(740) 925-4110

Tuscany Italian Restaurant
1308 Eastern Ave.
(740) 446-7800
tuscanygallia.com

LANCASTER

Ale House 1890
149 W. Main St.
(740) 277-6053
alehouse1890.com

Cherry Street Pub
202 N. Cherry St.
(740) 654-7828
cherrystreetpub.com

Fiesta Tropicana
1236 N. Memorial Dr.
(740) 687-5412

Kanji Japanese Steakhouse & Sushi Bar
1715 N. Memorial Dr.
(740) 687-1118
japanesesteakhouselancaster.com

The Mediterranean
1147 N. Memorial Drive
(740) 654-8237
medion33.com

O'Huids Gaelic Pub
167 W. Main St.
(740) 422-8850

Pink Cricket
929 E. Main St.
(740) 653-7300
pinkcricketrestaurant.com

Todd's Mountain View Restaurant
540 W. Fair Ave.
(740) 653-5973
toddsmountainview.com

LOGAN

58 West
58 W. Second St.
(740) 216-5360
58west.com

Kindred Spirits
Inn & Spa at Cedar Falls
21190 OH-374
(740) 385-7489
innatcedarfalls.com

Maya Burrito Co.
12 E. Main St.
(740) 380-9773
mayaburritoco.com

Millstone Southern Smoked BBQ
12790 Grey St.
(740) 385-5341
themillstonebbq.com

Pearl's Diner
12900 OH-664 Scenic B7
(740) 385-3663

MARIETTA

Austyn's Restaurant & Lounge
130 Front St.
(740) 374-8188
austyns.com

Galley
203 Second St.
(740) 374-8278
thegalleymarietta.com

Levee House Bistro
127 Ohio St.
(740) 371-7035
leveehousebistro.com

Spagna's
301 Gilman Ave.
(740) 376-9245

Riverfront Bar & Grill
101 Front St.
(800) 331-9336
lafayettehotel.com

MCCONNELSVILLE

Boondocks BBQ & Grill
4651 N. OH 60
(740) 962-4100

El Palenque Mexican Restaurant
205 W. Main St.
(740) 651-5206

Old Bridge Brewing Co.
281 W. Main St.
(740) 651-5042
oldbridgebrewing.com

NELSONVILLE

Rhapsody Restaurant
18 Public Square
(740) 753-5740
rhapsody.hocking.edu

Tammy's Country Kitchen
1333 E. Canal St.
(740) 753-2705
tammyscountrykitchen-nelsonville.com

The Mine Tavern
14 Public Square
(740) 753-3638
theminetavern.com

Southwest Ohio

Native Beauty

Two thousand years ago, along the rivers of what is now southern Ohio, a great civilization arose. The Hopewell culture flourished for more than 500 years, leaving behind extensive burial mounds, earthworks, and artifacts. They are preserved at the Mound City site of the ***Hopewell Culture National Historical Park***. Excavation and restoration work was conducted by the Ohio State Historical Society in 1920 and 1921, and the site was declared a National Monument in 1923. Additional excavations were conducted in the mid-1960s.

Some of the artifacts discovered and displayed here may have been used to establish trade and diplomatic ties between distant peoples. The territory we now call southern Ohio was the center of a network of peoples extending from Michigan to southern Florida, and from Kansas to the East Coast. The Hopewell included skilled artisans; they fished and hunted, gathered wild foods, and gardened. They lived along river valleys, in permanent or semipermanent villages near the mounds and earthworks they built. By about AD 500 the great Hopewell culture ended, perhaps because of social changes. In

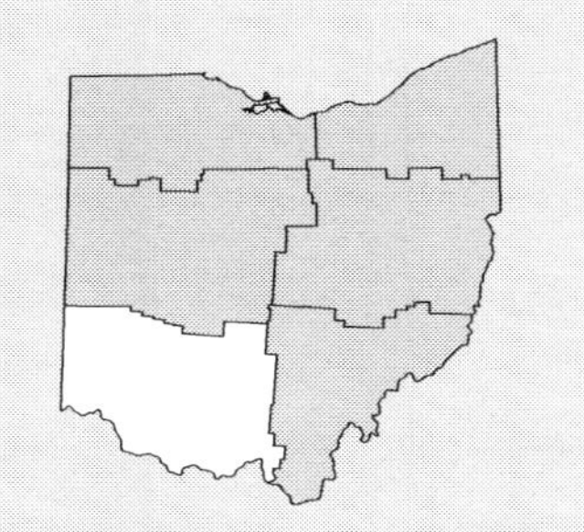

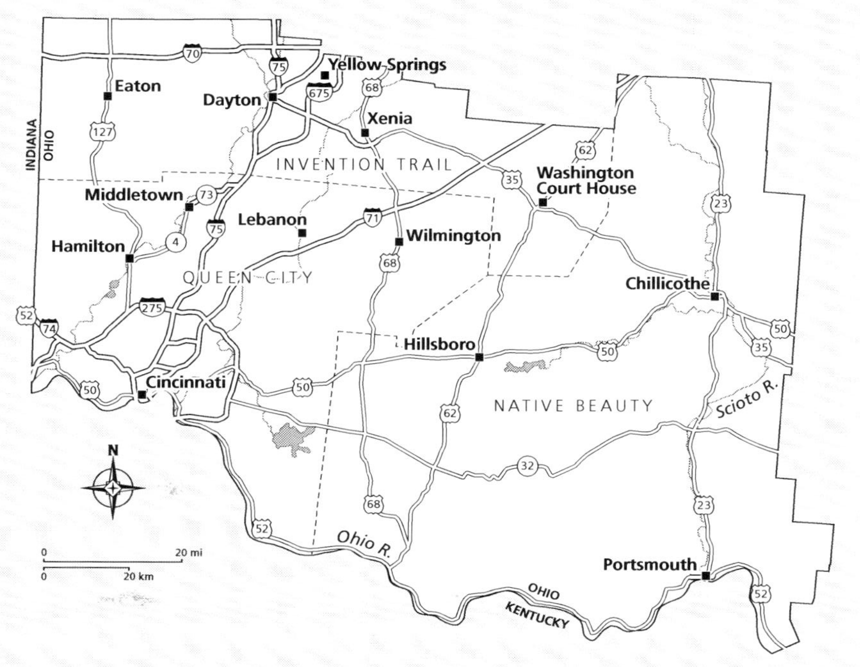
Yellow Springs
Eaton
Dayton
Xenia
INDIANA
OHIO
INVENTION TRAIL
Washington
Court House
Middletown
Lebanon
Wilmington
Hamilton
QUEEN CITY
Chillicothe
Hillsboro
Cincinnati
NATIVE BEAUTY
Scioto R.
N
Ohio R.
0
20 mi
0
20 km
Portsmouth
OHIO
KENTUCKY
70
75
68
675
127
62
35
73
71
4
68
275
52
74
50
50
35
23
50
62
32
68
23
52
52
50

addition to the Mound City Group, Hopewell Culture National Historical Park preserves four additional Hopewell sites in Ross County: Hopewell Mound Group, Seip Earthworks, High Bank Works, and Hopeton Earthworks.

Hopewell Culture National Historical Park is 3 miles north of Chillicothe at 16062 OH 104; (740) 774-1126; nps.gov/hocu. Park grounds are open daily from dawn to dusk. The Visitor Center is open 8:30 a.m. to 5 p.m. Admission is free.

Thomas Worthington first came to Ohio from Virginia at the age of 23 in 1796, when he and a small band of men arrived to claim the land promised their fathers and friends after the Revolutionary War. Worthington permanently moved his family to Ohio in 1798 and quickly became active in the efforts to achieve statehood for the territory. He succeeded in that endeavor and served as a member of Ohio's Constitutional Convention in 1802. After being elected as one of the state's first U.S. senators, Worthington built his magnificent hilltop estate, ***Adena***. Worthington and his wife, Eleanor, raised their ten children at Adena and entertained distinguished guests such as President James Monroe, Henry Clay, Aaron Burr, and the Shawnee Indian chief Tecumseh. After building Adena, Worthington was reelected to the U.S. Senate in 1811, and later he served two terms as the governor of Ohio.

More than 300 of the estate's original 5,000 acres are now open to the public, and visitors may explore the spacious two-story sandstone home, the barn, the springhouse, and the smokehouse—all located in a rolling meadow above the Scioto River Valley. Self-guided tours of the 18-room home allow you to browse at your own pace, appreciating the fine antiques described on the fact sheet, which gives the styles and origins of the furnishings in the home. Although many of the pieces on display did not belong to the

BEST ATTRACTIONS

Hopewell Culture National Historical Park	Serpent Mound
Adena	Rankin House
Highlands Nature Sanctuary	Cohearts Riverhouse
Pike Lake State Park	Grant's Boyhood Home
Lake White Club	Grant Birthplace
Shawnee State Park	Valley Vineyards
Fort Hill State Memorial	Bethel Historical Museum

Worthingtons, they date from the 1780s to 1820s and are typical of the pieces used at Adena.

The large downstairs master bedroom, with its dark ash and oak floors, has a splendid view of the formal gardens. In an adjacent sitting room hangs a most unusual portrait of Thomas Jefferson, created not with paint, but with different colors of wool thread. The enormous state dining room features the actual dining table and chairs used at Adena in 1825. Two large portraits decorate the drawing room; one of Thomas Worthington at age 25 and the other of his sister, who married Edward Tiffin, Ohio's first governor.

Two of Adena's most interesting rooms are tucked away down the back stairs: the weaving room, with a large Virginia loom (ca. 1790) and wool and flax wheels, and Worthington's private study. On display in the study is a tomahawk given to Worthington by Chief Tecumseh in 1807. Worthington's musket and his father's sword still hang above the fireplace.

Across the meadow from the home is a scenic overlook of the Scioto River Valley—you can see for miles from this spot. In fact, the splendor of the sunrise over Mount Logan as viewed from Adena is said to have inspired the sunrise design incorporated in the seal of the state of Ohio.

Adena Mansion & Gardens Historic Site is off OH 104 and Pleasant Valley Road at 847 Adena Rd., 3 miles north of Chillicothe; (740) 772-1500, (800) 319-7248; adenamansion.com. Open from Apr through Oct, Wed through Sat,

State Motto/Animal

In 1866 the Ohio legislature passed a bill adding a motto to Ohio's Great Seal. The motto, Imerium in Imperio, translates from Latin to "an empire within an empire." However, the motto's life span was brief. Critics blasted it as pretentious and feudal, and in 1867 the law authorizing it was repealed. For the next 91 years, Ohio had no state motto.

Cincinnati sixth-grader Jimmie Mastronardo was disturbed in 1958 to learn that Ohio was the only state without a motto, and he set about to correct this omission. He decided on a biblical verse from Matthew 19:26: "With God all things are possible." He and his classmates launched a petition drive aimed at the legislature, a drive that succeeded in 1959 when the new motto officially was adopted.

Students also were the driving force behind the designation of the white-tailed deer as Ohio's state animal in 1988. In this case, it was a fourth-grade class at Worthington Estates Elementary School that lobbied lawmakers. The students argued that the white-tailed deer's abundance (there are more deer today in Ohio than there were at the time of settlement) and gracefulness warranted the recognition. The legislators agreed and deemed it so.

9 a.m. to 5 p.m.; Sun, noon to 5 p.m. Admission: adults $12 senior citizens $11; children (ages 6 to 12) $6.

Shawnee leader Tecumseh dreamed of banding together 50,000 warriors from all the western Indian tribes in a force that he hoped would end the white man's westward expansion. The plan obviously failed, and the whites eventually conquered the land north and west of the Ohio River and beyond. Tecumseh's story is portrayed nightly, except Sunday, during the summer at ***Sugarloaf Mountain Amphitheatre*** in the outdoor drama *Tecumseh!*. Immediately following the performance, cast members of *Tecumseh!* gather in the pavilion area to sign autographs and pose for photographs.

The ***Kenton House*** offers pub favorites each evening from 4:30 p.m. until showtime. Menu favorites include burgers, brats, pizza, pretzel bites with pub cheese, pub fries, and more. The Tecumseh! Snack Shack serves treats to enjoy during the show, such as buttered popcorn, Hawaiian shaved ice, and Dippin' Dots. Alcoholic beverages, including wine slushie, are offered for showgoers age 21 and older. The Snack Shack is open nightly from 4:30 p.m. until after intermission.

A "behind-the-scenes experience" tour is offered daily at 4 p.m., 4:45 p.m., and 5:30 p.m. The 45-minute tour features costumed cast members portraying characters from the world of Tecumseh and the early settlers, plus demonstrations of weaponry, stunts, and makeup used in the production. Admission is $10 for adults and children.

In the gift shop, visitors can purchase bags of mining "rough" for $15 that has been "seeded" with gemstones, minerals, fossils, or arrowheads. Some rough even contains emeralds. "Miners" then learn how to sluice in barrel sluices and get help identifying what they have found to take home.

feast of the flowering moon

What child hasn't played at being a Native American or a rugged mountain man? The Feast of the Flowering Moon brings reenactment teams together to bring the days of early Ohio back to Yoctangee Park in Chillicothe. During the weekend festival you'll marvel at the skills of artisans and feel the beat of drums that fire the performance of Native American dancers.

The feast got its name from the American Indian tradition of using 13 lunar months instead of 12 months. At the end of May, tribes would celebrate the end of winter and the annual rebirth of the world. The Shawnee in Ohio called it the Flowering Moon. It was a time to sing and dance and give thanks for surviving the cold and barren Starving Moon.

The Feast of the Flowering Moon is held Memorial Day weekend in Yoctangee Park; no admission charge; feastofthefloweringmoon.org.

Sugarloaf Mountain Amphitheatre is at 5968 Marietta Rd., east of OH 159, 6 miles northeast of Chillicothe; (740) 775-0700, (866) 775-0700; tecumsehdrama .com. Performances take place from mid- June to early Sept. Admission from $31 to $51. Advance reservations required. The show is not recommended for children age 6 and younger due to some violent content and loud battle scenes.

"Lemonade Lucy" was the nickname ***Lucy Hayes***, the wife of President ***Rutherford B. Hayes***, was given while she lived at the White House because she would not serve alcohol at parties and receptions. Her birthplace, now the ***Lucy Hayes Heritage Center***, is modest compared to the president's official residence, but has much to teach us about the life of Lemonade Lucy and of families of the early 1800s. The two-story federal-style home houses period furniture as well as memorabilia from the president and the first lady.

Where's the Capital?

Congress divided the Northwest Territory in 1800 and designated Chillicothe as the capital of the eastern half. The territorial legislature met here in November 1800 in Abrams's Big House, a two-story log cabin and one of the few buildings in the four-year-old village large enough to accommodate the group. The main floor, where the legislature met, also was used for singing schools, dances, and religious services. Upstairs was a bar. Construction began on a statehouse built of stone taken from neighboring hills.

In 1802, when the population of the eastern division of the territory reached 45,000, Congress authorized the election of delegates to create a state constitution. Thirty-five delegates met in the new Chillicothe statehouse on November 4, 1802, and drafted the document in 25 days. Ohio's admission to the Union was in 1803, and the first Ohio General Assembly convened March 1, 1803.

The new constitution called for Chillicothe to remain the capital until 1808, starting an intense competition between towns wanting to be named the permanent capital. Zanesville went as far as building a statehouse and was named the temporary capital in 1809 for its efforts. The brick Zanesville statehouse served as the capital until 1812, when the seat of government was shifted back to Chillicothe.

Meanwhile, Worthington, Lancaster, Newark, Mt. Vernon, Delaware, Dublin, and Pickaway Plains all competed for the permanent site. Dublin was believed to be the front-runner, but legend has it that Dublin lost the favored spot as a result of a card game the night before the legislature was to act on the siting of the permanent capital. The winner was a plot of land across the Scioto River from the town of Franklinton.

The new capital site was heavily wooded and did not even have a name. Though Ohio City was the favorite name with many, the legislature designated the future capital as Columbus. State offices moved from Chillicothe to Columbus on October 1, 1816, and the legislature met for the first time in Columbus that December.

The Lucy Webb Hayes Heritage Center is at 90 W. Sixth St., Chillicothe; (740) 775-5829; ohio.org. Open Apr through Sept, Fri and Sat, 1 to 4 p.m. Open other hours by appointment. Admission $2.

In an area once inhabited by Shawnee and Delaware Indians, ***7 Caves Nature Preserve*** has intrigued visitors since the turn of the twentieth century. The park was established as 7 Caves in 1928 and was owned by the Miller family for decades, but went out of business in 2005. It is now part of the nonprofit ***Highlands Nature Sanctuary***.

Highlands Nature Sanctuary's Cave Canyon offers a scenic retreat with miles of hiking trails. In 1995 the Highlands Nature Sanctuary became the headquarters for the Arc of Appalachia Preserve System, whose mission is to reunite and preserve forestland in Ohio. The Arc purchased land that was once part of the 7 Caves tourist attraction. Highlands Nature Sanctuary, including Cave Canyon, now encompasses 2,000 acres, including the deep dolomite canyon known as the Rocky Fork Gorge. Cave Canyon is open to the public and provides nature lovers with access to three self-guided trails, a guided hike, and the Appalachian Forest Museum. The three self-guided trail walks provide views from the high bluffs and take hikers through an old-growth forest and past amazing rock formations.

To preserve these caves and the habitat they provide for bats, all the caves are now closed to the public. Additional trails into another 14-acre area are accessible.

Those interested in botany and horticulture will marvel at the more than 200 species of plants, thriving in environments from rock ledges to prairies. More than sixty types of trees can also be found in the preserve. The website provides information on special hikes for those particularly interested in flora.

Birders will also be attracted to this preserve. Multiple types of habitat support a wide variety of feathered residents and visitors. A sampling of the vast array includes wood ducks, great blue herons, osprey, cerulean warblers, hooded warblers, ovenbirds, kingfishers, orchard orioles, and barn owls.

Highlands Nature Sanctuary is 4 miles west of Bainbridge, off US 50 at 7660 Cave Rd.; (937) 365-1935. Open mid-Mar through mid-Nov daily from 9:30 a.m. to 4:30 pm. Entrance is by donation during regular hours only. Pets are not permitted.

When you're traveling through southern Ohio, you can't help but notice the dozens of lakes in the region—lakes providing boating, fishing, swimming, and other recreational activities. For this reason I heartily recommend that when you travel off the beaten path in southern Ohio, you always pack a swimsuit—particularly on hot summer days.

One of these alluring lakes is 13-acre Pike Lake in ***Pike Lake State Park***, which offers a delightful spot for swimming, rowing, fishing, or scuba diving. Lifeguards watch over the sandy beach and swimming area during the summer, and rowboats can be rented. Anglers enjoy catching the catfish, largemouth bass, crappie, and bluegill, and divers take advantage of the remarkably clear water.

Although the state park is a modest 600 acres, a densely wooded 10,600-acre state forest surrounds the park. There are numerous hiking trails in the state forest and 6 miles of trails in the park.

Up a shady hill from the lake sit the park's twenty-four rental cabins—twelve basic cabins, four standard, and eight preferred cabins. Some are pet friendly. All are set in secluded locations, and the preferred deluxe cabins offer completely equipped kitchens, baths, living areas, linens and screened porches. The standard cabins contain a single large sleeping and living area with four bunks and a fold-out couch, a kitchen, and a bath. Standard and preferred cabins sleep six. Basic sleeps four and provides no linens. A group lodge sleeps sixteen for a rate of $150. A new handicapped accessible cabin sleeps five. Pike Lake also has eighty campsites, and a park naturalist conducts nature programs during summer months.

Pike Lake State Park is at 1847 Pike Lake Rd., 7 miles south of Bainbridge; (740) 493-2212, (866) 644-6727; ohiodnr.gov/go-and-do/plan-a-visit/find-a-property/pike-lake-state-park. Rates for the cabins range from $75 to $125 per night. Early reservations recommended.

The Lake White Club dates back to 1936, but the building housing the club was a log cabin on Pee Pee Creek long before construction of the dam and spillway that created Lake White. The lobby of the restaurant contains the original rough-hewn wooden beams of the cabin, which was built on this spot in the 1820s. The Ohio and Erie Canal could be seen from the windows of that cabin; the canal followed the creek on its way south to Portsmouth. Pee Pee Creek received its name for the initials of Peter Patrick, which he carved in the trunk of a large beech tree beside the stream as a claim on this land in 1785, when this area was still Shawnee country.

The club specializes in down-home country cooking, and the chicken dinners are a house specialty. Other entrees include half a dozen cuts of steak, roast turkey, hickory-smoked ham in raisin sauce, and ham and turkey smothered with a cheese sauce. If the 180-degree view of the lake whets your appetite for seafood, try the broiled or fried pickerel, the lobster tail, the scallops, or the fried shrimp. The club offers prime rib as a special dinner every Saturday night.

The Lake White Club serves generous portions of all its entrees, and the light-wood paneling and bentwood chairs give the dining room a pleasant, not-too-formal atmosphere.

The Lake White Club is at 1166 OH 552, 2 miles south of Waverly; (740) 947-5000, (800) 774-5253; thelakewhiteclub.com. Upstairs dining open Wed and Fri 5 to 9 p.m.; Sat 4 to 9 p.m., Sun buffet from noon to 3 p.m. The Lake White Club downstairs lounge is open Wed through Sat from 5 p.m. to midnight and serves appetizers and bar food.

Shawnee State Park, with more than 60,000 acres of parkland and adjoining state forest, consists of ridge upon ridge of thick woods in the splendid southern Ohio countryside. To get perspective on the size of this stunningly beautiful acreage, note that the park contains over 130 miles of roads, not to mention miles of hiking and bridle paths. Shawnee is particularly popular in October, when the changing leaves produce hillsides bursting with reds, oranges, and golds. A 5,000-acre section of the park has been set aside as the Shawnee Wilderness Area, preserving the unspoiled natural beauty of the land. The park's two small lakes, Turkey Creek Lake and Roosevelt Lake, both have sandy swimming beaches.

A modern stone-and-timber 50-room lodge provides overnight accommodations in this peaceful park, as do twenty-five deluxe two-bedroom cabins. Facilities at the lodge include an indoor and outdoor pool, tennis courts, a restaurant, a game room, and an 18-hole golf course with putting green, restaurant, and game room. Lodge rates are $114 to $155, double occupancy. Campsite rates are $12 for nonelectrical and $26 for sites with electricity. The cabins are tucked away in an isolated section of the park and come equipped with all kitchen utensils, linens, and blankets. Cabin rates range from $139 to $229 per night, $985 to $1,200 per week. Numerous campsites are also available. Some cabins are pet friendly.

Shawnee State Park is at 4404 OH 125, 12 miles west of Portsmouth; (740) 858-6621, (866) 664-6727; gov/wps/portal/gov/odnr/go-and-do/plan-a-visit/find-a-property/shawnee-state-park. Open year-round; reservations recommended.

Fort Hill Earthworks & Nature Preserve offers the traveler a chance to

the cradle of american dentistry

Bainbridge was a trendsetter in the early 1800s, when Dr. John Harris opened the first school in the United States for teaching dentistry. Thanks to Harris, the town has been recognized as the "Cradle of American Dentistry." Harris founded the first U.S. dental school in 1825 in a modest one-story brick building on Main Street. The building today houses a dental museum.

see one of the best preserved Native American earthworks in all North America. Archaeologists believe that the 1½-mile-long earthen enclosure on the hilltop was constructed by the Hopewell people between 100 BC and AD 500. Experts believe that this area also contained at least two ceremonial buildings, and probably a village located in the Brush Creek Valley.

This 1,200-acre preserve lies just at the edge of the glacial boundary and has 11 miles of hiking trails. The hilly region is home to a wide variety of flowers and plants. Along with the hiking trails, visitors can take a break at the picnic grounds. A museum also offers information and exhibits on the area's geology and on the archaeological findings around the region.

Fort Hill Earthworks & Nature Preserve is located at 13614 Fort Hill Rd., Hillsboro; (937) 588-3221, (800) 283-8905; ohiohistory.org/visit/browse-historical-sites/fort-hill-earthworks-nature-preserve/. Open daylight hours (closed during deer hunting season, generally Nov through Jan). The museum is open May through Oct, Sat noon to 5 p.m. No admission charge.

Impressive but still shrouded in mystery is the ***Serpent Mound State Memorial*** in southwest Ohio. This huge snake built of mounded earth stretches for nearly a quarter of a mile. The Serpent Mound is the largest serpent effigy mound in the United States and one of the few effigy mounds in Ohio. Experts believe that the Adena people built this and other mounds, and lived in this area in Ohio from 800 BC to AD 100. Just what purpose the giant prehistoric mound played in the life and the culture of the Adena remains a mystery. However, archaeologists believe that the uncoiling snake symbolized some mythical or religious principle. Also on this site are smaller conical mounds that contain artifacts from the Adena people and also appear to serve as burial sites.

The Serpent Mound State Memorial located at 3850 OH 73, Peebles; (937) 587-2796, (800) 752-2757; ohiohistory.org/visit/browse-historical-sites/serpent-mound/. Park and earthworks are open daily, dawn to dusk. Museum and gift shop are open in Mar, Sat and Sun, 10 a.m. to 4 p.m.; Apr daily 10 a.m. to 4 p.m. May through Oct Mon through Thurs 10 a.m. to 4 p.m., Fri through Sun 9 a.m. to 5 p.m. Nov through Dec 21, Sat and Sun only, 10 a.m. to 4 p.m. Admission: per car, $8; bicycles, pedestrians, motorcycles, $4; RVs with 8 or more people, $9.

Rare plants and impressive geological features are waiting to awe the casual hiker or the serious botanist or geologist at the ***Davis Memorial Nature Preserve***. This 88-acre site was donated by Davon Inc. and bears the name of its chairman of the board, Edwin H. Davis.

Visitors enjoy two hiking trails in the preserve. Dolomite cliffs, an impressive geological fault, and a cave are among the geological points of interest.

The heavily wooded trails give hikers a chance to see bamboo grass, purple cliff brake ferns, great cane, and a rare plant called Sullivantia, which grew here in preglacial times.

The Davis Memorial Nature Preserve is located at Township Roads 126 and 129 at 3677 Davis Rd., 3 miles east of Peebles; (614) 265-6453; ohiodnr.gov/discover-and-learn/safety-conservation/about-ODNR/nature-preserves. Open daylight hours. No admission charge.

The redbrick two-story house, with its shake roof and white trim, does not at first appear in any way extraordinary. It does offer a marvelous view down the steep hill to the Ohio River, and across the river into northern Kentucky, but there is no outward evidence of this house's role in history. But 150 years ago, rickety wooden steps led from the river up the hillside to this modest home. Those steps became known as the "stairway to liberation," and on moonless nights slaves escaping from plantations in the South crossed the Ohio River and climbed those weathered steps to the ***Rankin House***, home of the Reverend John Rankin.

Rankin and his wife, Jean, were conductors on the Underground Railroad, which transported thousands of slaves to freedom in Canada. Rankin's battle against slavery began with his abolitionist preaching as early as 1815, and a series of his letters on the subject were published in a book in 1826. The home he built on "Liberty Hill" protected runaway slaves from the day it was completed in 1828 until 1863. Rankin used an elaborate set of signals, using lanterns in his windows, to communicate the "all clear" message to Dr. Alexander Campbell and other abolitionists in town.

birth of the women's christian temperance union

On Christmas morning 1873, Eliza Jane Thompson and seventy-five other women temperance activists visited every Hillsboro saloon and drugstore that sold alcohol. Thompson, daughter of a former governor and wife of a judge, led the charge into those businesses, where the protestors would kneel, pray aloud, and sing hymns. They informed the shocked owners they'd be back the next day and every day until they stopped selling the devil's brew.

The result: They stopped liquor sales in every Hillsboro store but one. Eliza Jane Thompson's protest movement became the Women's Temperance Crusade, which in turn evolved into the Women's Christian Temperance Union.

Designated a National Historic Landmark in September 1997, and now open to the public as a museum, the Rankin House contains some of Rankin's possessions, including his personal Bible, published in 1793. The house has dark hardwood floors and high ceilings typical of the period, as well as completely furnished bedrooms and a kitchen stocked with cooking utensils and equipment used in the mid-1800s.

One upstairs room houses a small abolitionist museum, which tells of the more than 2,000 slaves who stayed at Rankin House (often as many as twelve at a time) on their way to freedom. It was Rankin who told Harriet Beecher

TOP ANNUAL EVENTS

Feast of the Flowering Moon
Chillicothe, May
(740) 702-7677
feastofthefloweringmoon.org

Yellow Springs Street Fair
Yellow Springs, June
(937) 767-2686
yellowspringsohio.org/street_fair/s

***Tecumseh!* Outdoor Historical Drama**
Chillicothe, June to Sept
(740) 775-0700, (866) 775-0700
tecumsehdrama.com

Montgomery County Fair
Dayton, July
(937) 224-1619
montcofair.com

Greene Countrie Towne Festival
Greenfield, July
(740) 572-6737

Fayette County Fair
Washington Court House, July
(740) 335-5856
lafayettecofairoh.com

Sweet Corn Festival
Fairborn, Aug
(937) 305-0800
fairbornsweetcornfestival.org

Ohio Renaissance Festival
10542 E. State Route 73.,
Waynesville, weekends Sept to Oct
(888) 695-0888
renfestival.com

Highland County Fair
Hillsboro, Sept
(937) 393-9975
highlandcountyfair.org

Circleville Pumpkin Show
Circleville, Oct
(740) 474-7000
pumpkinshow.com

Sauerkraut Festival
Waynesville, Oct
(513) 897-8855
sauerkrautfestival.waynesvillohio.com

Hallzooween
Cincinnati, Oct
(513) 281-4700, (800) 944-4776
cincinnatizoo.org/events

Fall Festival of Leaves
Bainbridge, Oct
bainbridgeoh.com

Springboro Christmas Festival
Springboro, Nov
springborofestivals.org

Historic Clifton Mill Light Display
Clifton, late Nov to Dec
(937) 767-5501
cliftonmill.com/christma-lights/

Historic Lebanon Horse-Drawn Carriage Parade & Christmas Festival
Lebanon, Dec
(513) 932-1100
lebanonchamber.org

Stowe the account of a slave named Eliza who carried her children across the frozen, but thawing, Ohio River. Her bravery was rewarded—the bounty hunters pursuing her found the ice broken up by the time they reached the river the next morning, forcing them to abandon their chase. Stowe immortalized the story of Eliza in her book *Uncle Tom's Cabin*. Because of his influence in the abolitionist movement and his work as a conductor on the Underground Railroad, southern plantation owners offered a bounty for Rankin's life.

The John Rankin House is just off US 52, west of the central business district in Ripley at 6152 Rankin Hill Rd.; (800) 752-2705; ohiohistory.org/visit/browse-historical-sites/john-rankin-house/. Open Apr through Oct, Wed through Sun, 10 a.m. to 5 p.m.; closed Mon and Tues. Admission: adults $8; children $5.

For lunch or dinner in Ripley, stop by ***Cohearts Riverhouse***. Sisters Joanne May and Roberta Gaudio, veterans of the Cincinnati restaurant scene, restored this 1840s structure and opened for business in 1989. The second-floor screened porch offers a great view of the river. Cuisine uses produce from local farms, handmade pasta, and Amish cheeses. Dinner selections range from pasta and barbecue ribs to chicken, fish, and steaks. Lunch options include soups, salads, and sandwiches.

Cohearts Riverhouse is at 18 N. Front St., Ripley; (937) 392-4819; cohearts-riverhouse.edan.io. Open Fri 4:30 to 9 p.m.; Sat, 11:30 a.m. to 9 p.m.; Sun, 11:30 a.m. to 7 p.m. Personal checks accepted.

The modest but solid roots of Ulysses S. Grant (known as Hiram Ulysses Grant as a boy), commander of the Union forces during the Civil War and 18th U.S. president, are obvious when you visit ***Grant's Boyhood Home*** in rural Georgetown. Built by his father, Jesse Grant, in 1823, the home is designated a National Historic Landmark. The Grants expanded the home in 1825 and again in 1828. Grant lived here from the time he was a year old until he left to attend West Point at 17, the longest period spent at any residence during his lifetime.

Early nineteenth-century furnishings and Grant memorabilia are on display. The white gloves President Grant wore to his inaugural ball and a velvet dress belonging to his wife, Julia Dent Grant, are among the more noteworthy items.

A multiyear $1.4 million restoration of Grant's Boyhood Home was completed in 2013. The restoration returned the home to its appearance in 1839, the year Grant left for West Point. The two-room school attended by Grant can also be toured with the homestead. Built in 1829, the schoolhouse served as Georgetown's school until it was replaced in 1852.

U.S. Grant Boyhood Home & Schoolhouse at 219 E. Grant Ave., Georgetown; (877) 372-8177; usgrantboyhoodhome.org. May 1 to Oct 31, Wed through

Sun, noon to 5 p.m., Also open by appointment. Rates: adults $5; children (ages 6 to 12) $3.

Queen City

A three-room cottage was the birthplace of a man who would become the highest elected official in the land. The ***Grant Birthplace*** is a simple one-story home built in 1817. Hiram Ulysses Grant was born in the humble home five years later, on April 27, 1822. (Grant did not become "Ulysses S." until his application to West Point incorrectly identified him as such, a mistake with which he concurred.) Grant's father worked at a tannery, which was next to the Grant home.

Before the home was restored and preserved for all of us to visit, it was loaded on a railroad flatcar and transported on a tour around the United States. Now returned to its original site, it is open to the public and furnished in the style of the early 1800s.

The Grant Birthplace is at 1551 OH 232, Point Pleasant; (513) 497-0492; ohiohistory.org/visit/browse-historical-sites/u-s-grant-birthplace/. Open Apr through Sep, Wed through Sat, 10 a.m. to 12:30 p.m. and 1 to 5 p.m.; Sun, 1 to 5 p.m. Admission: adults $3; senior citizens $2; children (ages 6 to 12) $1.50.

Take time to walk through the historic Milford central business district. Housed in restored commercial buildings, stores on Main Street include early antiques and gift shops.

Valley Vineyards offers special holiday meals and cookouts on Friday and Saturday nights. In the warmer weather, July through October, they add Sunday dinners as well. In cold weather, the cookouts are actually cook-ins, using a huge indoor grill. The rest of the year, Valley Vineyards produces almost fifty fine wines from its 50 acres of American and French hybrid and vinifera grapes.

Grape growing and winemaking have been popular in southern Ohio for more than 150 years, and Ken Schuchter planted his first vines at Valley Vineyards in 1969. (Today, Valley Vineyards in managed by Ken's son and daughter-in-law, Kenny Joe and Dodie Schuchter, and his grandson, Joe Schuchter.) The winery, in a recent chalet-style building, offers a tasting tray with 1-ounce servings of nine wines—the perfect way to investigate and appreciate the vineyard's quality blends. I particularly enjoyed the Vidal blanc, the winner of many awards.

The winery has indoor and outdoor seating, with cookout dinners every Friday and Saturday throughout the year and on Sunday from July through October on the large patios. Reservations are required. Cheeseplates, pizzas

Ulysses S. Grant, First Ohio-Born Man to Become U.S. President

The president who gave America the federal Christmas holiday now has a special day of his own. In 2023, April 27 was officially named Ulysses S. Grant Day in his Ohio home state. Grant was born on that date in 1822.

Grant was born in Point Pleasant, Ohio, and originally named Hiram Ulysses Grant. A quiet, unassuming, and keenly intelligent man, Grant—at his father's urging—went to West Point when he was 17 years old.

Of his early cadet years, Grant wrote: "A military life had no charms for me, and I had not the faintest idea of staying in the army even if I should be graduated, which I did not expect."

It was at West Point that Hiram Ulysses Grant became Ulysses S. Grant due to a clerical error. In 1843, Grant graduated 21st out of 39 and planned to resign from the military after he served his mandatory four years of duty. During those years, Grant fought in the Mexican-American War where he was credited for bravery under fire.

Returning to civilian life, Grant moved his wife, Julia Dent Grant, and children to Missouri where he tried various jobs, including selling firewood on a St. Louis street. Eventually, Grant went to work in his father's tannery business as a clerk.

However, when Confederate troops attacked Fort Sumter on April 12, 1861, Grant answered the call of patriotism and volunteered for military service. He eventually was entrusted with the command of all U.S. armies in 1864. On April 9, 1865, Confederate General Robert E. Lee surrendered his army to Grant, marking the end of the Civil War.

The two generals met at a farm near Appomattox where a peace agreement was signed. In a magnanimous gesture, Grant allowed Lee's men to keep their horses and return to their homes, taking none of them as prisoners of war.

and other snacks are always available. The Schuchter family also creates craft beers under its label Cellar Dweller.

Valley Vineyards is on combined OH 22 and OH 3 at 2276 E. OH 22 and OH3, Morrow; (513) 899-2485; valleyvineyards.com. Open Mon and Tues, 11 a.m. to 6 p.m.; Wed, 11 a.m. to 9 p.m.; Thurs, 11 a.m. to 10 p.m.; Fri and Sat, 11 a.m. to 11 p.m.; and Sun, 1 to 6 p.m. Private cookouts year-round both indoor and outdoor. The House Dinner ($40 for adults) includes choice of NY strip, salmon, shrimp, or crab cakes, plus a bountiful buffet, dessert, and two drink tickets for any house wine, beer, or wine slushes. The Vintner Dinner for $50 includes a filet mignon with two premium drink tickets.

If you are looking for a unique shopping experience or for handcrafted eighteenth- or nineteenth-century reproduction furniture, then a trip to the

Hailed as a Civil War hero, Grant rode his popularity to the White House where in 1868 he was elected the 18th president of the United States. When he entered the White House, the Republican president was 46 years old, the youngest president up to that time. He went on to be elected president twice.

Although known as a man of honesty, Grant seemed to not be a good judge of character in others. As a result, his presidency was plagued by corruption. But as president, Grant also created the first National Park, pursued civil rights for African Americans, suppressed the Ku Klux Klan, and signed legislation in 1870 to create a federal Christmas holiday.

The move to celebrate Christmas was viewed as a way to unify the North and the South. At the time, some southern states had already embraced Christmas traditions while northern states generally ignored it as a result of their Puritan roots.

After leaving the White House, Grant again showed poor judgment by becoming a partner in a financial firm which went bankrupt. About that time, Grant was diagnosed with throat cancer. To pay off his debts and provide for his family, Grant began writing his memoirs. Racing against death, Grant died on July 23, 1885, just days after completing his last page.

Published by Grant's friend and admirer Mark Twain, the two-volume "Personal Memoirs of U.S. Grant" was immediately successful and earned more than $400,000 for his family. Grant's memoir is considered the finest military autobiography ever written.

Mourned by the nation, Grant was laid to rest in New York's Riverside Park, overlooking the Hudson River. Over 1.5 million people attended Grant's public funeral. Union, Confederate, and African American regiments marched in his honor. Stretching for miles, the procession took five hours to reach the burial site.

Five years later, Julia Dent Grant died and was placed in a matching sarcophagus inside the mausoleum beside her husband. The largest mausoleum in America, the facade of the tomb is inscribed with a quote attributed to Grant: "Let us have peace."

Workshops of David T. Smith should be on your itinerary. The site actually features many buildings housing woodworking and pottery areas. Visitors are welcome at the showroom and design center.

Each piece of furniture is unique and reflects a period of American furniture building. You can buy a simple table that looks like something the Pilgrims would have used during the first Thanksgiving or a Windsor chair with delicately turned legs. You could go home with a decorative spoon holder or contract to have your entire kitchen renovated with handmade cabinetry.

Pottery is also produced in the workshops. The potters specialize in Redware Pottery, formed from slabs of red clay that is either pressed into molds or thrown on a potter's wheel. Collectors will find a variety of pots, plates, lamps, and sculpture pieces from which to choose.

The Workshops of David T. Smith are at 3600 Shawhan Rd., Morrow; (513) 932-2472; davidtsmith.com. Open Tues through Sat, 10 a.m. to 5 p.m.

On December 23, 1803, Jonas Seaman received a license to operate a "house of public entertainment" at the site today occupied by one of Ohio's premier historic hotels, the ***Golden Lamb***. The present building replaced Seaman's cabin in 1815, and the Lamb now provides travelers with fine dining and period accommodations in picturesque Lebanon.

During its nearly two centuries, distinguished guests at the Golden Lamb have included ten American presidents, Henry Clay, Mark Twain (who performed at the Lebanon Opera House in the late nineteenth century), and Charles Dickens, who, it is told, complained vociferously during his visit in 1842 when informed the inn did not serve "spirits." Dickens would maintain his composure if he visited the Golden Lamb today, for the Black Horse Tavern provides complete bar service at the inn. And after some "refreshment," he might well enjoy browsing in the extensive gift shop on the lower level.

notsogoldrush

You missed the Ohio gold rush of 1868? Well, you didn't miss much. The discovery of what was thought to be gold at Batavia right after the Civil War set off a panic and prompted the establishment of the Batavia Gold Mining Company. Speculators sold shares in this venture for $100 each—big money in those days. Oh, there was gold here, but just minute traces too small to ever be profitably mined. The Batavia gold rush was over as quickly as it started.

With a reputation for serving challenging dishes, the Lamb offers a dinner menu that includes delights such as timbale of fillet of sole and salmon mousse with lobster sauce; roast duckling; broiled veal medallion topped with asparagus, crabmeat, and béarnaise sauce; and roast leg of spring lamb with mint jelly. More traditional entrees include steaks, ham, roast pork loin with dressing, and baked salmon. Lunch is also served at the Golden Lamb, with tasty soups, salads, and sandwiches, plus luncheon entrees including broiled petite filet mignon with béarnaise sauce and roasted chicken with dressing.

After eating in one of the four cozy downstairs dining areas, venture past the classy blue-gray lobby and up the stairs to the second floor. There you will discover five opulent private dining rooms. One is the Henry Clay Room (he visited the inn frequently on his trips between Kentucky and Washington, DC). Decorated in greens and pinks, this room is furnished with a gorgeous dark hardwood table and matching chairs for ten. With their splendid period pieces, these private dining rooms truly conjure up images of a bygone era.

The second floor also has the most expensive guest room at the inn—the Charles Dickens Room. The massive carved headboard towers 12 feet in the air, as do the mirror and frame on the marble-topped washstand. The third and fourth floors contain the other seventeen guest rooms, each unique in its appointments and named for one of the noteworthy guests who have stayed at the Golden Lamb. The De Witt Clinton Room, for example, is named for the New York governor who traveled to Lebanon in 1825 to attend the opening of the Ohio canal system, and it is furnished with a canopied four-poster bed and antique maple chests.

Ohio Renaissance Festival

Once upon a time in a kingdom about 5 miles east of Waynesville there was held the Ohio Renaissance Festival. In some ways, to call this a festival is a great understatement. From humble beginnings, a village of sorts has grown up in a farm field. Several streets of a 16th-century English village have evolved—and continue to evolve—into a real town of make-believe.

A king and queen reign over the town and over amazingly realistic jousting matches. Combatants actually mount horses and, in full armor, race toward each other and attempt to knock the opponent from his mount. One generally ends up bouncing on the ground (although we suspect that they probably decided who was going to take the blow before the match began). No blood is spilled, and no bones are broken, although falling from a galloping horse is a little rough on the body, even with choreography.

Throughout the village are more than 150 costumed shopkeepers and entertainers. Modern times do occasionally intrude in interesting ways. There is something a little odd about seeing a gentleman in tights and tunic holding a crossbow in one hand and a soft drink can in the other. A comical and talented array of performers entertains on several stages scattered throughout the village. Jugglers, tightrope artists, and a variety of clowns, magicians, and musicians take turns entertaining the crowds.

If you want to participate in medieval activities, you can buy a ticket and try the ax throw or spear chuck, or toss overripe tomatoes at the guy in the medieval equivalent of a dunk tank. There are plenty of unusual craft and artisan shops. Buy a talisman or a fake sword or a pouch to hang at your waist to hold your ducats. More modern souvenirs such as jewelry, glass art, and candles also are plentiful.

The Renaissance Festival is open weekends from September through October at 10542 E. State Route 73 from 10:30 a.m. to 7 p.m. Adults, $28; senior citizens, $25; children (ages 5 to 12), $10. A season pass is $80. Be prepared to park in a farm field and walk a bit to the "village gates." For specifics, call (513) 897-7000 or for tickets, (888) 695-0888. The website also provides a good deal of information: renfestival.com.

The fourth floor of the Lamb also houses the inn's Shaker museum, which is full of pieces collected from the former Shaker community called Union Village.

The Shakers migrated to Warren County from New Lebanon, New York, and established a religious communal village. But one of their religious convictions was celibacy, which doomed the sect to a relatively short existence.

Shaker furnishings are simple and functional, devoid of ornamentation. The Shaker Pantry has the characteristic wall pegs for hanging utensils, herbs, and even chairs not in use. The Shaker Retiring Room contains a simple rope-spring bed with trundle, a maple rocker, a pine cupboard, and a very rare Shaker embroidery hoop. Perhaps the most interesting display room—Sarah's Room—belonged to Sarah Stubbs, a young girl who came to live in the hotel with her aunt and uncle after the death of her father in 1883. The room has the furniture that was Sarah's more than 140 years ago.

The Black Horse Tavern menu features a wide array of delicious dishes, including sauerkraut balls—hand-rolled balls filled with a secret blend of spices and pork roasted with savory kraut and served with cocktail sauce and house mustard for an appetizer. "Historic Dining" choices include classic shepherd's pie with lamb, roasted local mushrooms, garlic, edamame, pearl onions, lamb stock reduction baked with goat cheese, and herb potatoes. Or try the Golden Lamb roast turkey dinner with brined and slow-roasted turkey breast, sage sausage and apple dressing, seasonal vegetables, cranberry chutney, mashed potatoes, and turkey gravy. The chateaubriand has slow-roasted beef tenderloin sliced and served with crushed red potatoes, sautéed leeks, bacon, aged white cheddar, roasted broccolini, and cabernet jus. (No reservations.)

The Golden Lamb is at 27 S. Broadway, Lebanon; (513) 932-5065; goldenlamb.com. Open daily for lunch and dinner except Christmas Day and the first week of January. Lodging rates: $129 to $169 per night.

If you are fascinated with unraveling the riddles of prehistory, you should visit ***Fort Ancient***. This prehistoric settlement is a significant archaeological site in North America. Two thousand years ago, Native Americans during the Hopewell culture built a walled enclosure, probably with crude digging tools, such as deer antlers or shoulder bones. The walls, which are earthen, run for 18,000 feet, and consist of 550,000 cubic yards of soil, which was transported in baskets, each capable of holding 35 or 40 pounds of earth. From the site, archaeologists have determined that parts of the walls were actually designed and constructed to align with the sun and the moon to create a calendar for the community. They believe that Fort Ancient served as a ceremonial and social center.

Visitors enjoy hiking the trails not only for the historic value of the site, but also for the beauty of the natural surroundings. The site also features the

Museum at Fort Ancient, which has numerous interactive exhibits and highlights 15,000 years of Native American history in the Ohio valley. A prehistoric garden demonstrates crops grown 2,000 years ago.

Fort Ancient is at 6123 OH 350, Oregonia; (513) 932-4421, (800) 283-8904; ohiohistory.org/visit/browse-historical-sites/fort-ancient-earthworks-nature-preserve/. Open Apr through Nov, Tues through Sat, 10 a.m. to 5 p.m.; Sun, noon to 5 p.m.; Dec through Mar, Sat, 10 a.m. to 5 p.m.; Sun, noon to 5 p.m. Admission: adults $7; senior citizens $6; children (ages 6 to 17) $6. Grounds only, $8 per vehicle.

With more antiques shops per square mile than any other city or town in Ohio, Waynesville is a browser's paradise. It has more than forty individual shops, plus three large buildings where dozens of dealers display their goods on consignment, and it has become a major antiques marketplace, attracting out-of-state buyers and Ohioans alike. Waynesville's antiques boom started inauspiciously in the mid-1960s with the opening of a handful of shops, but the number has grown steadily ever since. Now many of the town's commercial buildings, a substantial number of former residences, and even one of the town's churches house antiques stores—in fact, on one block on Main Street, there are nine shops in a row!

Among the many quality shops, one favorite is at 105 S. Main St.: ***Lilly's Corner Mall***. Originally Waynesville's first automotive garage and movie theater, the building was constructed in 1917. The Kilpatrick Garage and the Miami Theater shared the space. When the theater opened to much fanfare on February 16, 1918, movie fans flocked to see *A Poor Little Rich Girl* starring Mary Pickford. Admission was a dime, plus a penny "War Tax." Lilly's Corner Mall still has the original 22-foot-high wood ceiling as well as the original wood cornices. Lilly's Corner Mall is open Tues through Sat 11:30 a.m. to 5 p.m.; Sun noon to 5 p.m.; lillys-corner-mall.business.site; (513) 897-0388.

Caesar Creek Lake and the surrounding recreation area are managed by the Army Corps of Engineers primarily as a flood-control project. However, the 2,830-acre lake provides terrific recreation opportunities. The 1,200-foot-long beach welcomes swimmers, and the lake is a great place for fishing or boating. Remember to bring your fishing license if you want to try your luck at hooking bluegill, saugeye, crappie, largemouth, smallmouth, white, or spotted bass.

The visitor center is a good place to begin your trip to Caesar Creek Lake. It provides an overlook of the park and the dam and has lots of educational information about various features of the lake and the recreation area, including trail maps. The more than 10,000 acres of wildlife area include forests, meadowlands, and the Caesar Creek Gorge with rushing waters. Visitors enjoy day hikes. Trails range from a 3-mile, easy-to-moderate hike to a 13-mile trek for the serious hiker. Backpacking in the park area is allowed, but you need to stop at the visitor center and get a permit first. The area is also a favorite for bikers and horseback riders.

You can also pick up a free permit and directions to prepare you for a fossil hunt. The fossils here date back to the Ordovician age, when Ohio was covered by a shallow ocean. When a spillway was excavated, the area that was disturbed became a great fossil-hunting zone. Brachiopods (which look like seashells) and the remains of cephalopods (which resemble today's octopuses) are chief among the fossils you can discover on your hunt. This is one of the only areas where you can legally remove fossils and keep them as souvenirs of your adventures. If you are planning to bring a group along for picnicking, five shelters are available for $75 for weekends and federal holidays and $35 for weekday. Be sure to call ahead to check availability and to reserve the shelter. To reach Caesar Creek Lake recreation area, take exit 38 west off I-71 or exit 45 east from I-75. The visitor center is at 4020 N. Clarkesville Rd., Waynesville; (513) 897-1050; caesarcreekstatepark.com. While recreation may be the current focus of the Caesar Creek Lake area, its history is rich and long. This region was home to the prehistoric Native American tribes, the Hopewell and Adena, and later to the Miami and the Shawnee.

According to local historians, Caesar Creek was named for a Black slave, Caesar, who was captured by the Shawnee. The Shawnee must have been favorably impressed by Caesar—they gave him the area around Caesar Creek as his hunting ground. The villages that grew up in the area in the 1700s and 1800s became a Quaker settlement and an important stop on the Underground Railroad, supporting the flight of slaves on their way to freedom in the North.

When the Army Corps of Engineers was clearing land and preparing to dam the river in 1978, log homes dating back to the 1700s were found in the woods. These historic buildings were moved to the ***Caesar's Creek Pioneer Village***. Some of the buildings in Pioneer Village were actually erected there and stand on their original sites. Walking through the reconstructed village, visitors can see the log cabins, as well as some of the homes built in the early 1800s, the Quaker meetinghouse, and the tollhouse. The grounds are open daily, but the houses are only open on special occasions or if you prearrange a tour. Pioneer Village is in Waynesville, on the southeast side of Caesar Creek Lake. From Waynesville, go east on Route 73 for about 1 mile. Turn right on Clarksville Road, then left on Oregonia Road, then left again on Pioneer Village Road. The Village is at 3999 Pioneer Village Rd., Waynesville; (937) 705-0785; ccpv.us.

It will take a little effort to visit the ***Harveysburg Free Black School***. The school is not regularly open to the public, but tours can be arranged by calling (513) 897-6195.

This unassuming one-room schoolhouse has a special place in Ohio history. It was the first free school for Black children in the state. Jesse and Elizabeth Harvey, the founders of Harveysburg, founded the school in 1831 after finding out there were no educational opportunities for Black children. The Quaker community supported the school that allowed Black and Native children the then-rare opportunity to enter elementary school and continue in that tiny schoolhouse until they received a high school diploma.

The schoolhouse is a simple brick structure with a modest cupola on the roof to house the school bell. The school was acquired by the Harveysburg bicentennial committee in 1976 with a mission to preserve it as a part of the community's history. Primers, historical documents, and slate blackboards remain from this important chapter in the history of education and the search for freedom in Ohio.

The school, at 23 North St., serves as the Harveysburg Community Historical Society's headquarters. Contact the Harveysburg Historical Society at (513) 897-6195; ohiolha.org/member organization/harveysburg-community-historical-society/. Open by appointment. Admission is $5 for adults and $3 for children.

Many visitors to Warren County are attracted to the area because of southern Ohio's most popular amusement park complex: ***Kings Island***. Its eight themed areas, dozens of rides (including fourteen coasters!), live shows, international shops, and restaurants delight the millions who visit the park during its late-April-through-October season.

Soak City is a 30-acre water park with a massive 650,000-gallon wave pool and more than fifty water activities.

Planet Snoopy is a fun collection of rides and attractions with the theme of Peanuts cartoon characters for every age, including four kids' roller coasters. Planet Snoopy also features a live stage show and daily times to meet beloved Peanuts characters Charlie Brown, Linus, Peppermint Patty, and, of course, loveable beagle Snoopy.

Adventure Port, added in 2023, features two new family rides, Enrique's quick service restaurant, and the Mercado. The theme of Adventure Port involves the myths of an ancient civilization and its mighty city carved out of stone. Included is the Sol Spin ride, which looks like an immense sun disk created by an ancient civilization. Guests are welcome to climb aboard the open-air, suspended vehicle to experience the thrill of flying 60 feet through the air at 25 mph.

Kings Island is at 6300 Kings Island Drive, Mason; (800) 288-0808; visit kingsisland.com. Admission starts at $44.99.

A 1930s train station that houses three superior museums and an OMNIMAX theater? That's the incomparable ***Cincinnati Museum Center***. This magnificent, 500,000-square-foot Art Deco railroad station, built in 1933 as a center of regional travel, is now a center of fine exhibits and spectacular film showings. During its heyday as a rail hub, hundreds of trains arrived and departed from here each day. And while it is still an Amtrak station (one eastbound and one westbound daily, both in the middle of the night; call Amtrak at 800-872-7245), the crowds gather now not to greet passengers, but rather to discover the past.

One attraction at the Cincinnati History Museum is the world's largest S-scale city model, called "Cincinnati in Motion." It combines model trains with trolleys, homes, and city buildings. Interpreters help take the visitor back in time and tell the story of Cincinnati and its early days as a bustling river town. Children will find their own kind of fun at the Duke Energy Children's Museum, where they can explore interactive exhibits that use simple machines, balls, and a water play area to stimulate young imaginations. The Museum of Natural History and Science has walk-through re-creations of limestone caves and an Ice Age exhibit, as well as a Fossil Prep Lab that lets visitors observe scientists at work.

The Robert D. Lindner Family OMNIMAX Theater wraps you in sight and sound, highlighted by a five-story, 72-foot, domed screen. Dramatic films that depict flight and rapid travel appear to pull you into the action, while spectacular landscapes completely surround you.

In 2016, a $212.7 million restoration project began at the museum. The two-year restoration made repairs to the interior and exterior. As part of the project, The Center for Holocaust and Humanity Education was moved into Union Terminal.

Cincinnati Museum Center is at 1301 Western Ave., Cincinnati; (513) 287-7000, (800) 733-2077; cincymuseum.org. Open Thurs through Mon, 10 a.m. to 5 p.m. Closed Tues and Wed. Admission: adults $17.50, senior citizens $13.50; children (ages 3 to 12) $13.50. The OMNIMAX Theater requires a separate ticket, or the purchase of a ticket that combines the entrance fee for the museum and the theater. Call for OMNIMAX show times and ticket prices.

European elegance with a musical backdrop graces the intimate ***Symphony Hotel and Restaurant***. The full-service bed and breakfast welcomes guests into a graceful 1871 building, furnished in turn-of-the-twentieth-century antiques but modernized to provide private baths, telephones, televisions, and air-conditioning. A European-style breakfast also is included in the room rate.

The Symphony Hotel is across the street from the Cincinnati Music Hall, which was constructed in 1878. The musical theme continues into the hotel. Each of the nine guest rooms is dedicated to a composer, including Mozart, Brahms, Bach, and Beethoven. The dining room serves a special fixed-price,

ALSO WORTH SEEING

Cincinnati Art Museum

Cincinnati Zoo and Botanical Gardens

Irwin M. Krohn Conservatory, Cincinnati

Dayton Art Institute

3- or 5-course meal prior to performances at the music hall. Dinner guests must make reservations in advance. Reservations can also be made for special events such as parties, meetings, or luncheons.

The Symphony Hotel is at 210 W. 14th St., Cincinnati; (513) 721-3353; symphonyhotel.com. Rates: $161 to $259. Complimentary parking for guests.

One of the finest small art museums in the nation, the ***Taft Museum of Art*** is a National Historic Landmark. Built in 1820, this federal-period building is home to nearly 700 works of art, including the work of European and American Masters. However, this stunning building served first as a residence for Martin Baum. During his ownership of the property from 1829 to 1863, Nicholas Longworth began a tradition of artistic patronage that was expanded by the last private owners of the house, Charles Phelps Taft and Anna Sinton Taft. They acquired and decorated their home with treasures ranging from French Renaissance enamels and Italian decorative arts to Chinese porcelains and European and American oils.

The home and collections were donated as a gift to the people of Cincinnati in 1927, and the house opened as a museum in November 1932. With its slender Tuscan columns, the Taft Museum is a federal-period country villa. The central section of the structure features delicate elliptical windows, while the southeast facade has a distinctive upper and lower columned porch.

The collection includes works by such masters as Rembrandt, Hals, Gainsborough, Sargent, Ruisdael, Turner, and Corot. There's an extensive presentation of French Renaissance Limoges enamels and watches of the seventeenth and eighteenth centuries.

The Lindner Family Cafe at the Taft Museum offers light lunches as well as wine and beer. The exhibitions provide inspiration for the cafe's culinary staff. For example, the Louis Comfort Tiffany art exhibition inspired the Smoked Trout Mousse, a tasty combination of mousse of smoked trout, Neufchatel cheese, and caramelized onion accompanied by crostini, egg, capers, and pickles. The menu description notes it is the sort of lunch that could have been enjoyed at the Waldorf-Astoria a hundred years ago. "Imagine overhearing

Home of Baseball's First Professional Team—The Cincinnati Reds

"People will come, Ray. The one constant through all the years, Ray, has been baseball."

—James Earl Jones' character in *Field of Dreams*

Hearing the number of hits that Pete Rose made during his baseball career is impressive. Seeing them is mind boggling.

A 50-foot-tall "wall of balls" at the Cincinnati Reds Hall of Fame and Museum brings home that staggering fact. Arranged in rows, the three-story wall has 4,256 baseballs for the record set by Rose in 3,562 games over 24 seasons.

"Each ball represents one of Pete Rose's record number of hits," said Mark Harlow, ticket operations manager at the museum.

Although the legendary Rose is not included in the Baseball Hall of Fame, he was inducted into the Cincinnati Reds Hall of Fame in 2016. Rose spent most of his career with the Reds and was their manager when he agreed to a baseball ban in 1989 following an investigation into his gambling. Investigator John Dowd detailed 412 baseball wagers by Rose between April 8 and July 5, 1987, including 52 on Cincinnati to win.

Growing up in Ohio with the Reds as my home team, I was looking forward to seeing the renovated museum and the Great American Ball Park. However, the place is not only for Reds' fans. It is for anyone who loves baseball.

"It all started in 1869 when the Cincinnati Red Stockings emerged as baseball's first team of professional ballplayers," Harlow said. "Some cynics said it wouldn't last."

But the Red Stockings conducted themselves in such a gentlemanly fashion and played at such a remarkable level of skill—they boasted a 57-0 record—that professional baseball soon spread throughout the country.

That's not the only first for the Cincinnati Reds. They also hosted the first night game. On May 24, 1935, President Franklin Delano Roosevelt threw the light switch from the White House 600 miles away and the Reds beat the Philadelphia Phillies at Crosley Field. Although the first class of Hall of Fame inductees was enshrined nearly 50 years ago, the hall never had a real home until 2004. The facility opened to the public in 2004, and has been drawing fans ever since.

Located next to the Great American Ball Park—the Reds' home—in downtown Cincinnati, the museum is a great place to spend an afternoon. The ball park itself is something to see and park tours are offered. Situated on the winding banks of the Ohio River, the park has a pair of smokestacks, a salute to the Queen City's riverboat heritage.

"The smokestacks shoot off fireworks for a Reds home run and when the Reds win a game," Harlow said. "The smokestacks shoot out flames when the opposing team strikes out."

The stacks also serve as one of many tributes throughout the park to fallen Reds hero Rose. Seven bats bending outward are atop each stack. That makes 14 bats atop the stacks, the number on Pete Rose's uniform.

A large statue of Rose sliding into base also honors "Charlie Hustle" in front of the stadium located on Pete Rose Way. Born April 14, 1941, in Cincinnati, the story goes that Rose got his nickname during a spring training game against the New York Yankees in his 1963 rookie season.

Rose drew a walk and sprinted to first, prompting Whitey Ford and Mickey Mantle to yell from the dugout, "There goes Charlie Hustle." Rose was an integral part of the famed "Big Red Machine," the Reds team that from 1970 to 1976 won five division titles, four National League pennants, and two World Series championships.

Historic artifacts include the final-out baseballs from the Reds first (1919) and most recent (1990) World Series championships. Caught by Todd Benzinger as the Reds swept the Oakland A's in four games, the 1990 ball usually draws admirers.

The 1919 ball, however, is the most valuable artifact on display, according to Harlow. "That's a ball that 'Shoeless' Joe Jackson hit," he said. "The last one."

Shoeless Joe of the Chicago White Sox was accused of taking part in throwing the 1919 World Series against the Reds, along with seven of his teammates. Jackson reportedly accepted an envelope containing a $5,000 payoff and, although he could not read or write, signed a confession that he later refuted. Acquitted by a jury of his peers, Jackson was still banned from baseball and, ultimately, the Hall of Fame.

Jackson obtained the nickname "Shoeless" because he once had a pair of spikes that were too tight during a game so he took them off and played the game in his socks. Jackson died of a heart attack in 1951 at the age of 64.

On display are the design and various styles of uniforms during the years of both the Reds and their opponents, including a jersey belonging to Ted Kluszewski with its cut-off sleeves. The popular slugging first baseman who played for the Reds in the 1950s claimed the tight sleeves constricted his swing.

An extensive baseball card archive draws a great deal of interest. A fun interactive for visitors is getting to make a baseball card with the visitor's photo. An interactive in the broadcast section of the museum includes a Marty Brennaman and Joe Nuxhall feature where visitors can sit at a studio desk and feel like they are on TV and record calling a highlight and have the recording emailed to them.

The focal point of the Hall of Fame is a 360-degree interactive theater and gallery that honors all 89 inductees and trophies from the Reds' five World Series wins. Visitors can select and play rousing profiles of each honoree.

"We get visitors from everywhere," Harlow said. "Baseball fans are all ages and never outgrow that love."

Contact the Cincinnati Reds Hall of Fame & Museum at (866) 800-1275, mlb.com/reds/hall-of-fame

Tiffany himself, the next table over, discussing his plans to install windows at William James's house," the menu said. When the weather is good, dine on the garden patio. The cafe is open Wed through Sun from 11 a.m. to 2:30 p.m. Reservations recommended. Call the cafe at (513) 352-5140.

The Taft Museum of Art is at 316 Pike St., Cincinnati; (513) 241-0343; taftmuseum.org. Open Wed through Fri, 11 a.m. to 4 p.m.; Sat and Sun, 11 a.m. to 5 p.m. Admission: adults $12; college students, teachers, and senior citizens $10; children (ages 18 and under) free. Admission is free every Sun. The museum has free on-site parking.

Letters from President ***William Howard Taft's*** mother to her relatives in the east proved invaluable in the restoration of Taft's childhood home. The ***William Howard Taft National Historic Site*** was the childhood home of the 27th U.S. president. It is Greek revival in design; square and symmetrical with decorative trim. The home has been restored and is much as it must have been in the mid-1800s. The Taft family has provided many personal effects, including portraits and books that would have been in the Taft household when the young William was growing up.

Congress designated the house a National Historic Site and monument to the president in 1969, and placed it under the administration of the National Park Service. The William Howard Taft National Historic Site is at 2038 Auburn Ave., Cincinnati; (513) 684-3262; nps.gov/wiho. Open daily 8:30 a.m. to 4:45 p.m. Guided tours are every 30 minutes. The last guided tour of the day starts at 3:45 p.m. Closed on holidays. Free parking. No entrance fee.

In 1833, the daughter of the new president of Lane Seminary moved into a stately residence on the campus. This house, the ***Harriet Beecher Stowe House***, has now been renamed to acknowledge the legacy of the former resident.

Harriet Beecher Stowe wrote the landmark story *Uncle Tom's Cabin*, which dramatically portrayed the cruel and dehumanizing effects of slavery. The Stowe House is now a Black history, education, and cultural center.

The Harriet Beecher Stowe House is located at 2950 Gilbert Ave., Cincinnati; (513) 751-0651, (800) 847-6057; stowehousecincy.org. Open Fri and Sat, 10 a.m. to 4 p.m.; Sun, noon to 4 p.m. Hours are expected to be expanded. Check for operating hours before visiting. Admission: adults $6; senior citizens, $5; children (ages 6 to 17) $3.

If you're in the mood for mouth-watering barbecued ribs and chicken, plus ice-cold beer, try Ted Gregory's ***Montgomery Inn***. This popular restaurant claims to serve the "world's greatest ribs," a designation with which few customers would argue. Although the menu at the Montgomery Inn does include selections such as steaks, pork chops, and fillet of sole, the restaurant is known for tender ribs and chicken dripping with a zesty sauce.

While waiting in the bar for your table, you'll see photographs of the likes of Tommy Lasorda and Billy Carter displayed on the wall, each autographed and extolling the virtues of Ted Gregory's barbecue. On the rough wood paneling in the comfortable dining rooms are photos and paintings of Gregory's other passion—horse racing. You'll even find some bridles and jockeys' shirts displayed throughout the inn.

For those unable to decide between barbecued ribs and barbecued chicken, try some of each with the half-and-half dinner, which is served with crisp tossed salad and the inn's famous Saratoga chip potatoes. The management thoughtfully provides bibs for those partaking of the sauce-laden barbecue.

If you're not hungry for barbecue (which seems inconceivable once you experience the aroma in this restaurant), other menu selections include Cantonese-style fried Oriental shrimp with sweet 'n' hot sauce, Wisconsin's Pride duckling, and a number of sandwiches (including a barbecued beef sandwich).

The Montgomery Inn is at 9440 Montgomery Rd. (exit 12 off I-71), Montgomery; (513) 791-3482; montgomeryinn.com. Open Tues through Thurs, 4 to 9 p.m.; Fri, 4 to 10 p.m.; Sat, 3 to 10 p.m.; Sun, 3 to 9 p.m. Founded in 2003, the ***Tri-State Warbird Museum*** set lofty goals for itself, including being recognized as one of the most-admired museums dedicated to military and historic aviation. This museum honors both the pilots and planes that defended America during wartime, particularly during World War II. The planes and exhibits on display pay tribute to our rich military aviation history, recognizing the creativity, commitment, and sacrifice of so many during the crucial conflict in the 1940s.

Among the collection are such treasures as the P-51D Mustang, Cincinnati Miss. Smartly painted with a black-and-yellow checkered nose and yellow tail sections, she represents the definitive version of the P-51 single-seat fighter. Powered by a supercharged Merlin engine to a single prop, the D version delivered 1,695 horsepower, had a maximum speed of 437 miles per hour, a service ceiling of 41,800 feet, and a combat range of 1,000 miles. This long-range fighter aircraft entered service in 1943, featured six .50-caliber machine guns, and is still regarded as one of the best piston-engine fighters ever built. Nearly 8,000 P-51 D/K Mustangs were built.

Another mid-war entrant was the TBM-3 Avenger. Aptly named, the Avenger was designed and built to retaliate against the Japanese Navy after its attack on Pearl Harbor. Grumman and General Motors produced 9,836 Avengers, equipping them with a power-operated gun turret, heavy 22-inch torpedoes, bombs, rockets, and depth charges. The Wright Cyclone 14 engine delivered 1,726 horsepower, giving the Avenger a maximum speed of 276 miles per hour, a ceiling of 30,100 feet, and a range of more than 1,000 miles. It was a torpedo attack by British-flown Avengers that sank two of the world's largest

Unusual Swing House B&B Recalls Joyful Childhood Pastime

With a strong push, I soared higher and higher. Zoomed over the kitchen. Glided over the bedroom.

For real.

The Swing House is one of the most unusual places I have ever seen. On the outside, the blue 1880 house in the Camp Washington neighborhood of Cincinnati looks like most of the other historic homes around it. Inside is a different story.

Smack dab in the middle of the living room is a swing attached by 30 feet of natural fiber rope to a metal beam in the home's three-story ceiling. To make it even more fun, guests are invited to visit and stay in this swinging house.

Who in the world thought of this and how did he turn it into a reality?

A local artist named Mark de Jong says it took him three years to build the Swing House. But it had been his dream for decades. De Jong just took a detour into the construction business to earn a living before heading to his true passion for art.

"I stopped making art for 20 years and worked in construction instead, so this house was my leap back into the art world," he said.

De Jong did seem destined to become an artist. Born in the Netherlands, de Jong moved to Cincinnati with his family when he was a child. "My mom was a potter," he said. "She was in art school and always brought me around to her studio and art school. Being around my mother and other artists was my real inspiration point."

His mother also bought a warehouse in 1980 for use as her studio across the street from the house that de Jong would later turn into the Swing House. "I helped her work on that warehouse when I was 14 years old and that's what started my love for houses and buildings," he said. "

In his 20s, de Jong took classes at the University of Cincinnati's prestigious School of Design, Architecture, Art, and Planning (DAAP). He also graduated from Alfred University in New York. After years in the construction business, de Jong decided it was time to meld his construction and artistic skills to create the Swing House, which he opened to the public in the summer of 2017. "I could fix up a house and sell it as I had done, but the Swing House was a conscious decision not to sell it, to share it with people," he said.

battleships, the Japanese Musashi and Yamato in October 1944 and April 1945, respectively.

An equally proud member of the museum's collection is its twin-engine B-25 Mitchell bomber. Approximately 10,000 of these bombers were built by North American Aviation. Although designed for bombing runs at medium altitudes, they frequently were used for treetop-level missions against Japanese airfields

Today, guests can rent the one-bedroom, one-bathroom house for overnight stays.

For the unusual project, de Jong removed the house's interior wall and upper floors. The swing is made from pine that de Jong salvaged from third floor joists. On the ceiling, de Jong painted a black-and-white hourglass shape, a reminder of the passing of time in the pendulum-like swing.

Part of the fun of the swing is bending backwards to enjoy looking at the hourglass while, perhaps, remembering the freedom and joy of childhood swings. The light and airy main floor of the home is an immense open space with a kitchen, living area, and bedroom that flow from one to the other.

De Jong planned very carefully for the movement of the swing in the middle of the room. "The kitchen is in the front of the house," he said. "Somebody could be making dinner while someone was swinging overhead and never bother the kitchen. Or somebody could be sleeping in the bed and not be interrupted by somebody swinging over the bed."

The wood furniture in the house was constructed by de Jong from reused house material and other sources. Finding wall outlets and power switches along the walls is easy because de Jong used red-pigmented plaster to trace pathways to them.

A staircase leads to the basement where the bathroom and art gallery are located. Some of the artistic sculptures in the gallery were constructed by de Jong from remnants of the house. A series of children's drawings made by former residents were found by de Jong during the renovation. The drawings are now framed with material from the house and hanging on a gallery wall.

Also discovered in the house, Super 8 video footage of the same family is projected on another wall. During the demolition process, a stuffed Kermit the frog dropped out of the ceiling. Due to the top-heavy imbalance of his eyes, Kermit landed on his head, which is why de Jong displays Kermit upside down in the art gallery.

As for the future, de Jong has other special house projects in mind. "I absolutely love what I am doing," he said. "Every day is enjoyable to me because I am satisfied to be doing what I love."

Contact the Swing House at 513-325-6625, swing-house.com. The second Saturday of each month, the Swing House is open to the public from noon to 4 p.m. No admission fee.

and shipping in the Pacific. Powered by twin Wright Cyclone engines, each producing 1,850 horsepower, the B-25 had a top speed of 275 miles per hour, a combat range of 1,350 miles, and a ceiling of 25,000 feet. The most famous wartime use of B-25s was the 1942 Doolittle Raid, where pilots flew off the aircraft carrier USS *Hornet*, bombed Tokyo, and then crashed in China. It was also a B-25 that collided with the Empire State Building in New York City in 1945.

Many pilots in the US Navy, Air Force, and Marines and the British Royal Air Force learned to fly at the controls of a T-6 Texan. A total of 15,495 Texans, a single-engine, advanced trainer aircraft designed by North American Aviation, trained tens of thousands of wartime pilots. The museum's yellow and red Marine AT-6D version—Tweety—features a 600-horsepower radial engine, with a maximum speed of 208 miles per hour and a range of 730 miles.

Another common trainer was the Stearman Model 75 biplane. The museum's bright blue and yellow one is an excellent example of this popular trainer, originally built during the 1930s. Its rugged construction and open-air dual cockpit seating made it a popular crop duster and leisure aircraft once the war concluded.

One of the most intriguing exhibits at the 20,000 square-foot Tri-State Warbird Museum is not even an airplane. It's the ANT-18 Link Trainer. This was the first flight simulator trainer, built of wood in 1932 by Edwin A. Link, who used bellows and other parts from his father's Link Piano and Organ Company.

World War II produced a tremendous demand for new pilots, and cadet pilots could become proficient in instrument flying in fifty hours using the ANT-18. By the end of the war, 10,000 of the trainers had been built, teaching many of the 190,000 pilots trained in the United States during World War II.

The museum also honors Cincinnati-area military aviation veterans, such as Tom Griffin, who flew with Lieutenant Colonel Jimmy Doolittle, and Russell B. Witte Jr., a B-25 bomber pilot with more than fifty missions flying from North Africa over Sicily and Italy. He was awarded the Distinguished Flying Cross and nine Air Medals. Many of the museum's aircraft are still airworthy and can often be found at regional air shows and similar events.

The Tri-State Warbird Museum is at 4021 Borman Dr., Batavia; (513) 735-4500; tri-statewarbirdmuseum.org. Open Wed, 4 to 7 p.m.; Sat, 10 a.m. to 3 p.m. Admission is $12 for adults, $7 for students and veterans. Admission is free for World War II veterans and all veterans in uniform.

The founders of the Mariemont Company designed and constructed the village of Mariemont as a totally planned community modeled after the "garden city" villages in England. In the 1920s, they envisioned Mariemont as a rural alternative to bustling Cincinnati nearby.

Although it's no longer in the country (Mariemont is now in the suburban ring surrounding Cincinnati), this quaint village, with its Tudor commercial buildings and peaceful, tree-lined residential neighborhoods, does provide the tranquil existence sought by its founders. The entire village is listed on the National Register of Historic Places.

The ***Mariemont Inn***, a member of Historic Hotels of America, offers visitors a charming place to imbibe, dine, and spend the night. It is set facing the circle in the center of the commercial business district, and the striking Tudor exterior is rivaled by the interior decor in this classic structure. Each of the 45 guest rooms contains the dark, heavy woods and rich colors typical of the Tudor period; the spacious suites come furnished with ornate canopy beds, and there are antiques throughout the inn. Your day starts off with complimentary coffee or juice, delivered to your room at your convenience.

Visitors unwind in Southerby's Pub, a cozy old-English pub. The popularity of the National Examplar dining room for breakfast, lunch, and dinner with area residents and businesspeople speaks for the excellent food. An innovative breakfast-brunch-lunch menu featuring omelets, homemade soups, fine salads, and a wide selection of sandwiches is served from 7 a.m. until 2:30 p.m. Dinner is served Mon through Thurs, 5 p.m. to 9 p.m.; Fri and Sat, 5 p.m. to 10 p.m.; Sun, 5 p.m. to 9 p.m. The varied dinner selections include fresh seafood, pasta, veal, and many great steaks, with appetizers and desserts to accompany these dishes. The inn is now part of the Best Western hotel group.

The Mariemont Inn is at 6880 Wooster Pike (US 50), Cincinnati; (513) 271-2100, (877) 271-2211; bestwesternmariemontinn.guestreservations.com. Lodging rates: from $185 to $259 per night.

After your meal, enjoy a stroll, jog, or bike ride in the picturesque village, or stop by the gift shop, bookstore, ice-cream parlor, or other shops adjacent to the inn. Though downtown Cincinnati is only 15 minutes from Mariemont, when you're walking through this peaceful community, the big city seems worlds away.

It is the last of its kind in Clermont County. The ***Stonelick Covered Bridge*** has become not just an icon of a bygone era but a magnet for tourists and the inspiration for local artists. This covered bridge, also known as the Perintown Covered Bridge, was built in 1878, restored in 1971, and placed on the National Register of Historic Places in 1974. The 140-foot-long bridge is supported by an impressive 12-panel Howe Truss system, patented by William Howe in 1840. This system uses vertical iron rods instead of vertical timber posts, and crossed timber members forming the familiar X-shaped supports. The bridge spans Stonelick Creek.

The bridge is home to an urban legend where the apparition of a hanging man can be summoned. Legend says that to do the summoning, a motorist must stop on the bridge near its only window, turn off the vehicle's engine, and flash the vehicle's headlights three times. Then look out the window to see the apparition of a man hanging by his neck in the trees. Supposedly, the vehicle will not start again until the hanging man disappears.

It is said that motorists flash their vehicle headlights when crossing the bridge to warn other motorists about oncoming traffic on the one-lane bridge.

It is also rumored that drivers ensure their vehicle windows are securely rolled up before entering the bridge.

The Stonelick Covered Bridge is on Stone-Williams Corner Road (CR 116) in Clermont County, 0.2 mile west of the junction of US 50 and OH 222 (go north on Stone-Williams Road).

Take a drive off the beaten path to the small Clermont County town of ***Bethel***, population 2,635. Founded in 1798 by Obed Denham in what was then the Northwest Territory, the settlement was called Denham Town. In 1802, the name was changed to Bethel after a city in the Bible where Jacob built an altar to God. The name Bethel means "House of God."

Grant Memorial Building Honors U.S. President Ulysses S. Grant

Smack dab in the middle of Bethel is the Grant Memorial Building at 235 W. Plane St. The Grant Memorial Building was dedicated in 1930 to the memory of Civil War hero Ulysses S. Grant who served two terms as U.S. president from 1869 to 1877.

Born April 27, 1822, in Point Pleasant, Grant was appointed as a 17-year-old to West Point in 1839. In 1841, Grant's father, Jesse Grant, bought a house on the northwest corner of Water and Charity streets in Bethel. Jesse then opened a tannery on the southwest corner of Charity and Water streets.

In the summer of 1841, Ulysses spent his furlough from West Point with his family in Bethel. "Those ten weeks were shorter than one week at West Point," Grant later wrote.

In 1851, Jesse Grant became the first mayor of Bethel. A year later, Ulysses' son, Ulysses S. Grant, Jr., was born on July 22, 1852, in Bethel. At the time of his son's birth, Ulysses had been ordered to move with the 4th U.S. Infantry to the west coast so his pregnant wife, Julia Grant, was making her way back to her childhood home in St. Louis.

When Julia stopped to visit her husband's family in Bethel, her baby chose that place to be born. Ulysses Jr. was given the nickname "Buck" for his birth in the "Buckeye State" of Ohio. Serving in the Army, Ulysses would not get to see his son until the baby was more than one and a half years old.

Inside the Grant Memorial Building is an interesting museum operated by the Bethel Historical Society. Of course, many photos and other items honor Ulysses S. Grant who led the Union army to victory in the Civil War. Other Civil War items in the museum include photos of Clermont County soldiers, an ammo box, and a plate honoring Newark, Ohio, drummer boy, Johnny Clem. Born Aug. 13, 1851, Clem was the Union army's youngest recruit.

The museum's other military items include World War II artifacts, such as a Japanese flag and sword from a Japanese prisoner and a German officer's weapon and holster. The

To learn more about Bethel history, visit the Bethel Historical Society Museum in the Grant Memorial Building. For a relaxing picnic or leisurely walk, stop by Burke Park at 120 N. Main St. The grounds for Burke Park were donated in 1923 by Edmund Glenn Burke who made his fortune selling real estate.

A stone shelter house with a stone fireplace in Burke Park was built by the Works Progress Administration (WPA), a program created by President Franklin Delano Roosevelt in 1935 to employ men to build public works projects. The park also was a Civilian Conservation Corps camp during the 1930s when the government program was created to give men a job during the Great Depression. The land reverted to a park in 1937.

museum also features local businesses, schools, and churches, as well as exhibits on some prominent citizens through the years.

A well-worn backpack honors a local Bethel man, Steven M. Newman, who set out to walk the world. At age nine, Newman had dreamed of such an exploit. At age 28, a journalist and onetime oilfield worker, Newman set out to make his dream a reality. Leaving from his Bethel home on April 1, 1983, Newman walked the world, unsponsored, paying his own way. Four years later in 1987, he had achieved his goal - hiking about 15,500 miles across 21 nations on five continents to become the first man to ever walk the globe.

Newman is listed in the Guinness Book of World Records for being the first person documented to walk solo around the world. Along the way, he endured life-threatening episodes – a blizzard in the Pyrenees, wild boars in Algeria, a flash flood in Australia – and he was arrested in Algeria, Yugoslavia, and Turkey.

Newman has written numerous magazine and newspaper articles about his adventures, plus several books including the popular 1989 *Worldwalk*. The book title was taken from the nickname bestowed upon Newman during his long trek.

Other museum items donated by local townspeople include a large Native American ax head formed from a big rock. Donated by my younger brother, Joe Michael Poynter, the ax head was given to Joe by our father, Smiley Jack Poynter, when Joe was seven years old. Dad had found the ax when he was doing local construction work in 1957/58. As an adult, Joe felt the relic belonged in the Bethel museum.

Joe now lives on the Ute Indian Reservation in Colorado where he served as director of Bayfield Early Education Programs. "Living on a Native American reservation, I have learned to respect relics," he said. "The first settlers in Bethel were the Native Americans. It was one of their favorite hunting grounds so I gave the relic to the museum for the public as part of our local history."

The museum is open 1 to 4 p.m. the first and third Saturday of the month or by appointment. Call (513) 734-0145 or visit bethelohiohistorymuseum.com. Free Admission.

The historic ***Benninghofen House*** on North Second Street was built in 1862 for Hamilton lawyer Noah C. McFarland, who served as district senator from 1866 to 1868. He lived in the house 12 years, then sold it to John Benninghofen in 1874. Built of brick with iron elements, the Benninghofen House is a high-quality Italianate structure. The home was placed on the National Register of Historic Homes in 1973.

The Beninghofen House itself is a wonderful reflection of the times, but the visitor also will find various collections in the home noteworthy. Civil War enthusiasts will want to note the field desk, sword, and flag from the Ohio Volunteer Infantry. Dolls, surveying equipment, pottery, and vintage furniture all provide color and life to this slice of Ohio history. The Benninghofen House is at 327 N. Second St., Hamilton; (513) 896-9930; bchistoricalsociety.com. Guided tours are available Tues through Fri, 10 a.m. to 4 p.m.; Sat, 9 a.m. to 2 p.m. Admission: $5 adults.

For a bit of confusion, the city of Hamilton boasts another Benninghofen House located at 807 Dayton St. Built in 1892 by Christian and Anna Benninghofen, the stunning home has intricate woodwork, beautiful fireplaces with Hamilton and Rookwood tile, and wonderful stained-glass windows. Michael and Bekki Rennick bought the home in 2015 and transformed it into a boutique hotel with an event space and four short-term rental spaces. It's definitely worth a drive by to see this remarkable house. Call (513) 275-9990, benninghofenhouse.com.

When most of us think of a museum of sculpture, we don't even begin to imagine what awaits us on a visit to the ***Pyramid Hill Sculpture Park and Museum***. Yes, there are 60 interesting pieces to view and ponder, but they are set in a 355-acre arboretum. This is one of the four largest sculpture gardens in the nation. Your leisurely walk down three well-marked trails takes you past gardens, seven lakes, and a wide variety of trees. You'll even see the remains of a nineteenth-century stone pioneer home.

These outdoor features provide a backdrop for the nearly three dozen

mt.healthy

In 1817, John La Boiteaux and Samuel Hill founded Mt. Pleasant in Hamilton County. Although the town was known as Mt. Pleasant for years, the post office urged the residents to rename it, to avoid confusion with the "other Mt. Pleasant." They did, choosing Mt. Healthy as the new name in gratitude for being spared the cholera epidemic that struck Cincinnati in the late 1840s.

Cincinnati lost 7 percent of its population to cholera in 1849, during the nineteenth century's second global epidemic of this once-terrifying disease. Ohio had become vulnerable for the first time due to increased contact with travelers from other parts of the country and the world.

sculptures. Some, like *Eve* by Marc Mellon, are traditional. *Age of Stone* by Jon Isherwood evokes the feeling of a mystic place filled with ancient druids. The park also features a series of one-way roads that allow visitors to view the art from their private cars. The park provides bus tours, but you need to make a reservation for this guided tour. Pyramid Hill offers many special children's programs in the summer months, as well as music programs that provide a blending of arts that will enchant the entire family.

The park also features a 10,000-square-foot Ancient Sculpture Museum with Etruscan, Greek, Egyptian, and Roman sculpture thousands of years old. The Ancient Sculpture Museum is open daily, noon to 5 p.m.

The Pyramid Hill Sculpture Park and Museum is 3 miles southwest of Hamilton on OH 128 at 1763 Hamilton-Cleves Rd.; (513) 861-1234, (513) 868-8336; pyramidhill.org. The park is open daily from 9 a.m. to 5 p.m. Museum hours are daily from noon to 5 p.m. Admission: adults $10; children (ages 6 to 12)

Sorg Opera House Ghost

Since 1891 the Sorg Opera House has been a place where the starstruck come and linger. More than 100 years ago, a wealthy entrepreneur, Paul Sorg, built the theater. Famous actors and grand productions were invited to the Middletown stage to perform with Jeannie Sorg, Paul's wife and a great fan of the performing arts.

Over the life of the theater, the likes of George M. Cohan and Bob Hope have taken their place on center stage. It became a movie house in the 1920s and hosted the first "talkie" shown in town. A fire damaged the building in 1935, but it was renovated and reopened four years later.

The legend of the theater centers on Paul Sorg. As owner, the well-dressed business baron is reported to have always claimed the best seat in the house when he attended performances. In the 1890s those seated in the orchestra or the first balcony arrived at the opera house in full evening dress. Paul Sorg was a fixture at his theater, dressed in fashionable garb and seated in his favorite seat in the first row of the first balcony.

Through the years and even today, staff and patrons sometimes claim they catch a glimpse of the nattily attired Sorg taking his place in the first balcony. When asked to describe the man, many ghost spotters have described him as he appears in his portrait, which hangs in the theater lobby. Sometimes only his footsteps are heard crossing the stage or walking overhead on the catwalks. So, while actors and actresses have come and gone, the first owner maintains his star status as the legend of the Sorg Opera House.

The Sorg Opera House is located at 63 S. Main St., Middletown; sorgoperahouse.org. Musical events are scheduled throughout the year.

$5. Known as "Art Carts," golf carts can be rented to tour Pyramid Hill. Cost is $25 for the first hour and $20 each additional hour.

Picture a thoroughfare of pumpkins. In the autumn, you can walk past hundreds of pumpkins at the ***Barn 'n' Bunk Farm Market***. In warmer weather, the market is filled with bedding plants, hanging baskets, and Amish-made lawn furniture, as well as farm-fresh produce. The market grew out of the family farm of Bev and Tom Theobald.

The century-old barns now house a variety of shops. More than fifty local crafters provide items from candles and baskets to birdhouses and furniture pieces. On the sweeter side, you can also indulge in honeys, jellies, candies, Amish baked goods, and even ice cream. Weekends in September and October feature special fall displays and events, and the market puts on its finest for visitors in the days before Christmas.

The Barn 'n' Bunk Farm Market is on OH 73 and Wayne Madison Road at 3677 Wayne Madison Rd. in Trenton; (513) 988-9211; barnnbunk.com. Open Mar 22 to Dec 23, Mon through Sat, 10 a.m. to 5 p.m.; Sun, 10:30 a.m. to 5 p.m.

Invention Trail

The community of Miamisburg has the largest conical burial mound in Ohio—the ***Miamisburg Mound***. Artifacts excavated from this 68-foot-high mound, which contains 54,000 cubic yards of earth, indicate the Adena Indians built it sometime between 1000 BC and AD 100. With a circumference of nearly 900 feet at the base, the mound had two burial vaults: one 8 feet from the top of the mound containing a bark-covered skeleton, the other 36 feet down and surrounded by logs but without any skeletal remains.

Visitors to the mound, which today is overgrown with brush and trees, can climb 116 steps to the top of this impressive earthwork for a splendid view of the Miami Valley. A 36-acre park encircles the mound, with picnic tables, barbecue grills, and shelter houses.

The Miamisburg Mound is 1 mile south of OH 725 at 900 East Mound Rd., Miamisburg; (866) 580-6508; ohiohistory.org/visit/browse-historical-sites/miamisburg-mound/. Open daylight hours; no admission charge.

Just south of downtown Dayton, along the Great Miami River, is the landmark ***Deeds Carillon***, a 151-foot-high, 57-bell carillon that stands at the entrance to ***Carillon Historical Park***. Dedicated in 1942, the carillon was given to the people of Dayton by Colonel Edward Deeds and his wife, Edith. Concerts delight audiences from May through October.

In addition to the bells, this 65-acre park has an outstanding group of exhibit buildings, primarily dedicated to Dayton's invention, transportation, and settlement history. The museum's crown jewel has to be the 1905 Wright Flyer III in Wright Hall, a National Historic Landmark and part of the Dayton Aviation Heritage National Historic Park. Weighing 855 pounds, this plane was the world's first practical aircraft and was described by Orville Wright as the plane in which he and Wilbur learned to fly. Two years after their historic 1903 flights at Kitty Hawk, Wilbur stayed aloft in the Flyer III for 39 minutes at an average speed of 38 miles per hour. Orville Wright later supervised the initial restoration of this aircraft.

Deeds Barn, a replica of the carriage house that stood behind Colonel Deeds's home, houses exhibits that underscore the contributions of Deeds and his friend and contemporary Charles F. Kettering. It was on the second floor of the original barn that Kettering and his "barn gang" revolutionized automobile ignition and lighting systems, and the barn contains a 1912 Cadillac, the first production auto to feature these innovations. Kettering and Deeds went on to found Dayton Engineering Laboratories Company (later called Delco). Kettering's early inventions at National Cash Register Company and Deeds's later accomplishments in developing the Liberty aircraft engine also are displayed.

The two-story log building called ***Newcom Tavern***, Dayton's oldest existing building, was the home of George Newcom. It also served as Dayton's first courtroom. The tavern includes many of its original items, such as the china used by Colonel and Mrs. Newcom, and the colonel's favorite rocking chair.

Other displays in Carillon Historical Park include locomotives and railroad cars, a restored canal lock and covered bridge, a working 1930s print shop, and a replica of the Wright brothers' bicycle shop. The Dayton Sales Company automobile showroom has a 1910 Speedwell, a 1923 Maxwell, and a very rare 1908 Stoddard-Dayton.

Carillon Historical Park is at the intersection of Patterson and Carillon Boulevards, east of I-75 at the Edwin Moses/Nicholas Road exit, Dayton; at 1000 Carillon Blvd; (937) 293-2841; daytonhistory.org. The park is open Mon through Sat, 9:30 a.m. to 5 p.m.; Sun, noon to 5 p.m. (Closed on major holidays.) Admission: adults $14; senior citizens $ 12; children (ages 3 to 17) $10.

Dayton's historical sites provide interesting glimpses into the lives and work of some of its most famous citizens. The final resting place of some of these notables, ***Woodland Cemetery and Arboretum***, is also a quiet spot to reflect on their contributions. This cemetery is one of the five oldest rural garden cemeteries in the country. The 100-acre arboretum and cemetery was planned as the city of Dayton grew, and opened in the 1840s. Such places provided a peaceful alternative to burial in highly populated urban centers. In this cemetery are the graves of poet Paul Laurence Dunbar, both Orville and Wilbur Wright, Ohio governor James Cox, and writer and humorist Erma Bombeck.

Visitors enter the cemetery through the impressive Romanesque gateway and chapel. This imposing structure was built in 1889, has an original Tiffany stained-glass window, and is listed on the National Register of Historic Places. This structure also houses the administrative offices where visitors can find walking tour maps or borrow a CD player and headset that provides an audio tour of Woodland's highlights. Special tours can be arranged by calling ahead; special events are listed on the website. More than 3,000 trees and 10,000 monuments are found on the grounds. Some memorials are modern in design, such as the 29,000-pound structure forming the monument for writer Erma Bombeck. Others are more traditional, with statuary of angels, cherubs, and urns or replicas of Greek or Egyptian temples. Some, like the grave of the child Johnny Morehouse, reflect poignant stories. This memorial pictures the faithful dog that pulled the child from a river after he had fallen in, but too late to save him.

Victoria Theatre

Some of the attractions of the historic Victoria Theatre in Dayton are easy for the visitor to see and appreciate. The turn-of-the-twentieth-century building is graced by lavish period touches, such as gilt trim and green marble pillars. But another attraction is a bit more elusive.

According to legend, the ghost of a young actress occasionally makes an appearance behind the glass and bronze doors of the Victoria. The young lady is winsome, wearing a 1900s black taffeta dress nipped in at the waist and draped softly to the floor. She has a penchant for appearing in the mirror of one of the third-floor dressing rooms.

It is from that dressing room, the legend says, that the ghost, nicknamed Vickie, made her final dramatic exit. In the middle of a production, Vickie is supposed to have forgotten a fan she needed in the next scene and so told the other actors she was returning to the dressing room to get it. She was last seen climbing the stairs. She never returned to the stage. She just vanished.

Did Vickie sneak out of the theater to join a lover? Did she meet with foul play? No one knows for sure, but theatergoers and staff say that she still remains, in spirit.

The door to the fabled dressing room seems to have a mind of its own, and feminine footsteps sometimes can be heard tripping lightly on the stairway. If you hear the rustle of taffeta, detect the scent of rose perfume, or feel the light brush of a young lady passing close to you, then you, too, have experienced the continuing performance of Vickie. Check the website at daytonlive.org/venues/Victoria-theatre/

Woodland Cemetery and Arboretum is located at 118 Woodland Ave., Dayton; (937) 228-3221; woodlandcemetery.org. Open daily, 8 a.m. to 7 p.m. in the summer; daily 8 a.m. to 6 p.m. in the winter. No admission charge.

Art lovers, families, art historians, and those just looking for a glimpse of the unusual can find just what they're looking for at the ***Dayton Art Institute***. Located in downtown Dayton, overlooking the Great Miami River, the impressive Italian Renaissance–style museum features an extensive collection of more than 12,000 objects spanning 5,000 years of art history. Highlights include an outstanding Asian collection, seventeenth-century Baroque paintings, and eighteenth- and nineteenth-century American art collections. In addition, the institute features innovative exhibits, including a hands-on family "Experiencenter," which let visitors experience art in a new and participatory manner.

The Dayton Art Institute also exhibits some objects never before seen in galleries dedicated to Native American and Oceanic art forms. In addition to the extensive permanent collections, the institute hosts world-class special and traveling exhibits, and art-related educational and cultural events. The historic building also houses an education resource center and an art reference library.

The Dayton Art Institute is located at 456 Belmonte Park North, Dayton; (937) 223-4278; daytonartinstitute.org. Open Wed, Fri and Sat, 11 a.m. to 5 p.m.; Thurs, 11 a.m. to 8 p.m.; and Sun, noon to 5 p.m. Closed Mon and Tues. Admission: adults $15; senior citizens $10; college students (with ID) and children (ages 7 to 17) $5; free for children 6 and under. Visitors unable to pay the admission are welcome to tour the museum's permanent collection galleries free of charge.

The ***Paul Laurence Dunbar House*** was the first state memorial in Ohio dedicated to an African American. This distinction seems fitting, since Paul Laurence Dunbar is often referred to as the poet laureate of African Americans. The turn-of-the-twentieth-century home of Italianate design was the poet's final residence.

The son of former slaves, Dunbar used his writing to portray the dilemmas faced by a recently freed but still disenfranchised people. Dunbar died at age 34 in 1906, but his mother lived in the Dunbar House until 1934. Thanks to her care in preserving her son's belongings, visitors can view many of his original works and personal items as well as many of the family furnishings.

The Paul Laurence Dunbar House is located at 219 Paul Laurence Dunbar St., Dayton; (937) 225-7705, (800) 860-0148; ohiohistory.org/visit/browse-historical-sites/paul-laurence-dunbar-house/. Open Fri, Sat and Sun, 10 a.m. to 4 p.m., or by appointment. Free admission.

Making science fun is the mission of the ***Boonshoft Museum of Discovery*** in Dayton. Formerly the Dayton Museum of Natural History, today

Boonshoft uses a hands-on, interactive environment to foster interest in and understanding of all things scientific.

Travel through time and space at the Caryl D. Phillips Space Theater, where an advanced computer graphics system projects stunning skylines and impressive galaxies. On stage at the Oscar Boonshoft Science Central's Science Theater are live performances showcasing mind-boggling scientific stunts. The Boonshoft also houses an extensive collection of 1.4 million real animal specimens and artifacts, including live animals at the indoor Charles Exley Jr. Wild Ohio Zoo, complete with a variety of native Ohio wildlife such as coyotes, river otters, and bobcats. Other favorite exhibits include the Tidal Pool and the Sonoran Desert. For a bird's-eye view of the museum's outdoor amphitheater and lush woodland trails, kids climb the MeadWestvaco Treehouse.

The Boonshoft Museum of Discovery is at 2600 DeWeese Parkway, Dayton; (937) 275-7431; boonshoft.org. Open Mon through Sat, 9 a.m. to 5 p.m.; Sun, noon to 5 p.m. Admission: adults $14.50; senior citizens $12.50; children (ages 3 to 17) $11.50.

For a look at more modern modes of transportation, be sure to see the more than 300 aircraft and missiles displayed at the impressive ***National Museum of the United States Air Force***. With 17 acres of exhibit space in the three main hangar-type buildings, plus the Presidential and Research/Development Galleries, this may be the world's most complete aviation museum. From a Wright Brothers original to an Apollo space capsule, the museum contains an incredibly comprehensive collection of flying machines. Spads, Camels, Spitfires, Mustangs, the B-29 that dropped the atomic bomb on Nagasaki in 1945, and the enormous Strategic Air Command B-36 bomber—all these are in one museum.

Located only 3 miles from where the Wright Brothers tested their early designs, the museum, in addition to the aircraft, balloons, and missiles, has hundreds of exhibits that chronicle the history and milestones of military aviation. The newest hangar focuses on the Cold War era to the present day, and features a B-1B bomber, an F-117 Stealth fighter, and a B-2 Spirit stealth bomber. Also new is the Hall of Missiles, including a collection of intercontinental ballistic missiles. And there is an outstanding IMAX theater, which shows spectacular aviation-related films.

For dining, the museum offers the Valkyrie Café and the Refueling Café. Both are open daily from 10 a.m. to 4:30 p.m. Named after the legendary XB-70, the Valkyrie Café offers salads, pizza, and other light snacks. The Refueling Café is known for its three new Signature Dogs–100 percent, ¼-pound hot dogs nestled in a warm pretzel bun and topped either with mac and cheese, coleslaw, or chili with cheese, peppers, and onions.

The National Museum of the United States Air Force is at Wright-Patterson Air Force Base, off OH 4 northeast of Dayton at 1100 Spaatz St.; (937) 255-3286; nationalmuseum.af.mil. Open daily except Christmas, Thanksgiving, and New Year's Day, 9 a.m. to 5 p.m. No admission or parking charge except for the Museum Theater and flight simulators.

The newest addition to the National Park System's Dayton Aviation Heritage History Park is the ***Huffman Prairie Flying Field***. While the Wright Brothers may have taken that first flight at Kitty Hawk, this field was where they tested and perfected their flying machines and their flying skills. The experimental planes, the Flyer II, built in 1904, and the Flyer III, built in 1905, were tested on this prairie land. Along with testing airplanes, this plot of land was also home to the Wright Company flying school from 1910 to 1916, the first flight school in the world. A hangar, similar to the one you would have seen if you visited the Wright brothers, has been erected on the site. In addition to the historic value of the field to flight buffs, this area is also the largest remaining remnant of prairie land in Ohio.

Huffman Prairie Flying Field is located at Gate 16A of Wright-Patterson Air Force Base off OH 444; (937) 225-7705; nps.gov/daav. Open Wed through Sun, 9 a.m. to 4 p.m. Closed Thanksgiving, Christmas, and New Year's Day. Admission: free.

Ohio is rich in ancient cultures. One of the best ways to learn more about one of these cultures is to visit ***SunWatch Indian Village/Archaeological Park***, a reconstructed Native American village. This twelfth-century village was rebuilt based on the archaeological findings discovered on this site. You'll see pottery and other artifacts typical of the village's era.

The village is named SunWatch because of the advanced system of charting time developed by the village's original inhabitants. During summer months, reconstruction continues at the site, in search of more clues to the past. In season, you'll observe planting, harvesting, house construction, and the manufacture of various artifacts.

SunWatch Indian Village/Archaeological Park is at 2301 W. River Rd., Dayton; (937) 268-8199; boonshoft.org/sunwatch-2/. Open Apr through Nov, Tues through Sat, 9 a.m. to 5 p.m.; Sun, noon to 5 p.m. Open Dec through Mar, Sat and Sun, 10 a.m. to 4 p.m. Admission: adults $7; senior citizens $6; children (ages 6 to 16) $6.

Daniel Arnold established his 158-acre family farm in 1830 and constructed a farmhouse six years later. The Arnold family worked the farm until 1910, and today this entire farmstead is being restored to its appearance in the 1880s. It's called ***Carriage Hill Farm Museum***, and it is part of Carriage Hill MetroPark.

The farmhouse contains furnishings typical of a nineteenth-century conservative farm family—quilting frame, wood-burning cook stove, and firebox—while bubbles and imperfections in the house's window glass identify it as original. During hot weather, the Arnolds prepared their meals at the outdoor "summer kitchen" to avoid further heating the farmhouse; on many weekends, volunteers now use the cookstove in the summer kitchen to bake fresh bread.

Other demonstrations at Carriage Hill include a blacksmith who operates the old blower, and a woodworker who shapes furniture on a foot-powered lathe.

Like any 1880s farm, Carriage Hill has a variety of farm animals: cattle, chickens, horses, sheep, and pigs. The horses are used to giving hayrides through the reserve's lush meadows and woods. Hiking and bridle trails also wind through the park's acreage. Special events such as square dances, cider pressing, and old-fashioned wheat threshing take place throughout the year at Carriage Hill.

Carriage Hill MetroPark is at 7800 E. Shull Rd., north of I-70 off OH 201, Dayton; (937) 278-2609; metroparks.org/places-to-go/CarriageHill.

The park is open daily Apr through Oct, 8 a.m. to 10 p.m. and Nov through Mar, 8 a.m. to 8 p.m. Closed Christmas and New Year's Day. The farm museum is open Apr through Oct Tues through Sat, 10 a.m. to 5 p.m.; Sun, noon to 5 p.m.; and Nov through Mar, Tues through Sun, noon to 4 p.m. Closed on Thanksgiving, Christmas, and New Year's Day. No admission charge.

You have to give ***Historic Clifton Mill*** credit—it has burned down twice, but it has always come back. The first water-powered gristmill at this site on the Little Miami River was built in 1802. Called Davis Mill for its founder, Owen Davis, this first mill prospered until destroyed by fire in the 1840s. But a year or two later, a second mill was erected here, a mill that did its part for the Union army by providing cornmeal and flour to federal troops during the Civil War.

This mill, however, burned down about the time the Confederacy was defeated. In 1869 the Armstrong family built a third mill on this site, which they sold to Isaac Preston twenty years later.

Three generations of Prestons operated the mill until 1948. And although it avoided catching fire again, Clifton Mill did sit idle, deteriorating for fifteen years, until Robert Heller bought it and breathed life into it once again. The Satariano family acquired the mill in the mid-1980s, expanding it. A covered bridge now spans the gorge, providing spectacular views.

Today visitors enjoy self-guided tours of this impressive six-story powerplant. The huge James Leffel Company turbine on the lowest level, installed in 1908, once provided electricity for farms, homes, and businesses in Clifton, Cedarville, and Yellow Springs at a very modest $1 per month per customer.

Clifton Mill grinds flour, cornmeal, and pancake mix as it has for decades, a process you observe during your tour. And meal and flour, along with home-made breads, pies, and other pastries, are available for purchase, as are fine jams, jellies, syrups, teas, spices, and other specialties. Clifton Mill also serves breakfast, soups, sandwiches, and salads, plus ice cream. On a nice day, take your meal or snack out on the Millrace Deck, and listen to water rushing under your feet on its way to the turbines. At Christmastime the mill is radiant with 2.6 million lights. There's an enormous collection of Santa Clauses and a 100-foot waterfall of lights.

Historic Clifton Mill is at 75 Water St. (OH 72), Clifton; (937) 767-5501; cliftonmill.com. Mill tours at $3 are offered Mon through Fri during spring and summer from 10 a.m. to 2 p.m. The restaurant and gift shop are open Mon through Fri, 9 a.m. to 2 p.m.; Sat and Sun, 8 a.m. to 3 p.m. Closed on Thanksgiving, Christmas, and New Year's Day.

Designated a National Natural Landmark by the National Park Service, the ***Clifton Gorge Nature Preserve*** rates as some of Ohio's most beautiful public land. Over the years, the swift Little Miami River has carved a deep gorge through the thick forest, a process started by the raging meltwaters of the last retreating glacier. The power of the river once turned the wheels of two gristmills in the area—Clifton Mill (described above) and a second mill, the remains of which are still visible in the gorge.

Given the clean vertical drops of the limestone cliffs, Clifton Gorge ranked high with rock climbers until that activity was banned in 1982. Concern for the nearly 350 different wildflowers in the park, which provide an unparalleled spring display, prompted the rock-climbing prohibition.

The preserve has miles of hiking trails along both rims of the gorge and following the river at the floor of the canyon. The adjacent John Bryan State Park contains eleven additional hiking trails, campsites, and picnic areas.

Clifton Gorge Nature Preserve is on OH 343, just west of Clifton at 2331 OH 343. The entrance to John Bryan State Park is on OH 370, near Clifton; (937) 767-1274; https://ohiodnr.gov/go-and-do/plan-a-visit/find-a-property/clifton-gorge-state-nature-preserve. Open daylight hours; no admission charge.

Another fabulous natural area is Antioch College's ***Glen Helen***, a 1,000-acre preserve and outdoor education center adjacent to the college's Yellow Springs campus. Designated a National Natural Landmark by the National Park Service in 1965, Glen Helen has a thick regrown forest canopy, a full array of woodland wildflowers, and undisturbed native wildlife. Scenic features include valleys carved by glacial meltwater, ledges, potholes, cascades, and the Yellow

Spring, from which the village gets its name. Flowing at 70 gallons per minute, the spring has built a distinctive hill of travertine deposits that extends from the cliff line down to the valley floor. Numerous hiking trails permeate the landscape.

Nearly two-thirds of Glen Helen is thickly wooded, and the balance is mowed meadow and planted prairie—a diversity that creates varied habitats for many species of animals and birds. A 2½-mile stretch of the beautiful, free-flowing Little Miami River courses through the glen.

One unique feature of this preserve is its Raptor Center. Here injured birds of prey—hawks, owls, falcons, eagles, osprey, and vultures—are nursed back to health for their return to the wild. The center also serves as a public education facility, permitting visitors to view and better understand these marvelous creatures. The website for the Glen Helen Ecology Institute at Antioch University posts a calendar of events that are open to the general public. These events include wildflower walks, birding walks, and reptile feeding adventures.

Glen Helen is accessible from OH 343 just east of Yellow Springs, or from the Trailside Museum, 405 Corry St., Yellow Springs; (937) 769-1902; glenhelen.org. Open year-round, daylight hours. No admission charge.

Known as a hotbed of antiwar and counterculture activity in the 1960s and early 1970s, Yellow Springs remains slightly eccentric. The marchers and demonstrators have been replaced by potters and shopkeepers, but Antioch College still provides the youthful emphasis of this uncommon community.

Ohio is home to the ***National Afro-American Museum and Cultural Center***, a repository for preservation, study, and interpretation of the traditions, values, social customs, and experiences of African Americans. The museum's permanent exhibit, From Victory to Freedom, chronicles the period from 1945 to 1965—from victory in World War II to freedom through the passage of federal civil rights legislation. Photographs and artifacts re-create a period of social struggle and dramatic change. Particularly impressive is the award-winning film *Music As Metaphor*, which presents the inspiring African-American music of the period and features artists such as Paul Robeson, Fats Domino, Dizzy Gillespie, and many others.

The first phase of this museum opened in 1988, and it is bordered by a scenic wooded area. Additional phases of development are planned. In 2013 a new art exhibit opened that showcases how African Americans have used art to mobilize communities to action in civil rights efforts. The title, "How I Got Over," is from a song sung by Mahalia Jackson after Dr. Martin Luther King Jr. gave his "I Have a Dream" speech in 1963.

The National Afro-American Museum and Cultural Center is at 1350 Brush Row Rd., Wilberforce; (937) 376-4944, (800) 752-2603; ohiohistory.org/visit/

browse-historical-sites/national-afro-american-museum-cultural-center/. The museum is open Wed through Sat, 9 a.m. to 4 p.m. Admission: adults $6; senior citizens $5; college students with ID $3; children (ages 6 to 17) $3.

Places to Stay in Southwest Ohio

CHILLICOTHE

Atwood House Bed & Breakfast
68 S. Paint St.
(740) 774-1606
atwoodhousebandb.com

Christopher Inn & Suites
30 N. Plaza Blvd.
(740) 774-6835
christopherhotels.com

The Willis-James Bed & Breakfast
58 W. Fifth St.
(740) 229-9019
thewillisjames.com

CINCINNATI

Gaslight Bed & Breakfast
3652 Middleton Ave.
(513) 861-5222
gaslightbb.com

The Clifton House
500 Terrace Ave.
(513) 221-7600
thecliftonhouse.com

Graduate Cincinnati
151 Goodman Dr.
(513) 487-3800
graduatehotels.com

The Inn of Hyde Park
3539 Shaw Ave.
(513) 321-2824
innofhydepark.com

Kinley Cincinnati Downtown
636 Race St.
(513) 381-1100
marriott.com

The Lytle Park Hotel, Autograph Collection
311 Pike St.
(513) 621-4500
marriott.com

The Mariemont Inn
6880 Wooster Pike
(513) 271-2100
bestwesternmariemontinn.com

Renaissance Cincinnati Downtown Hotel
36 E. Fourth St.
(513) 333-0000
marriott.com

Six Acres Bed & Breakfast
5350 Hamilton Ave.
(513) 541-0873
sixacresbb.com

The Summit Hotel
5345 Medpace Way
(513) 527-9900
thesummithotel.com

The Symphony Hotel and Restaurant
210 W. 14th St.
(513) 721-3353,
(888) 281-8032
symphonyhotel.com

21c Museum Hotel
609 Walnut St.
(513) 578-6600
21cmuseumhotels.com

DAYTON

Inn Port Guesthouse
22 Brown St.
(937) 224-7678
innport.com

LEBANON

Brian Manor
129 W. State Route 122
(513) 836-3071
brianmanor.net

Golden Lamb
27 S. Broadway St.
(513) 932-5065
goldenlamb.com

MASON

Great Wolf Lodge Water Park
2501 Great Wolf Dr.
(800) 913-9653
greatwolf.com

HELPFUL WEBSITES

Ohio Division of Travel and Tourism
ohio.org

Cincinnati Convention and Visitors Bureau
visitcincy.com

Cincinnati Enquirer
cincinnati.com

Dayton Convention and Visitors Bureau
daytoncvb.com

Kings Island
visitkingsisland.com

PORTSMOUTH

Shawnee State Park
OH 125, 12 miles west of Portsmouth
(740) 858-6652,
(800) 217-2481
shawneeparklodge.com

WEST UNION

The Murphin Ridge Inn
750 Murphin Ridge Rd.
(937) 544-2263
themurphinridgeinn.com

XENIA

John Allen House Bed & Breakfast
209 E. Second St.
(937) 347-3203
johnallenhouse.com

WILMINGTON

General Denver Hotel
81 W. Main St.
(937) 383-4141
generaldenver.com

YELLOW SPRINGS

Arthur Morgan House
120 W. Limestone St.
(937) 761-1761

Grinnell Mill Bed & Breakfast
3536 Bryan Park Rd.
(937) 767-0131
grinnellmillbandb.com

Jailhouse Suites
111 N. Winter St.
(937) 319-1191
jailhousesuites.com

Mills Park Hotel
321 Xenia Ave.
(937) 319-0400
millsparkhotel.com

Three Ten Bed & Breakfast
310 Dayton St.
(937) 546-0184
threetendbedandbreakfast.com

Places to Eat in Southwest Ohio

CHILLICOTHE

Hana Japanese Steakhouse
1015 N. Bridge St.
(740) 779-9009
hanasteakhouse.com

Hometown Hibachi
59 N. Paint St.
(740) 771-4705
hometownhibachi.net

Old Canal Smoke House
94 E. Water St.
(740) 779-3278
oldcanalsmokehouse.com

7 Miles Smokehouse
285 E. Seventh St.
(740) 851-4015
7milessmokehouse.com

The Pour House at Machinery Hall
25 E. Second St.
(740) 771-4770
pouronchillicothe.com

CINCINNATI

Abigail Street
1214 Vine St.
(513) 421-4040
abigailstreet.com

Bakersfield
1213 Vine St.
(513) 579-0446
bakersfieldtacos.com

The Capital Grille
3821 Edwards Rd.
(513) 351-0814
thecapitalgrille.com

Goose & Elder
1800 Race St.
(513) 579-8400
gooseandelder.com

Krueger's Tavern
1313 Vine St.
(513) 834-8670
kruegerstavern.com

Maplewood Kitchen & Bar
525 Race St.
(513) 421-2100
maplewoodkitchenandbar.com

Moerlein Lager House
115 Joe Nuxhall Way
(513) 421-2337
moerleinlagerhouse.com

Montgomery Inn The Boathouse
925 Riverside Dr.
(513) 721-7427
montgomeryinn.com

Nicola's
1420 Sycamore St.
(513) 721-6200
nicolasotr.com

Pepp & Dolores
1501 Vine St.
(513) 419-1820
peppanddolores.com

Salazar Restaurant
1401 Republic St.
(513) 621-7000
salazarcincinnati.com

Sotto
118 E. Sixth St.
(513) 977-6886
sottocincinnati.com

DAYTON

Amber Rose Restaurant & Catering
1400 Valley St.
(937) 228-2511
theamberrose.com

Dublin Pub
300 Wayne Ave.
(937) 224-7822
dubpub.com

Grist
46 W. Fifth St.
(937) 802-4544
eatgrist.com

Jollity
127 E. Third St.
(937) 938-9089
jollitydayton.com

Lily's Dayton
329 E. Fifth St.
(937) 723-7637
lilysdayton.com

Oakwood Club
2414 Far Hills Ave.
(937) 293-6973
theoakwoodclub.com

Pine Club
1926 Brown St.
(937) 228-7463
thepineclub.com

Roost Modern Italian
525 E. Fifth St.
(937) 222-3100
roostitalian.com

Salar Restaurant & Lounge
400 E. Fifth St.
(937) 203-3999
salarrestaurant.com

Wheat Penny Oven & Bar
515 Wayne Ave.
(937) 496-5268
wheatpennydayton.com

HAMILTON

Basil 1791
241 High St.
(513) 883-1019
basil1791.com

Billy Yanks
205 Main St.
(513) 844-0130
billyyanks.com

Fretboard Brewing & Public House
103 Main St.
(513) 737-1111
fbpublichouse.com

Hyde's Restaurant
130 S. Erie Blvd.
(513) 892-1287
hydesrestaurant.com

LEBANON

Broadway Barrel House
402 N. Broadway St.
(513) 934-7799

The Golden Lamb
27 S. Broadway St.
(513) 932-5065
goldenlamb.com
Lodging is also available.

Greenhouse Café
105 E. Mulberry St.
(513) 934-7248
greenhousecafeohio.com

Toki Japanese Steakhouse
726 E. Main St.
(513) 409-5571
tokilebanon.com

MIDDLETOWN

Bandanas Italian Eatery
2200 Central Ave.
(513) 422-9922

Bourbon's Craft Kitchen & Bar
2231 N. Verity Pkwy.
(513) 217-0099
bourbonskitchen.com

Combs BBQ Central
2223 Central Ave.
(513) 849-2110
combsbbq.com

Veracruz Mexican Restaurant
1230 Elliott Dr.
(513) 422-4271
veracruzrestaurant.com

MONTGOMERY

Artemis Mediterranean Bistro
7791 Cooper Rd.
(513) 802-5500
artemisbistro.com

Montgomery Inn
9440 Montgomery Rd.
(513) 791-3482
montgomeryinn.com

Carlo & Johnny By Jeff Ruby
9769 Montgomery Rd.
(513) 936-8600
jeffruby.com

Stone Creek Dining
9856 Montgomery Rd.
(513) 489-1444
stonecreekdining.com

PORTSMOUTH

Fork & Finger Restaurant
232 Second St.
(740) 353-8500
fork-and-finger-restaurant.business.site

Maestro's Mexican Grill
836 Fourth St.
(740) 660-4287
mhme.nu

Scioto Ribber
1026 Gallia St.
(740) 353-9329
thesciotoribber.com

RIPLEY

Cohearts Riverhouse
18 N. Front St.
(937) 392-4819
cohearts-riverhouse.edan.io

WAVERLY

Lake White Club
OH 552, 2 miles south of Waverly
(740) 947-5000,
(800) 774-5253
thelakewhiteclub.com

WILMINGTON

Beaugard's Southern Bar "B" Que
975 S. South St.
(937) 655-8100
beaugardsbbq.com

General Denver Hotel
81 W. Main St.
(937) 383-4141
generaldenver.com
Lodging is also available.

XENIA

Acapulco Restaurant
88 Xenia Towne Square
(937) 374-0582
acapulcoxenia.com

Nick's Restaurant
1443 N. Detroit St.
(937) 372-3202
gotonicks.com

YELLOW SPRINGS

Aahar India
101 S. Walnut St.
(937) 532-5667
aaharindia.net

Current Cuisine
237 Xenia Ave.
(937) 767-8291
currentcuisine.com

Ellie's Restaurant & Bakery
321 Xenia Ave.
(937) 319-0402
millsparkhotel.com
Lodging is also available.

Winds Café
215 Xenia Ave.
(937) 767-1144
windscafe.com

Ye Olde Trail Tavern
228 Xenia Ave.
(937) 767-7448
oldetrailtavern.com

West Central Ohio

Rural Roots

Just up the road from Yellow Springs' Antioch College (and across the Greene County–Clark County line) is a most remarkable store—***Young's Jersey Dairy***. Located at a working dairy, Young's caters to the nearby college crowd and the area's year-round residents with fresh breads and pastries, fountain service, and homemade ice cream.

Young's bakes its vast selection of doughnuts and pastries—turnovers, brownies, pies, cream horns, pecan rolls, coffeecake, fudge, and cookies, plus glazed, whole-wheat, powdered, jelly-filled, and cinnamon doughnuts—from scratch. The fountain offers shakes, splits, sundaes, and ice-cream sodas created with Young's homemade ice cream. The shakes are particularly good—made in every flavor imaginable. Served regular or extra thick, the calf shake has two scoops of ice cream, the cow shake comes loaded with four scoops, and the diet-busting bull shake contains five scoops.

They also serve country breakfasts and a full lunch menu of sandwiches and side orders. After you eat, check out the farm animal petting zoo, wagon rides (Sat and Sun during

WEST CENTRAL OHIO

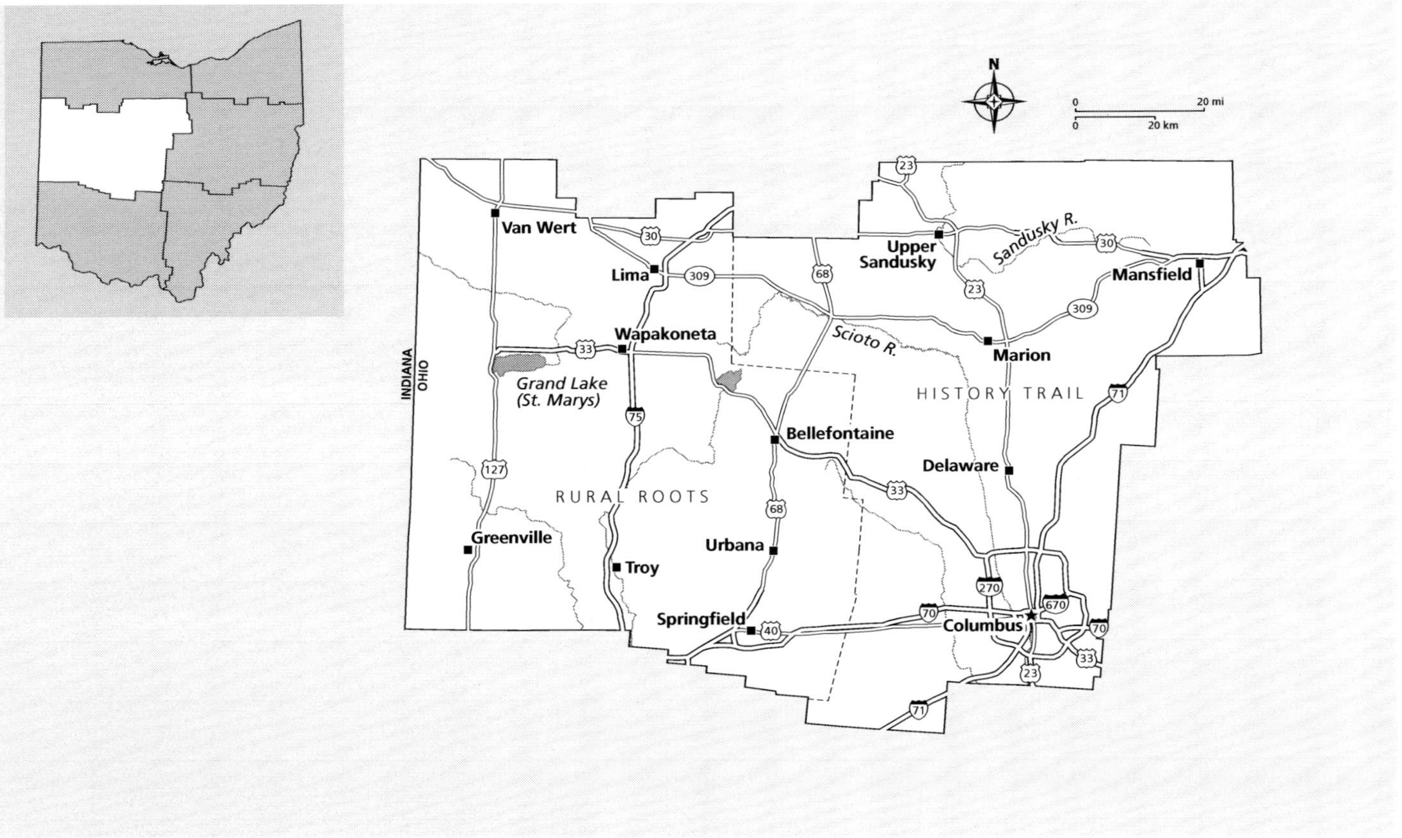

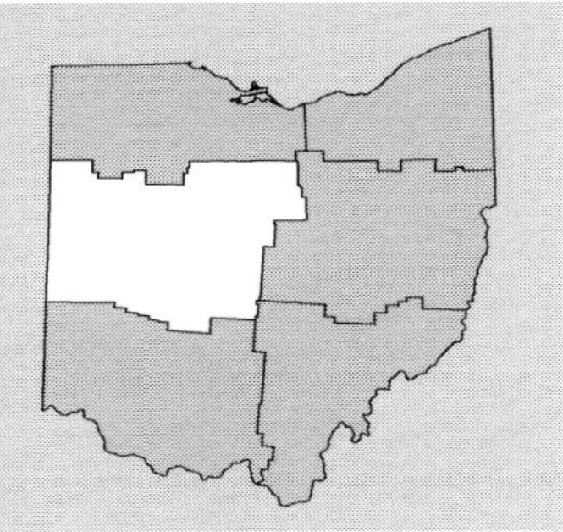

warmer months), and Young's farm-themed miniature golf course, Udders and Putters.

Young's Jersey Dairy is on US 68 just north of the Greene County–Clark County line at 6880 Springfield-Xenia Rd., Yellow Springs; (937) 325-0629; youngsdairy.com. Open Mon through Thurs, 11 a.m. to 8 p.m.; Fri, 11 a.m. to 9 p.m.; Sat, 9 a.m. to 9 p.m.; Sun 9 a.m. to 8 p.m. Dine-in breakfast available on Sat and Sun from 9 a.m. to 2 p.m.

With 165 acres and more than 6 miles of trails, the ***Brukner Nature Center***'s mission is to preserve and present to the public the splendor of the outdoors. Hardwood and pine forests, ridges, and ravines—all are accessible by the center's nature trails. Visitors observe the flora and fauna while hiking by Cattail and Catface Ponds and while following the banks of the Stillwater River.

The spring woodland flora delights visitors with displays of bluebells, trillium, Dutchman's breeches, and delphinium. In summer, Queen Anne's lace, thin-leaved coneflowers, butterfly milkweed, and prairie roses flourish along the trails. Occasional glimpses of hawks, garter snakes, cottontail rabbits, white-tailed deer, and chipmunks give visitors a sample of Brukner's diverse native fauna. No pets allowed. "They scare our wildlife," the center notes.

The wildlife rehabilitation unit nurses back to health injured animals brought to Brukner. Those unable to survive in the wild are kept in the animal

BEST ATTRACTIONS

- Young's Jersey Dairy Farm Store
- Brukner Nature Center
- Johnston Farm and Indian Agency
- Fort Jefferson State Memorial
- Bear's Mill
- Oak Island at Indian Lake
- Zane Shawnee Caverns and Southwind Park
- Mad River Mountain
- Piatt Castles
- Ohio Caverns
- Neil Armstrong Air and Space Museum
- Fort Recovery State Museum
- Allen County Museum
- Harding Home
- Indian Mill State Memorial
- Malabar Farm
- Kingwood Center
- Richland Carrousel Park
- BibleWalk & Living Bible Museum
- Ohio Statehouse
- North Market

room on display for visitors to the center. Brukner also hosts a variety of classes and seminars on topics such as quilting, wood carving, gems and minerals, stargazing, beekeeping, and natural history.

Brukner Nature Center is at 5995 Horseshoe Bend Rd., off OH 55 west of Troy; (937) 698-6493; bruknernaturecenter.com. Trails are open during daylight hours. The interpretive building is open Mon through Sat, 9 a.m. to 4 p.m.; Sun, 12:30 to 4 p.m. Admission is $2.50 per person or $10 for a family.

In 1804, for $5 an acre, John Johnston bought the 235 acres he called Upper Pickaway Farms. John and Rachel Johnston, along with their eleven children, lived in the family farmhouse from its completion in 1815 to the 1860s. This historic farm has been restored to its appearance in 1829 and is now the ***Johnston Farm and Indian Agency***.

The farmhouse is completely furnished with pieces dating from the early 1800s. The Johnstons used the outdoor fruit kiln to dry apple slices from the farm's two orchards. One feature that attracted Johnston to this property was the flowing spring, and he built a springhouse to utilize the cool spring water to refrigerate meats, milk, and produce. Inside the two-story structure, the clear water circles a stone island in the center of the floor. Items requiring cooling were placed either on the stones or in the flowing water. The spring also provided fresh drinking water for the family. When Johnston advertised the farm for sale in 1857, he estimated the spring's output at ten gallons per minute. The second floor of the springhouse originally contained accommodations for the farm's hired help, but today holds an oak loom (ca. 1750) on which rug making is demonstrated.

The Johnstons' enormous double-pen log barn, constructed in 1808, is the largest log barn in Ohio. Johnston used it for his flock of 100 sheep, and the original pens and beams are still plainly visible. Other attractions at the Johnston Farm and Indian Agency include canal boat rides on a restored section of the Miami and Erie Canal and an Indian museum dedicated to the tribes prevalent in Ohio from the seventeenth to mid-nineteenth centuries.

The Johnston Farm and Indian Agency is at 9845 N. Hardin Rd. east of OH 66, north of Piqua; (937) 773-2522, (800) 752-2619; johnstonfarmohio.com. Open from June through Labor Day, Thurs and Fri, 10 a.m. to 5 p.m.; Sat and Sun, noon to 5 p.m. Hours in Apr, May, Sept, and Oct, Mon through Fri, 9 a.m. to 2 p.m. or by appointment. Admission: adults $10; seniors $9; children (ages 6 to 12) $5.

In October 1791, the forces of General Arthur St. Clair built Fort Jefferson as an outpost, one of the chain of defensive forts constructed to protect army supplies from Indians. Named for Thomas Jefferson, then secretary of state, the fort served as a supply base for the campaigns of General St. Clair and General

"Mad" Anthony Wayne. It was abandoned in 1796, its location too accessible to the enemy and its water supply too vulnerable.

Today visitors to the ***Fort Jefferson State Memorial*** find a monument 6 feet square and 20 feet tall made of granite field boulders. The fort exists only in the imagination of those who travel here; none of the structure survived.

Fort Jefferson State Memorial is on CR 24 at OH 121 at 3981 Weavers-Fort Jefferson Rd. Fort Jefferson; (937) 547-7370; ohiohistory.org/visit/browse-historical-sites/fort-jefferson-memorial-park/. Open daylight hours; no admission charge.

The water of Greenville Creek meanders around a bend in the stream and pushes into a lake surrounded by lily pads. It then cascades over a dam or is forced into the millrace leading to historic ***Bear's Mill***.

In 1824 President James Monroe granted the site of the mill, as well as water rights, to Major George Adams. In 1849 Gabriel Bear constructed Bear's Mill. One hundred and thirty years later, Terry and Julie Clark, a local family, discovered the mill for sale while taking a leisurely drive in the country. Terry, having a fascination for anything old, immediately was drawn to the property. They decided this noble, rustic building and its adjoining property were perfect for them. After two years of renovation, the Clarks reopened Bear's Mill in 1981.

Today Bear's Mill is listed on the National Register of Historic Places and is an operating, water-powered, stone-grinding flour mill run by the nonprofit Friends of Bear's Mill. Clark Gallery offers a wide variety of art from a growing slate of regional artists.

The Clark Gallery was re-dedicated in 2015 to honor Terry and Julie Clark, who owned Bear's Mill for nearly three decades.

Located on the first floor, the Mill Store at Bear's Mill offers wholesome stone-ground flour, as well as a selection of home, gift, and gourmet items. These include organic grain products and cereals, pancake and soup mixes, gourmet coffees, preserves, and sauces. Handcrafted wood items, garden accessories, tableware, handmade jewelry, soaps, and candles are also available. Visitors are welcome to take a self-guided tour of the four-story mill.

Bear's Mill is off OH 36 at 6450 Arcanum-Bear's Mill Rd., 5 miles east of Greenville; (937) 548-5112; bearsmill.org. Open Tues and Wed 10 a.m. to 4 p.m.; Thurs through Sat, 11 a.m. to 5 p.m.; Sun 1 to 5 p.m.

General Anthony Wayne arrived in Greenville in 1793 and built the largest fortification on the western frontier. After the signing of the Treaty of Greenville between Wayne and representatives of the Wyandot, Delaware, Miami, Shawnee, Pottawatomi, Chippewa, Ottawa, Kickapoo, Kaskasia, Piankeshaw, Eel River, and Wea nations on August 3, 1795, the area opened for settlement. At the end of the War of 1812, and with the defeat of Indian chiefs Tecumseh and

The Prophet in 1813, a second treaty was signed with the Indians August 20, 1814, by William Henry Harrison, who served as Wayne's aide in 1795.

The buildings that constitute the ***Garst Museum*** preserve and present this region's rich history. In 1852 George Coover built the Garst House as an inn for travelers on the Dayton and Union Railroad. John Hufnagle purchased the property in 1861 as a gift to his daughter Miranda Garst. It remained in the Garst family until 1946, when it was converted into a museum. It is on the National Register of Historic Sites.

annieoakley

Back in 1875, a young lady used her marksman prowess to become a legend. That's when 15-year-old Phoebe Ann Moses, born in a log cabin near North Star, challenged champion marksman and showman Frank Butler to a shooting match and won. Annie, as she was called, prevailed over Butler at a place called Oakley near Cincinnati, and hence the legend of Annie Oakley was born.

Annie married Frank Butler a year later, and they began touring together and eventually were featured in Buffalo Bill's Wild West Show. Annie died on November 3, 1926, and she and Frank are still together, in North Star's Brock Cemetery.

Another son of Darke County is Lowell Thomas, one of the twentieth century's most notable newsmen, known for his wondrous tales of exotic lands. Built in the 1880s, the Lowell Thomas birthplace, a two-story in Gothic Victorian style, was moved from Woodington to the Garst Museum grounds and completely restored.

The museum's Coppock Wing houses its Lowell Thomas and Annie Oakley collections, including the largest known collection of Annie Oakley memorabilia. The Village Wing features items from Buffalo Bill Cody, Anna Bier paintings, as well as an old schoolroom, a post office, a print shop, a barbershop, and a doctor's office, among others.

The Garst Museum is at 205 N. Broadway, Greenville; (937) 548-5250; garstmuseum.org. Open Tues through Sat, 10 a.m. to 4 p.m. closed Sun, Mon, Easter, Independence Day, Thanksgiving, Christmas, and New Year's Eve and the month of Jan. Admission: adults $12; senior citizens $11; children (ages 6 to 17) $9.

Cedar Bog Nature Preserve has seen it all since its glacial upbringing—mastodons probably fed here and all of Ohio's Native American cultures lived in the area. The bog is the largest and best example of a boreal and prairie fen complex in the state, and as such it supports many rare plants as well as excellent orchid, prairie, and woodland wildflower displays. It is the artesian flow of cool water filtered through limestone gravel that makes this place environmentally unique. Spotted turtles and swamp rattlesnakes also call the bog home.

Cedar Bog Nature Preserve is at 980 Woodburn Rd., Urbana; (937) 484-3744, (800) 860-0147; cedarbognp.org. Open year-round. Cedar Bog Boardwalk is open daily, dawn to dusk; closed during deer gun-hunting season. The Nature Center is open Mar through Oct, Wed through Sun, 10 a.m. to 4 p.m. Rates: adults $5; students $4. If the Nature Center is closed, visitors may leave their admission money in the little blue box at the start of the boardwalk. Pets are not allowed on the boardwalk.

The Westcott House Foundation was established in 2000 to renovate a home designed by noted architect Frank Lloyd Wright. The ***Westcott House***, the only prairie-style home in Ohio designed by Lloyd Wright, was fully restored and opened as a museum and educational center in 2005. Construction on the home began in 1904 and ended four years later. Wright designed the home for the Ohio manufacturer Burton J. Westcott and his wife, Orpha. The home was converted into an apartment building in the 1940s, so the effort to return it to its original configuration took a great deal of research, effort, and millions of dollars.

The house was quite a break from the traditional architecture of the time. Wright focused on the horizontal lines of the land on the American prairie and replicated the flat, horizontal plains in the lines of this and other prairie-style designs. Rather than following the rising, skyscraping designs popular in U.S. cities prior to World War I, Wright created these low-rising structures, which gave a feeling of security and harmony with the land. To ground the home, he created a central hearth area. Surrounding benches create an inner room of sorts and a place of comfort. Rooms blend one into another, with a feeling of openness, and were designed as multipurpose areas.

The building materials and the design of the home reflect Wright's desire to blur the lines between interior and exterior, between nature and human construction. He built the home of wood and stucco, and he created connections with the surrounding landscape via a terrace, a pool, and gardens. Some have compared the home to a Shinto temple. A bank of divided windows stretches across an entire side of the house, creating an impressive vista, reminiscent of a shoji screen, perhaps inspired by Wright's trip to Japan shortly before he designed the home. These expanses of windows and skylights flood the entry and common areas with natural light. In addition, Japanese-inspired elements include sleeping porches, many restored lanterns, and a clay-tiled roof.

The Frank Lloyd Wright's Westcott House is at 85 S. Greenmount Ave., Springfield; (937) 327-9291; westcotthouse.org. Tours: Tues through Fri, 11 a.m. and 1 p.m.; Sat, 11 a.m., 1 p.m., and 3 p.m.; Sun, 1 and 3 p.m. Admission: adults $18; senior citizens and students $15. Reservations are strongly recommended.

To get a peek at what earned the Westcotts enough money to build this great home, head over to the center of the city of Springfield to the ***Heritage Center***. The center has a rare Westcott automobile on display. The center has permanent exhibits highlighting Ohio and regional history in its 13,000 square feet of permanent gallery space and uses an additional 3,000 square feet for a variety of temporary and traveling exhibits.

The Heritage Center building itself is impressive. The massive 53,000-square-foot brick and stone edifice is an imposing structure in the middle of downtown and is listed on the National Register of Historic Sites. The structure was constructed in 1890 to house city offices and a farmers' market. Along with the Heritage Center, the history society maintains an archive and library resource center for students, researchers, or those attempting to hunt down their family history.

The Heritage Center is at 117 S. Fountain Ave., Springfield; (937) 324-0657; heritage.center. The museum is open Tues through Fri, 9 a.m. to 4 p.m.; Sat, 9 a.m. to 3 p.m. The Research Library and Archives are open Wed through Fri, 10 a.m. to 4 p.m.; Sat, 10 a.m. to 3 p.m. Admission: free, but donations are accepted. Recommended donations are $5 for adults, $2 for children, and $10 for families.

Ready to sail away to your own private island? ***Oak Island at Indian Lake*** could be the place to live out that fantasy. This cottage getaway is a solitary retreat on Oak Island. You'll have to take a boat to reach your private sanctuary.

Whether you are looking for a romantic vacation, family reunion, or family getaway, you can relax at the private beach or on the cottage's covered patios. The cottage has 1.5 baths and three bedrooms, each with a double bed; two roll-away beds are also available. The kitchen comes equipped with a range, oven, refrigerator, and freezer, as well as cooking and serving utensils.

Around the area of Indian Lake, you'll find restaurants, sailing, waterskiing, golf, and plenty of natural areas for walks, hikes, and exploring. At the close of summer, generally in the first week of September, the residents around the lake set off flares around the rim of the lake to create a "Ring of Fire." This is a reenactment of a Native American tradition that welcomed the coming of autumn.

Oak Island at Indian Lake is accessible only by boat from Russells Point; (614) 560-3859; indianlake.com/oak-island. Open May through Sept. Rates vary by season, day of the week, and length of stay.

The 6,000-acre Indian Lake, with its shady islands, peninsulas, and lakefront homes, attracts recreation seekers for fishing, boating, and waterskiing.

Fifteen miles southeast of Indian Lake, a private park, ***Zane Shawnee Caverns and Southwind Park***, offers a fascinating cavern, camping, and accommodations. A swift underground river eroded the 11 million-year-old cavern from the limestone, leaving a labyrinth of caves and tunnels and unusual crystal formations. Water seeping through the rock and dripping down on limestone boulders has created distinctive beehive crystals and, in one case, rare cave pearls. These pure white crystal balls formed in a small pool of water around tiny pieces of rock and dust. The only other set of similar pearls in existence is in a cave in Switzerland.

Zane Shawnee Caverns, with its many "rooms," splendid colors, and clear pools of 40-degree water, was discovered by a young boy in 1892 when his dog fell in a hole and dropped down into the cavern. Early visitors entered through that same hole (which is still visible from inside the cavern); they were lowered in a basket and given a kerosene lamp. In the early 1900s, these self-guided tours cost 10 cents. The Shawnee Nation United Remnant Band of Ohio purchased the caverns in 1996.

Today it takes about 40 minutes for guides to lead a group from one end of the cavern to the other. The tour reaches a depth of 132 feet below the surface, but various tunnels and crevasses shoot off from the main cavern to even greater depths. The caverns are open year-round. Tours are $16 for adults and $7 for children (ages 5 to 12).

The park's 200 acres of woods, ridges, and ravines also offer camping and lodging for overnight guests at the Southwind Campground. If you're not a tent camper, Zane Shawnee Caverns and Southwind Park; (937) 592-9592; zaneshawneecavernsandsouthwindpark.com has seventeen RV sites with electricity and ten RV sites with electricity and water. The campground also has twelve permanent campsites for cold-weather camping, eight with electricity and water and four with electricity only. Another delightful place to rest one's head is the Eagles' Nest. Set on stilts in a heavily wooded ravine, this screened sleeping shelter contains a double bed, with a picnic table and barbecue grill adjacent. Six more summer cabins offer accommodations, each with electricity, a table and chairs, a screened porch, and a fire ring in front. Owl's Nest has bunked double beds; Hawk's Nest has one double bed and single bunk beds. Campsites are $20 to $75 per night. Cabins are $40 to $60 per night.

Other attractions at the caverns include the Shawnee Woodland Native American Museum (admission is $11 for adults and $5 for children) and the Zane/LaBelle Trading Post 1830s Pioneer Village and Historic Shawnee Village (admission is $10 for adults and $5 for children).

Zane Shawnee Caverns is on OH 540, 5 miles east of Bellefontaine; (937) 592-9592; zaneshawneecaverns.net. Reservations and a deposit are required for accommodations.

Winter recreation in Logan County is centered at ***Mad River Mountain*** ski resort, with twenty slopes and trails for skiers and snowboarders, and ten runs for snow tubing. The 144 hilly acres of the resort are open Dec through Mar. Ski instruction and rental equipment are offered. Mad River Mountain is on US 33 at 1000 Snow Valley Rd., 5 miles east of Bellefontaine; (937) 599-1015, (800) 231-7669; skimadriver.com.

Rural Logan County might seem an unusual place for two brothers to build a pair of castles, but that is precisely what Colonel Donn Piatt and General Abram Sanders Piatt did during the mid-1800s. Members of the Piatt family came to America in the 1670s from southeastern France. Donn and Abram's grandfather, Jacob Piatt, served on George Washington's staff during the Revolutionary War. Jacob's son Benjamin, after fighting in the War of 1812, acquired 1,700 acres in the Mac-A-Cheek Valley, named after a local Shawnee settlement. It was Benjamin's sons, Donn and Abram, who built the two stone castles a mile apart in what is today Logan County.

america's first concrete street

Once the site of a Native American settlement, Bellefontaine (pronounced "bell-fountain") is most famous for something we take for granted today—paved roads. It was here in 1891 that the Buckeye Cement Company laid an 8-foot strip of concrete on Main Street, America's first concrete street. The company later paved around the courthouse, and this innovation attracted engineers from across the country. A section of the street was displayed at the 1893 Chicago World's Fair, winning a gold medal. We've been pouring concrete ever since.

Abram Sanders Piatt built the first of the ***Piatt Castles***, Castle Piatt Mac-A-Cheek, using an architectural style that blends Gothic revival and Second Empire. The three-story home (with five-story watchtower) has walls 2-feet thick made of locally quarried limestone, which was hand-chiseled on the site.

The castle has remained in the Piatt family since its construction, and all furnishings in the castle are family originals. The first stop on self-guided tours of Castle Piatt Mac-A-Cheek is the spacious drawing room, with its intricate oak, walnut, and cherry floors and splendid ash, pine, and walnut walls. Fine woodwork graces the entire castle, as do frescoed ceilings painted by French artist Oliver Frey in 1880. These ceilings have survived a century surprisingly well, without so much as a touchup.

The castle's furnishings include horsehair-stuffed couches and chairs, massive carved beds, and wardrobes—some dating as far back as the Revolutionary War period—plus a collection of Native American artifacts. The family's historic firearms collection and a private chapel, complete with altar and kneeler, are upstairs.

Down the road, Donn Piatt's Flemish-style ***Mac-O-Chee Castle*** (a variation of the name Mac-A-Cheek) contains impressive woodwork and ornately painted walls and ceilings throughout. The castle was completed in 1881, but the Piatt family lost ownership of this three-story, twin-spired structure in the mid-1890s, when Ella Piatt, Colonel Donn Piatt's widow, sold it. It served briefly as a health spa but eventually stood empty and was even used as a barn for more than a decade. Now it's back in the Piatt family and open to visitors. It is an excellent example of a late nineteenth-century estate.

The Piatt Castles are on OH 245, 1 and 2 miles east of West Liberty; (937) 465-2821; piattcastle.org. Mac-A-Cheek Castle is located at 10051 Township Road 47. Mac-O-Chee Castle is at 2319 OH 287. Both castles are open mid-Apr through mid-May on weekends from 10 a.m. to 4 p.m.; May 27 through Sept 4 daily from 10 a.m. to 5 p.m. Sept and Oct on weekends from 10 a.m. to 4 p.m. Admission: adults $13; senior citizens $11; children (ages 5 to 15) $7.

Caves and caverns are scattered across (and under) Ohio, but the largest of such caverns open to the public are at ***Ohio Caverns***. With a 54-degree temperature, a visit to Ohio Caverns can be enjoyed any time of year, no matter the weather on the "outside."

Inside, you'll discover exquisite crystal-white stalactite and stalagmite formations. Unique coloring and ever-changing shapes make this cave tour a treat. Like many such caverns, the more unusual formations have been named—the "Crystal King" and "Pathway through the Palace of the Gods." The real intrigue is not the clever designations, but rather the strange and natural beauty underground. Bring your camera and enjoy.

Ohio Caverns is at 2210 East OH 245, 4 miles east of West Liberty; (937) 465-4017; ohiocaverns.com. Open daily year-round: May through Sept, 9 a.m. to 5 p.m.; Oct through Apr, 10 a.m. to 4 p.m. The last tour starts an hour before closing. Ohio Caverns offers two tours—Natural Wonders Tour, available

america's first gasoline-powered automobile

It could have happened anywhere, but it happened here, in 1891. America's first gasoline-powered automobile chugged out of John Lambert's implement store and hit the roads in Ohio City, such as they were. No doubt this caused a stir, as the strange, noisy contraption tooled along, dodging trees and potholes. Lambert reportedly ran into a hitching post on one of his early forays, and this very first car was destroyed in a fire later that same year.

Lambert continued to tinker with automobiles and held 600 patents related to the invention.

year-round, and Historic Tour, available only Apr through Oct. The Natural Wonders Tour takes about 50 minutes and costs $24 for adults and $12 for children (ages 5 to 12). The Historic Tour lasts about 50 minutes and costs $24 for adults and $12 for children (ages 5 to 12). A combination fee for both tours, with a short break in between, is $36 for adults and $18 for children (ages 5 to 12).

On the afternoon of July 6, 1901, the town of Versailles suffered a disastrous fire. The epicenter of the blaze was the old Scheffel Mill, which had stood unused for many years and now burned like tinder as a fierce west wind pushed the flames into the heart of town. Six blocks of local businesses and thirty-eight homes were destroyed.

The ***Hotel Versailles***, formerly the Inn at Versailles, now occupies several of the structures built after the fire of 1901. The upstairs had been the Snyder Hotel, while the kitchen once housed the Beare's Coffee Shop. The lobby was the W.C. Beare Grocery Company, the Alsace Room was a drug store, and the Lorraine and Versailles rooms were a hardware store.

The hotel's modern life began in 1992, when, after sitting vacant for years, it was completely renovated in the style of a French country inn.

In October 2019, the former Inn at Versailles experienced a substantial fire that closed the business. In January 2020, the decision was made to rebuild even bigger, better, and more beautiful than ever on the site that holds more than 150 years of hospitality history. The new Hotel Versailles opened in 2022 with thirty guestrooms and suites, plus chef Aaron Allen's Silas Creative Kitchen + Cocktails and meeting and event space for up to 200 guests in the 1819 Room.

The Hotel Versailles is at 22 N. Center St., Versailles; (937) 526-3020; hotelversaillesohio.com. Rates: $259 to $279 per night.

At 10:56:20 Eastern Daylight Time on July 20, 1969, Neil Armstrong became the first man to step onto the lunar surface. "That's one small step for a man—one giant leap for mankind," crackled Armstrong's first radio transmission from Tranquility Base, as he accomplished the goal set by John Kennedy in the early 1960s. It was less than seventy years earlier that Dayton's Wright Brothers had conquered powered flight over

grandlake st.mary's

Stretching from Lake Erie to the Ohio River in western Ohio, the construction of the Miami & Erie Canal was a major catalyst in the state's development. For the canal to succeed, it needed a reliable water source at its high point, near Celina. Some 1,700 men, paid 30 cents a day, labored for years to create Grand Lake St. Mary's, the largest man-made lake in the world when it was completed in 1845. Today, with the canal long gone, the lake is a haven for recreation.

the sands of Kitty Hawk—from the first successful aircraft to lunar exploration in a little more than six decades.

The ***Neil Armstrong Air and Space Museum*** in Wapakoneta celebrates the achievements of local boy Armstrong and other Ohioans who contributed to the field of aviation.

A NASA F5D Skylancer aircraft flown by Armstrong in the early 1960s greets visitors, and from the Skylancer you simply follow the runway lights to the entrance of the futuristic exhibit building.

Sketches, models, and photographs trace the history of manned flight, from the earliest use of balloons to powered aircraft and space travel. The bright yellow, single-engine Aeronca Champion propeller plane flown by Armstrong at age 16, and his Gemini 8 space capsule, span his accomplishments as an aviator. Other exhibits include spacesuits from the Gemini and Apollo missions, a Jupiter rocket engine, and not particularly tempting packets of astronaut space food. One video projection room continuously shows marvelous footage of American astronauts from various Apollo missions walking, hopping, jumping, and driving on the lunar surface.

The Neil Armstrong Air and Space Museum is at I-75 and Bellefontaine Street at 500 Apollo Dr., Wapakoneta; (419) 738-8811, (800) 860-0142; armstrongmuseum.org. Open Wed through Sun 10 a.m. to 5 p.m., closed holidays. From April through Labor Day, the museum is open daily from 10 a.m. to 5 p.m. Admission: adults $12; senior citizens $11; children (ages 6 to 12) $7.50.

One location on the Wabash River was the site of both one of the worst defeats and one of the most important victories for American troops battling the Native Americans in the 1790s. Native warriors led by Little Turtle and Blue Jacket caught General Arthur St. Clair's forces in a surprise attack on November 4, 1791, killing or wounding three-quarters of the soldiers.

But two years after St. Clair's defeat, General "Mad" Anthony Wayne picked that spot on the Wabash to construct a fort consisting of four blockhouses connected by log stockade walls. Each blockhouse measured 20-feet square, and Wayne's troops finished ***Fort Recovery*** in less than a week. When the Native Americans attacked on the morning of June 30, 1794, Wayne's forces prevailed, setting the stage for the general's final victory over the natives at Fallen Timbers on August 20, 1794, and the signing of the Treaty of Greenville in 1795.

Visitors to Fort Recovery State Museum inspect the two reconstructed blockhouses and view artifacts from the original fort in the two-story stone museum. These artifacts include an army-issue felling ax, bottles, a skillet handle, and bone-handled knives and forks. The museum has other items used in battle here two centuries ago, such as howitzer shells, cannonballs, grapeshot, and parts of muskets and pistols.

One exhibit explains the construction of Fort Recovery, describing how 13-foot logs with one end axed to a point were placed on end in 3-foot-deep trenches to form the stockade walls. A gap approximately every 6 feet allowed the fort's defenders to point their rifles through the wall and fire on attackers. Other displays include mannequins of an army sergeant and a Native American brave clothed in their respective 1794 battle uniforms, a collection of muskets and military swords from the 1860s, plus Native American artifacts from Mercer County such as tomahawks, leather goods, and arrowheads.

Fort Recovery State Museum is near the intersection of OH 49 and OH 119 at 1 Fort Site St., Fort Recovery; (419) 375-4649, (800) 283-8920; fortrecoverymuseum.com. Open daily June through Aug, noon to 5 p.m., plus weekends in May and Sept, noon to 5 p.m. Admission: adults $5; children (ages 5 to 12) $2.

Lima residents boast of having one of the best county museums in the state—the ***Allen County Museum***—and it is. Two floors in a modern brick building contain hundreds of items. Its pioneer kitchen contains old-fashioned butter stamps, molds, and churns, while the pioneer bedroom has a corn-husk mattress on a primitive wooden bed. The mother of the Haller twins (Kathern and Sophie) rocked her infants on the rare double cradle bench during their first year in 1852.

treaty of greenville

In the summer of 1795, fresh from his victory at the Battle of Fallen Timbers, General "Mad" Anthony Wayne returned to Fort Greenville and waited. By July, twelve tribes with more than 1,300 braves arrived to hammer out a peace treaty with the whites.

On August 3, 1795, the Treaty of Greenville was signed, opening most of Ohio to white settlement. Outgunned, the Native Americans took cash and gave up two-thirds of what is today Ohio. For the native peoples, this was yet another sad chapter in their forced migration west.

The museum has collected a variety of wagons and buggies, including a covered wagon and a hearse, as well as antique cars such as a magnificent 1909 Locomobile Sports Roadster. Downstairs features a number of muskets and pistols and all manner of Native American items including arrowheads, beads, ornate Hopi dolls and masks, pottery, blankets, and a large ribbed canoe. A nineteenth-century doctor's office and a general store are completely stocked with items typical of the era.

One unusual item is the 1903 Kodak "mugging" camera, used by the Lima police department at the turn of the twentieth century (plus sample mug shots demonstrating the policemen's photographic abilities). Other collections include rocks, fossils, and minerals found in the county, and a group of antique farm implements.

Next to the museum is the Log House, furnished with primitive pioneer possessions, and the MacDonell House, a Victorian mansion renowned for its handsome woodwork, big-game trophies, and period pieces.

The Allen County Museum is at 620 W. Market St., Lima; (419) 222-9426; allencountymuseum.org. Open Tues through Fri, 1 to 5 p.m.; Sat, 1 to 4 p.m. Summer hours are Tues through Fri, 11 a.m. to 5 p.m., and Sat, 11 a.m. to 4 p.m. Admission is $3 for the MacDonell House, children (ages 8 and under) free. Admission to the museum is $5; children (ages 8 and under) free.

History Trail

In 1890 ***Warren G. Harding***, then 25 years old, and his fiancée planned and had built the dark-green home at 380 Mount Vernon Ave., Marion. From the ***Harding Home***, he conducted his famous "front porch" campaign in 1920 and won the presidency. The Harding years in the White House were turbulent ones—his administration was rocked by scandals, including the infamous Teapot Dome incident. Harding died in San Francisco in 1923, without completing his term of office.

The eldest son of a doctor, Harding was born in Blooming Grove, Ohio, on November 2, 1865. After working as a printer's apprentice, he bought the Marion Daily Star at the age of 19. In 1891, he married Florence Kling DeWolfe, daughter of one of Marion's wealthiest and most prominent Republicans, on the stairway of the home they had designed. Harding's election to the Ohio Senate in 1899, as lieutenant governor of Ohio in 1903, and to the U.S. Senate in 1914 laid the groundwork for his successful presidential campaign in 1920. He used the large front porch of his home—the porch he had expanded in 1900—to speak to the 600,000 voters who traveled to Marion in the summer of 1920 to hear the acclaimed oratory of the Republican candidate.

Inside the entryway sits the small wooden desk where Harding sat on election night reading the latest telegraphed election returns. Nearly all the furnishings and accessories in the Harding home are exactly as the Hardings left them when they went to Washington in 1921. Many of the art objects collected by the Hardings on their three trips to Europe are there, and so is the hat worn by the 29th president at his inauguration. The small building behind

porkrind, anyone?

It may not be exactly a celebration of health food, but Harrod festivities honoring pork rinds reflect the local popularity of this legendary snack. Of course, the Pork Rind Heritage Festival features this lip-smacking treat, but it also includes a hog roast and a variety of other food fare. And no pork rind fan could leave without cheering on the Pork Rind Parade or staying to enjoy the live entertainment.

The festival is held on Main Street, Harrod, in mid-June; visit the website, porkrindfest.com, for more information.

the Harding residence, which served as the press headquarters during the 1920 campaign, now is a museum.

The Harding Home is at 380 Mount Vernon Ave., Marion; (740) 387-9630, (800) 600-6894; hardingpresidentialsites .org. Open Thurs through Sat, 9 a.m. to 5 pm.; Sun, noon to 5 p.m. from Dec through Feb. Site returns to Wed through Sun hours in March. Admission: adults $16; senior citizens $15; children (ages 6 to 17) $8.

Not far from the Harding Home are the 10-acre grounds containing the ***Harding Tomb***. Constructed in 1927 of Georgia white marble, the 52-foot-tall memorial surrounds the graves of President and Mrs. Harding (she died in 1924, a year after her husband). Labrador granite tombstones cover the graves of the Hardings, who were buried here on December 21, 1927. The careful rows of maple trees on the grounds form the shape of a Latin cross.

The Harding Tomb is at the corner of OH 423 and Vernon Heights Boulevard, Marion at 966-870 Delaware Ave.; (740) 387-9630; hardingpresidentialsites .org. Open daylight hours; no admission charge.

Richard Hendricks purchased his dream in 1963—the 10,000-foot ***Indian Trail Caverns*** he had first visited as a child. Once called the Wyandot Indian Caverns, this bit of underground history first opened in 1927 but closed ten years later. Hendricks, the postmaster in nearby Vanlue, worked nights and weekends whenever the weather would permit, clearing glacial debris from the floor of the caverns, and reopened them in 1973.

The U.S. government constructed a saw- and gristmill for Ohio's Wyandot Indians in 1820 in gratitude for their support during the War of 1812.

The mill was on the Sandusky River, and government-appointed millers ground flour and cornmeal for the Wyandot reservation until the Indians were relocated to Kansas in 1843, putting the mill out of operation.

A second mill was built 300 feet downstream from the first in 1861 and operated until 1941. This mill had a reputation for particularly good stone-ground buckwheat and cornmeal, and has since become the country's first museum of milling—***Indian Mill State Memorial***.

TOP ANNUAL EVENTS

Columbus Arts Festival
Columbus, June
(614) 224-2606
columbusartsfestival.org

Peony Festival
Van Wert, June
vwpeonyfestival.com

Strawberry Festival
Troy, June
(937) 339-7714
troystrawberryfest.com

Pork Rind Heritage Festival
Harrod, June
porkrindfest.com

Rose Festival
Columbus, June
(614) 645-3300
columbus.gov

National Threshers Annual Reunion
Fulton County Fairgrounds
Wauseon, June
(517) 398-0152
nationalthreshers.com

London Strawberry Festival
London, June
(614) 787-1214
londonstrawberryfestival.com

Miami Valley Steam Threshers Show
Plain City, July
(614) 270-0007

Spend-A-Day Raft Off
Russells Point, Aug
(937) 843-5392
visitindianlakeohio.com

Bucyrus Bratwurst Festival
Bucyrus, Aug
(419) 562-2728
bucyrusbratwurstfestival.com

All Ohio Balloon Fest
Marysville, Aug
(937) 243-5833
allohioballoonfest.com

Dublin Irish Festival
Dublin, Aug
dublinirishfestival.org

Ohio State Fair
Columbus, Aug
(888) 646-3976
ohiostatefair.com

Miami County Fair
Troy, Aug
(937) 335-7492
miamicountyohiofair.com

Darke County Fair
Greenville, Aug
(937) 548-5044, (800) 736-3671
darkecountyfair.com

Reynoldsburg Tomato Festival
Reynoldsburg, Aug
reytomatofest.com

Marion Popcorn Festival
Marion, Sept
popcornfestival.com

Crestline Harvest–Antique Festival
Crestline, Sept
(419) 683-3800
crestlineharvestfestival.org

Harvest and Herb Festival
Ada, Sept
(419) 788-9459
adaareachamber.org

Ohio Heritage Days Festival
Lucas, Sept
(419) 892-2784
malabarfarm.org

Ohio Gourd Show
Greenville, late Sept, Oct
(937) 547-0025
ohiogourdsociety.com

The museum includes a detailed explanation of the four types of mill waterwheels: the overshot, undershot, breast, and horizontal wheels. Exhibits explain the history of gristmills and sawmills and their importance to early Ohio settlements. Perhaps the most intriguing feature of the museum is the working model of a water turbine mill. This model demonstrates the complex system of "flights" that transported grain and milled meal from floor to floor in the mill—from its entry down a chute to the grinding stones on the lower level to the upper floors for sifting, separating, and sacking. Outside the mill, a 3-acre park across the river bridge is a tranquil and picturesque spot for a picnic or just relaxing.

Indian Mill State Memorial is at 7417 CR 47, off OH 67 or US 23 northeast of Upper Sandusky; (419) 294-3857, (800) 600-7147; visitwyandotcounty.com/indian-mill. Open May through Oct, Thurs through Sun, 1 to 4 p.m. Admission: adults $2; children (ages 4 to 12) $1.

Strange as it may seem, ***Malabar Farm***, the 914-acre farm of Pulitzer Prize–winning novelist ***Louis Bromfield***, was once the vacation destination of Hollywood royalty, including ***Humphrey Bogart*** and ***Lauren Bacall***. Bromfield was born in nearby Mansfield in 1896 and graduated from Mansfield Senior High School. Though he studied agriculture at Cornell and journalism at Columbia, this prominent author and screenplay writer never received a college degree.

After driving ambulances in World War I, Bromfield remained in Europe and published his first novel, *The Green Bay Tree*, in 1925, launching a literary career that would produce thirty-three books over the next thirty-three years, as well as a number of screenplays. Although dedicated to his writing, Bromfield never lost his interest in agriculture. In 1939, when the outbreak of World War II forced Bromfield and his family to flee France, he began searching Ohio for suitable farm acreage to practice the conservation techniques he had learned from his grandfather and French farmers. He found Malabar—or, more accurately, created Malabar (which means

thecrawford incident

Ohio was the site of many conflicts between white settlers and Native Americans. One of the most gruesome was the execution of Colonel William Crawford by Delaware and Indot Indians. In 1782 Crawford, a friend of George Washington, led a force of 480 men bent on attacking Native American villages along the Sandusky River.

Not only did his campaign fail, but Crawford was captured and held responsible for the atrocities by whites at Gnadenhutten. Crawford literally was burned alive at the stake after being beaten and tortured. Today,Crawford County bears his name as a reminder of this incident.

"beautiful valley" in a Native American dialect) by purchasing four adjacent farms in the lush, rolling hills of Richland County. Saving only four rooms of the original farmhouse, Bromfield added twenty-eight others, including nine bedrooms, six full baths, and four half baths, producing the airy, rambling estate where he entertained family and friends.

Among the many visitors to Malabar were Hollywood celebrities such as William Powell, Errol Flynn, Dorothy Lamour, and Shirley Temple—all friends of Bromfield's from his work in motion pictures. Bromfield explained his innovative "grass farming" method of agriculture to them, a system of planting grasses in critical areas to arrest soil erosion and reinvigorate the earth. Bromfield distrusted the effects on the soil of using every available acre for grain production; instead he cultivated only enough acreage to support his dairy operation.

The Bromfield home is furnished exactly as it was when the family lived here, with many of the pieces brought back from France in 1939. Bromfield also imported the bright wallpapers from France, and all the oak floors and walnut doors are original. Two Grandma Moses paintings hang in the house, and, because of Bromfield's love of the outdoors, every room on the first floor has an outside door. Bromfield had the 29-drawer desk in his study custom-built, only to discover he was unhappy with the way it "felt." He actually worked at a card table behind the desk.

The family's boxer dogs were important members of the household, and the doors of the house were equipped with special latches that the dogs could open, giving them free run of Malabar. In addition to guided tours of the house, self-guided tours of the barns, chicken coop, smokehouse, and the farm's active dairy operation are also offered. Cross-country skiing is popular at the farm in the winter, with rental equipment available.

"salesday"

Talk about a tradition. London has held a livestock auction the first Tues of every month since 1856. In all those years, only four sales have been canceled: two in 1863, one in 1865, and one in 1868. Farmers bring their herds in for the 10 a.m. sale, and then spend the day "in town." Crowds often number 2,000 to 3,000 people on Public Square for a "sales day."

Malabar Farm is at 4050 Bromfield Rd., west of OH 603 off Pleasant Valley Road, south of Lucas; (419) 892-2784; malabarfarm.org. Tours are conducted from Memorial Day to Labor Day at 11 a.m. and 2 p.m. Mon through Thurs, plus 11 a.m., 2 p.m., and 4:30 p.m. on Fri and Sat.

Tours of the house are $6 for adults and $4 for children (ages 6 to 17). Wagon tours and hayrides of the farm are conducted at 12:30 and 3:30 p.m. on weekends from Memorial Day to Labor Day; rides are $3 per person (ages 6 and up), free to children (ages 5 and under).

The late Charles Kelley King, chairman of the board of Mansfield's Ohio Brass Company, spent $400,000 building and furnishing his palatial French provincial estate in 1926—an estate now dedicated to the study and display of gardening, horticulture, birds, and related subjects, and called ***Kingwood Center***.

King joined Ohio Brass in 1893, working his way through the ranks from chief engineer to sales manager, and later from vice president and president to chairman. After his death at age 84 in 1952, his will established an endowment for the development and perpetual maintenance of Kingwood.

Two of the three floors of the mansion are open to the public. Perhaps the most impressive room is the formal dining room, with its hand-painted French wallpaper, delicate crystal chandelier, and antique chairs and table—a room that any monarch would proudly claim. The mansion also houses an extensive library on horticulture, landscaping, and related topics.

The grounds of the estate include twelve distinct gardens, each designed and arranged by the staff. The center plants 55,000 tulips each year, with the peak blooming season for these during the first two weeks in May. The tulips are replaced with 35,000 annuals to create a summer display. The paths also take you past Kingwood's collections of trees, shrubs, and ferns, and nature trails allow you to enjoy the abundant wildflowers. A variety of ducks and ornamental birds freely roam the grounds, and 130 species of native birds have been sighted on the premises. The greenhouse and orangery feature displays of seasonal flowering plants, cactuses, orchids, and tropical plants.

Kingwood Center is at 900 Park Ave. West (OH 430), in Mansfield; (419) 522-0211; kingwoodcenter.org. Grounds and greenhouse are open daily, 10 a.m. to 5 p.m., Mar through Dec. Kingwood Hall is open May through Sept, with tours every Sat at 11 a.m. and 2 p.m. Kingwood Hall admission is $8 per person, children (ages 12 and under) free.

keene's fireproof house

Fred Sharby was afraid of fire. Two of the theaters he owned burned flat, and he had a terror of dying in a fire. So he tore down his house on the north side of Roxbury Street in Keene and built a new one, all of fireproof materials. Steel girders, stucco, plaster, and fireproof floor tiles, doors of solid metal, and a furnace enclosed in cement walls have indeed lasted to this day without a fire.

Fred wasn't so lucky. He chose the night of November 28, 1942, to go to the Cocoanut Grove in Boston and died in that fire.

ALSO WORTH SEEING

Franklin Park Conservatory and Botanical Gardens, Columbus

German Village, Columbus

Short North arts and entertainment district, Columbus

Columbus Zoo

Columbus Museum of Art

COSI, Center of Science and Industry, Columbus

Ohio Historical Society and Ohio Village, Columbus

Wexner Center for the Arts, Columbus

Wyandot Lake, Columbus

The modern carousel emerged in the 1870s, when an English engineer-manufacturer named Frederick Savage applied steampower to these marvelous devices. Within a few years of this enhancement, Robert Tidman, an amusement ride manufacturer from England, designed one of the first up-and-down cranking devices that gave the horses their now-familiar galloping motion. Machines could now support two and three (eventually up to five) concentric rows of elaborately carved wooden horses and various other menagerie figures, as well as the many decorative panels and trimmings that were used to give the carousel a grand appearance by hiding its mechanicals. Musical accompaniment also evolved, from the simplicity of a drum or set of bells to the rich sounds of a band organ.

Consequently, public demand for carousels reached new heights in much of Europe and America, rising steadily in the years approaching the turn of the century and then truly booming in the two decades following 1900. This demand was further driven by the increased number of amusement parks built on both continents. Wherever it was, the carousel became a central part of a magnificent social event, as crowds of people in their Sunday best would climb aboard a favorite steed or just sit and listen to the lively music while enjoying the breeze generated by the machine.

Unique carving styles emerged from each of three regions producing carousels. English carousel figures were the easiest to identify because their "romance" side (the side that faced out and thus received more detailed carving) was on the left, unlike most other European and all American figures, whose outer side was on the right. This difference stemmed from the clockwise direction of English carousels, which encouraged riders to mount their horse properly from the left and was a result of the fact that the ring-catching game so popular in continental Europe and America never caught on in England.

Conversely, carousels in the US and the rest of Europe rotated counterclockwise to leave the right hand free to reach for the ring.

With tools in hand, gifted craftsmen gave us what has come to be known as the "golden age" of the wooden carousel in America, which extended from around 1880 to the early 1930s. During this time, carousels became evermore artistically grand and technologically advanced, with electricity replacing steam and the development of an overhead cranking mechanism, still in use today, that produced a smoother galloping motion.

Mansfield is home to the first new hand-carved wooden carousel built since the 1930s. Reminiscent of a turn-of-the-twentieth-century Philadelphia-style carousel, the main attraction at ***Richland Carrousel Park*** features fifty-two distinctive wooden animals and two chariots. The carousel has thirty

Lincoln's Last Journey

Abraham Lincoln journeyed across Ohio in life and death, and some say the slain president still travels Ohio's railways. Between the time of the popular vote and the formal vote of the Electoral College in 1860, Lincoln visited Ohio. It was, we are told, in the office of Ohio governor William Dennison that Lincoln actually heard he had won the presidency. Visitors to the Ohio Statehouse can see the desk at which the governor and President-elect Lincoln sat that day. The desk has been preserved and the current governor uses it as part of his working office. The rest of the rooms and chambers have also been restored to the style, color, and furnishings that Mr. Lincoln saw during that happy visit.

Lincoln journeyed back across Ohio on the trip that marked the close of his presidency and the end of his life. The funeral train for the slain president stopped in Columbus, and the body of Lincoln lay in state in the statehouse rotunda. The educational center in the lower level of the building documents that sad event, describing the crowds that packed the statehouse and grounds to pay their respects to the fallen leader.

The Lincoln funeral train also gave people in farming and rural regions the chance of a glimpse of their assassinated president. A special lead engine, or pilot car, steamed down the rails in advance of the funeral train. People came to the tracks to wait in sad tribute. As the train, draped in black, passed by, some could see the ornate coffin and the men on guard around it.

The image of that somber journey burned itself into the memories of the adults and children who stood in a final tribute along the rail line. But some say that moment was also somehow burned into the fabric of time. Each April 27, legend has it that Lincoln's train again rolls down the track. The muffled sound of the steam locomotive passes through the quiet Ohio countryside. Those who tell the tale of the recurring trip say that the dim light from the funeral train illuminates the ever-vigilant guards who will forever stand over the last journey of their fallen leader.

The Lady in Gray

If you take a moment to stroll through the historic Camp Chase Confederate Cemetery in Columbus, some say the Lady in Gray may join you. A grieving young woman with her hair tied back in a bun and dressed in an 1860s-style gray traveling suit is fabled to walk among the gravestones there. Visitors to the site, which rests on what was Camp Chase Union Military Camp during the Civil War, have reported this sad woman, always looking down and weeping.

Adding to the legend, flowers have been placed on the grave of the Unknown Soldier and on the grave of Benjamin Allen, a Confederate soldier in the 50th Tennessee regiment. Since the site is also home to Civil War reenactments and commemorations, the legend grows. Those participating in the reenactments and dressed in period garb or uniform have reported either being joined by the Lady in Gray, hearing an otherworldly weeping, or having their commemorations disrupted by violent gusts of wind.

So as you stroll among the tombstones, the Lady in Gray could be lingering nearby, still grieving for a loved one lost in the great Civil War. The annual Camp Chase Memorial Service for fallen Confederate Soldiers is held at the cemetery at 2900 Sullivant Ave., Columbus. This commemoration has been held at this site since 1895.

horses and twenty-two menagerie figures including four bears, four ostriches, four cats, four rabbits, a goat, a giraffe, a lion, a tiger, a zebra, and a mythical hippocampus. The carousel is one the few which is wheelchair accessible. The horse in front of the chariot swivels and the chariot seat lifts up to accommodate a wheelchair.

These colorful figures were hand-carved and painted in Mansfield. Guarding the entrance to the carousel are two large bronze horses, cast from antique molds.

Music is provided by a Stinson organ, which helps conjure up childhood memories for many of the carousel's riders. Eighteen hand-painted scenery panels adorn the top of the carousel, depicting Mansfield past and present.

Richland Carrousel Park is at 75 N. Main St., Mansfield; (419) 522-4223; richlandcarrousel.com. Open Memorial Day through Labor Day, Mon through Sat, 10 a.m. to 5 p.m.; and Sun, 11 a.m. to 5 p.m. Every Fri from 4 to 8 p.m. is family night, with five rides for $2. Open the day after Labor Day until the day before Memorial Day daily 11 a.m. to 5 p.m. and the first Fri 11 a.m. to 8 p.m.; closed on holidays. No admission charge; rides are $1 or 6 for $5.

A walk through the Bible? That's what you'll find at ***BibleWalk*** dedicated to "bringing God's word to life." The vision for this unique museum—Ohio's only wax museum—dates back to the early 1970s, when pastor Richard

Diamond and his wife, Alwilda, toured a museum in Georgia that depicted the Ascension of Christ. Moved by the exhibit, the Diamonds started planning for a Bible museum. After years of work, the museum opened its doors for the first time on August 15, 1987.

The museum has more than 100 scenes and over 325 wax figures for vivid life-size re-creations of favorite Old and New Testament stories, including a wax re-creation of the Last Supper. From the Creation of Man to the Judgment of Man, these scenes are complete with narrative and special effects. BibleWalk now has seven museums—Life of Christ, Miracles of the Old Testament,

Shawshank Trail Showcases Ohio Filming

"Remember, Red, hope is a good thing, maybe the best of things, and no good thing ever dies."

Andy Dufresne (Tim Robbins) in *The Shawshank Redemption*

The heavy clank of the metal door echoes off the cold concrete and sends shivers down my spine. What a living death it must have been to be locked away in these dark prison cells.

But one man did escape, at least in the movie *The Shawshank Redemption*, filmed in the very prison where I am standing. Released in 1994 and based on a story by Stephen King, the movie traces the tale of mild-mannered banker Andy Dufresne (actor Tim Robbins), sentenced to two consecutive life terms in a horrendous prison for the murders of his wife and her lover – a crime he didn't commit.

Forming a friendship with fellow prisoner Red (actor Morgan Freeman), Andy suffers the brutality of prison life, ingratiates himself with the warden by running a money-laundering operation for the man in charge, and manages a daring escape after 19 years.

"I don't think anyone expected the movie to be as popular as it is," said Jodie Snavely, special projects director for Destination Mansfield Richland County (Ohio). "It remains one of the most loved and iconic movies of all time."

When the movie came out, Shawshank devotees began heading to Mansfield. "Visitors from all over the world started coming into our office asking where this Shawshank site was or that site was," Snavely said. "We decided to find those locations and make it easier for Shawshank fans. We created our Shawshank Trail."

The driving tour features fourteen filming sites with large red-and-white Shawshank Trail signs that visitors can enjoy at their own pace. Visitors often start their tour with that spookily magnificent prison nicknamed "Dracula's Castle." Built in 1886, the Gothic-looking Ohio State Reformatory is beautiful in a scary way.

"It was supposed to be menacing yet spiritual," said tour guide Ron Puff. "The idea was to encourage young inmates to turn away from their sinful pasts, to reform, and to start a new life when they left here."

Museum of Christian Martyrs, Amazing Grace–The Journeys of Paul, Kingdom of God, Museum of Woodworking, and Heart of the Reformation.

The "Museum of Woodcarving" is the largest collection of woodcarvings in the world created by one man. Joseph Barta took three decades to carve his vision of Bible stories into 100 life-size figures. To complete his life-sized carving of the The Last Supper, Barta spent more than four years, including two years on the face of Jesus. The collection also features more than 400 miniature carvings of wildlife, pets, and livestock. The collection was originally displayed in a museum in Spooner, Wisconsin, for more than 32 years. In

But as prison populations burgeoned in the twentieth century, the reformatory was forced to accept more violent criminals. By the 1960s, the reformatory was overcrowded and filled with disease, murder, and mayhem.

After a prison riot and complaints of atrocities, the Ohio State Reformatory was closed due to inhumane conditions on Dec. 31, 1990. About 154,000 inmates had passed through its gates. The reformatory was slated to be torn down and turned into a parking lot for the newer prison built nearby.

Instead the facility is now on the National Register of Historic Places and has its East Cell Block listed in the *Guinness Book of World Records* for the world's largest free-standing steel cell block–six terrifying tiers.

Shawshank fans touring the prison can experience the parole board room, Andy's cell, warden's office, sinister solitary confinement "hole," and Andy's escape tunnel that he secretly dug for years and through which he crawled to freedom.

One of the most poignant and important Shawshank sites is no longer there. On July 22, 2016, the famous Shawshank oak tree was toppled by high winds. Part of the tree had already fallen when it was split by lightning in a storm five years earlier.

In the film, the tree is where Red goes after his release from prison and finds a box buried under stones near the tree. The box contains a letter and cash to buy a bus ticket to see old friend Andy who fled to Mexico after escaping prison. The towering tree was where Andy had proposed to his wife.

"Promise me, Red, if you ever get out, find that spot," Andy told Red one day in prison.

I think what Snavely said after hearing that the tree had crashed to the ground is a perfect eulogy for the beloved white oak and a reminder of one of the most famous quotes from the film:

"I'm sure people will still come to see where the tree was because hope is a good thing," Snavely said. "And a good thing never dies."

Shawshank Trail brochures are available at the Mansfield Visitors Center at 124 N. Main St. (419) 525-1300, destinationmansfield.com.

1984, the owners moved the collection to Kissimmee, Florida. It was returned to Wisconsin in 1989 to Shell Lake. And, in August 2020, the collection moved to BibleWalk.

BibleWalk is at 500 Tingley Ave., Mansfield; (419) 524-0139, (800) 222-0139; biblewalk.us. Open Oct, Nov, and Dec, Tues through Sat, 10 a.m. to 4 p.m.; Jan through Mar, Sat 10 a.m. to 4 p.m.; Apr and May, Tues through Sat, 10 a.m. to 5 p.m.; June through Aug, Mon through Sat, 10 a.m. to 5 p.m.; Sept, Mon through Sat, 10 a.m. to 5 p.m.

Admission for each museum: adults $6.50; senior citizens $6.25; children (ages 9 to 18) $5; age 8 and under free. A package rate for all seven tours is adults $38; senior citizens $36.25; children (ages 9 to 18) $19. Dinner With Grace dinner theater offers a full-course meal with a portrayal on Sat during the summer at 12:30 p.m. At least two-week advance reservation required. Dinner: $20 adults, $5 students (ages 6 to 12), and free for children (ages 5 and under).

During the Civil War, the grounds were used as a Union army training facility because of a healthy spring located near the site. In the 1880s, Mansfield donated the land to the State of Ohio for a reformatory. Work began on the ***Ohio State Reformatory*** in 1885.

"Mansfield's Greatest Day," proclaimed the Richland Shield with a banner headline on November 4, 1886. The cornerstone laid that day evolved into a magnificent chateauesque structure. Noted architect Levi T. Scofield designed the Ohio State Reformatory to resemble medieval chateaus and castles. Spiritual and uplifting architecture was intended to provide a transcendent religious experience to help reform the behavior of young male prisoners. The East Cell Block houses the world's largest freestanding steel cell block, rising six tiers. After numerous delays, the first prisoners arrived at this turn-of-the-twentieth-century prison in 1896, and inmates passed time there for nearly 100 years, until its closing in 1990.

The Ohio State Reformatory is listed on the National Register of Historic Places and today welcomes visitors. It also welcomes film crews. *The Shawshank Redemption* with Tim Robbins and Morgan Freeman was shot here, and so were scenes from *Air Force One* with Harrison Ford, *Tango and Cash*, and *Harry and Walter Go to New York*. Special events at the reformatory include the always popular Ghost Hunts and the Haunted Prison Experience around Halloween.

The Ohio State Reformatory is at 100 Reformatory Rd., Mansfield; (419) 522-2644; mrps.org. The facility is open Apr through Sept, daily from 11 a.m. to 4 p.m.; Oct through Mar, Thurs through Sun, 11 a.m. to 4 p.m. A variety of guided and self-guided tours are offered; check the website. Admission for self-guided tours: adults $25; senior citizens $23; children (ages 7 to 17) $23.

Guided tours are an additional $10 per person. Audio wands are an additional $5 per person on self-guided tours.

On select days throughout the year, the Ohio State Reformatory also offers Ghost Hunts, which are informal attempts to document paranormal activity. Admission is $99 per person and includes access to the facility from 7 p.m. to 3 a.m. with complimentary water, coffee, and hot chocolate available throughout the night. Ghost Hunts are limited to ages 18 and over and are not sleepovers. Participants leave at 3 a.m. and do not have sleeping facilities. Participants have full access to the eight most haunted areas. Brave souls also can undergo a lone vigil in the Hole, the spooky site once used for solitary confinement. Check the website for other paranormal tours.

The Ohio State Fair

Perhaps the carnival rides on the midway aren't your idea of getting away from the crowds and onto the road less traveled. But visitors to the Ohio State Fair, as well as many of Ohio's county fairs, can find the simple pleasures of yesteryear if they look beyond the glare of the midway.

Visiting the animal exhibits takes you back to the time when fairs were truly a celebration of rural life. Here's an example: One of the most charming and whimsical animal competitions is found in the rabbit barn. There is something comical about a judge walking down a row of fluffy bunnies, noses wiggling, whiskers twitching, and tall rabbit ears standing up on alert. You may be amazed at just how many kinds of rabbits are shown at the fairs, from tiny dwarfs to those the size of the average dog, and some with ears that droop like those of a basset hound.

The more traditional farm animals also are a treat for all members of the family to observe. Check the daily schedule for the children's competitions. You'll be charmed by the spunk of a 3-foot-tall girl or boy showing a cow, goat, or pig that has to be twice the child's weight.

Just a trip through the barns can bring a smile to your face. The goats will greet you with grumpy bleats, and the sheep are forever being groomed and fluffed by their owners. To keep the animals clean and fresh looking, some owners will wrap them in blankets, often with a signature color and the name of the family farm. It looks, to the city dweller, as if they are uniformed and suited up for some kind of sheep football game.

The modern fair is awash with food wagons featuring fried just about anything. But if you want something that will keep you in that bygone, farm feeling, just keep walking past the wagons to the Dairy Barn. Not only can you see a huge sculpture of something (it changes every year) made out of pounds and pounds of butter, but you can get a scoop or a cone of some dairy-fresh ice cream, or a cheese sandwich that doesn't taste like it came out of a plastic wrapper.

Between 1839 and 1861, Ohio inmates constructed the foundation and ground floor of the ***Ohio Statehouse***. Built in the Greek revival style, the statehouse is situated on a 10-acre site donated by four prominent Columbus landowners. Greek revival was the architecture of choice in nineteenth-century America, with Greece representing one of the world's earliest democracies. The statehouse, with its center rotunda and cupola, mimics the stature of the Greek Parthenon. The large Doric colonnades are typical of Greek revival structures.

Construction of this significant building did not happen easily; it took seven architects more than twenty-two years, encompassing a cholera epidemic and an 8-year work stoppage. One of the most important architects on the

Ohio Veterans Plaza

The words of the unknown soldier speak across the years. Written to his son from overseas as a birthday letter to congratulate him on turning 8 years old, the soldier's sorrow and loneliness are etched between the lines.

"As I write this, I am in my 'office' about 300 feet under the ground," he writes. "Outside the tunnel, which is hewn out of solid rock, I can hear the air rushing. I have just come back from a long trip all along the front. I saw a few of my old friends. So many more are gone."

The soldier doubts the letter will even reach the boy until he is almost 9. He talks of the brave men he knew who were killed in the conflict. In signing off, he closes, "Be good, study hard and don't forget me."

The unknown soldier never came back from that conflict. But the words he wrote to his son are now preserved for all to read at the Ohio Veterans Plaza at the Ohio Statehouse in Columbus.

Dedicated in August 1998, the Ohio Veterans Plaza honors Ohio men and women who have served our country since the beginning of World War II.

The idea behind the letters is that visitors can't tell which war was going on when they were written. What was expressed in the letters was timeless. Literary consultant John H. Mitchell, a Navy and Vietnam war veteran from Greenfield, chose the letters based on their "timeless sentiments."

The letters were gathered from across Ohio. The Governor's Office of Veterans' Affairs got about 1,500 letters, and the Mitchell narrowed the selection to 250 letters.

A committee of veterans and Statehouse representatives then selected the final 70 letters written by Ohio soldiers to their loved ones back home in Ohio. Designed by John Schooley, the $1.9 million plaza features two curving, limestone walls on the north and south ends of the lawn on the east side of the Statehouse. Each wall contains 35 letters.

project was Nathan B. Kelly. He added many flourishes to the building, though his thanks was to be fired because the commissioners overseeing the project viewed these same flourishes as both too expensive and too lavish. To Kelly's credit, it was he who realized that the design contained no heating or ventilation system, an oversight he corrected.

During the twentieth century, growth in state government resulted in the building being continuously remodeled, with its magnificent high-ceilinged rooms slowly chopped up and subdivided with new walls and drop ceiling after drop ceiling. Heating and cooling systems produced a ground floor most notable for its exposed (and occasionally leaking) steampipes and wiring.

The Ohio Veterans Plaza has been positioned as the east entrance to the Capitol Complex. Officials say this positioning is a symbol that the government could not exist without the sacrifices Ohio's veterans have made.

Flags representing the 88 Ohio counties border the plaza. The site is landscaped with flowers, and each end features a lighted fountain. The grassy area between the two walls of letters was designed as a parade ground for military color guard marches and flag presentations on holidays.

The Ohio Veterans Plaza marked the completion of a $116.7 million Statehouse renovation project that took six years and was finished in 1996. Built between 1829 and 1861, the Statehouse is one of the oldest statehouses in continuous use in the United States, housing both the governor and the General Assembly.

Constructed in the Doric, Greek Revival architecture style, the Statehouse is built of Columbus limestone, taken from the west bank of the Scioto River.

You can see a stained-glass skylight of the Seal of Ohio that was not evident before the restoration began. In an attempt to fix a leak, the skylight had been covered years earlier on both the inside and outside with wood. Restorers were not even aware that the beautiful stained-glass skylight was there until they began restorations and removed the wooden cover.

Several months of cleaning was required to restore the marble Grand Staircase to its original white appearance. Years of coal, wood, and tobacco smoke had stained the marble to a dark yellow.

Light fixtures along the Grand Staircase are plumbed for both gas and electricity because the original designers did not know if electricity was going to catch on.

The Ohio Veterans Plaza has quickly become a popular gathering spot. No matter how many times people visit, they are often drawn to the words carved on the plaza walls.

Each letter tells the story of a real person with hopes and fears. Many of the writers never returned home. But one letter is filled with jubilation. It says simply: "This is it, Baby. I'm coming home!"

A comprehensive restoration of the statehouse and adjoining Senate Building in the 1990s was long overdue. This massive project, which required the Ohio house and senate to meet outside the statehouse complex for two years, restored Ohio's most significant government buildings to their earlier grandeur. The Capitol Atrium, which connects the two buildings, was added as well. It was on this site in 1859 that Abraham Lincoln spoke to a small group of Ohioans about the just-completed Lincoln-Douglas debates. The ground floor today hosts a museum and visitor center, with guided tours available.

Free guided tours are offered on the hour, Mon through Fri, from 10 a.m. to 3 p.m.; Sat, noon to 3 p.m. Tours last about an hour. Self-guided tours can be taken anytime during statehouse hours. Self-guided tour brochures are available at the Statehouse Museum Shop. The Statehouse also offers cell phone audio tours for free. Visitors can explore the 10 acres of Capitol Square and dial in on their cell phone to specific phone numbers to listen to information about monuments and sculpture. Audio tour signs are at the base of each monument.

The Ohio Statehouse is at the corner of Broad and High Streets at 1 Capitol Sq., Columbus; (614) 752-9777, (888) 644-6123; ohiostatehouse.org. Open Mon through Fri, 8 a.m. to 5 p.m.; Sat and Sun, 11 a.m. to 5 p.m.; closed holidays. No admission charge.

Looking for fresh food or just a fresh shopping experience? Try the ***North Market Downtown*** in Columbus. The market, in operation since 1876, is a celebration of food and fun. During the summer, there is an outdoor market showcasing the best from neighboring farms, as well as entertainment and children's activities. Gourmet cooks can find the freshest eggs, poultry, meats, seafood, cheeses, vegetables, and fruits. A Touch of Earth offers a large assortment of spices and herbs. Fresh herbs are also available at North Market Spices.

If you want to add specialty baked goods to your table, or just nibble on a delicious snack while you shop, stop

where the tomato is king

Tomato juice, tomato soup, tomato sauce—they all are standard fare at the annual Tomato Festival in Reynoldsburg. But you'll find some surprising and different tomato dishes, too, from fried green tomatoes to tomato brownies.

Reynoldsburg takes special pride in the red fruit—or vegetable, depending on your point of view. You'll see the lovely red round tomato on city signs proclaiming Reynoldsburg "The Tomato Capital."

It's certain that the tomato is king during the yearly celebration as the city welcomes farmers, cooks, and tomato lovers to town to eat and compete.

The festival is generally held in the early part of September. Visit reytomatofest.com for a tomato festival update.

Stroll through Historic German Village

They don't speak Deutsch in German Village anymore. But the neighborhood still has an Old World feeling of its own and is a popular attraction for residents and visitors. Its brick-lined streets feature shops, guesthouses, restaurants, and a bookstore that takes up an entire street block. The Book Loft offers thirty-two rooms of books, stacked from floor to ceiling. Opened in the late 1970s with just five rooms, the Book Loft is now said to stock more than 500,000 books, plus puzzles, stationery, cards, souvenirs, and much more.

Designated a National Historic District, German Village has its roots in 1814 when German immigrants settled in a village designed to be almost like home. After 1830, more Germans began to arrive in the area to escape wars, famine, persecution, and lack of opportunity in their homeland.

The streets are narrow, with houses made of handmade brick, built almost on the sidewalk. Surprisingly beautiful gardens have been created on the sides and in back of the homes. Today, German Village is 233 acres of "living" history filled with sturdy brick cottages, Dutch doubles, and two-story homes. You can see hand-cut limestone steps leading to heavy wooden doors, beautiful slate roofs, clay chimney pots, and other details that are reminders of another time.

The front steps, or "stoops," were an extension of a person's home into the public domain and played an important part in the village's social life in the nineteenth century. Constructed of gray limestone, they were a prominent feature on many homes.

About 4,000 people now live in German Village and many of them volunteer to keep their neighborhood a special place. Home and garden tours along with neighborhood strolls are offered throughout the year.

German Village is also home to a vibrant commercial community, including Schmidt's Restaurant Und Sausage Haus. A fifth-generation family-owned business since 1886, Schmidt's Restaurant still uses its original sausage recipe.

Stop by the German Village Visitors Center at 588 S. Third St., (614) 221-8888, germanvillage.com, to watch an award-winning 8-minute history video and pick up brochures and maps about what to see and do in German Village.

in at Pastaria, Omega Artisan Baking, or Fox's Bagel & Deli. You can even complete your table with fresh flowers from Market Blooms or a bottle of that special wine from The Barrel & Boar.

International specialties are also within easy reach at the North Market Downtown. ***Flavors of India*** stocks a full line of Indian foods and spices. ***Firdous Express*** serves Mediterranean foods, including a line of fresh baked goods. Sushi and Japanese groceries can be found at ***Nida's Sushi***. ***Hubert's Polish Kitchen*** serves delish pierogi, cabbage rolls, kielbasa, and more from authentic Polish recipes handed down for generations. ***Dos Hermanos*** will light your taste buds with authentic Mexican food, plus virtual cooking classes.

The North Market is located at 59 Spruce St., Columbus; (614) 463-9664; northmarket.org. Open Sun and Mon, 10 a.m. to 5 p.m. (optional merchant day; not all businesses are open); Tues through Sat, 9 a.m. to 7 p.m.

In 2020, North Market Bridge Park opened for business in the city of Dublin at the Bridge Park development. The new market offers about 20 of the finest tastemakers in the region. North Market Bridge Park is open Sun through Tues, 9 a.m. to 8 pm.; Wed, 9 a.m. to 9 p.m.; Fri and Sat, 9 a.m. to 11 p.m. Merchants include Bake Me Happy, Bubbles Tea & Juice Company, Falafel Kitchen, Galio's Pizzeria, Pablo's Havana Café, Saddleberk, and The Pit BBQ Grille.

The North Market sits in the midst of two of Columbus's best entertainment areas, the Arena District (named for Nationwide Arena, home of the Columbus Blue Jackets National Hockey League team) and the Short North.

Kelton House

Your tours in the Columbus area may take you to the lovely Kelton House. This grand and charming mansion was built in 1852 and is a fine example of Greek revival architecture. The home and its lovely Victorian garden at 586 E. Town St. are now a favorite spot, not just for tours, but for special events such as wedding and anniversary celebrations.

The Junior League operates the mansion, but legend has it that the home still feels the touch of the Kelton family. Fernando Kelton built the home in the mid-1800s, and it remained in the family until 1975. The last of the Keltons to occupy the home was Fernando Kelton's granddaughter, Grace Bird Kelton. She was nationally known in her own right as an interior designer. She preserved the lovely old home's furnishing in the graceful style of her grandfather's era.

The legend surrounding Kelton House is that though Ms. Kelton passed from this world on Christmas Eve 1975, she just couldn't leave the care of the family manse to outsiders. Tales tell of the former owner returning to rearrange the furniture or move objects or just walk through the house to make sure that the current caretakers don't forget who is really in charge of this piece of Kelton family history.

For self-guided audio tours, the Kelton House is open Thurs through Sun, noon to 4 p.m. Closed in January. Admission $7 adults, $5 senior citizens, $3 students kindergarten to grade 12. Sophia's Secret Tour features "Sophia Kenton" as personal guide, sharing her family's secret life as conductors on the Underground Railroad and may introduce visitors to a runaway slave making her way to freedom in Canada. Tours are $12 per person. Or choose Tour and Tea with Sophia where "Sophia Kenton" guides guests through the home and offers afternoon refreshments. Tour is $18 per person. keltonhouse.com, (614) 464-2022.

These commercial areas and residential neighborhoods just north of the heart of downtown are full of great restaurants, bars, clubs, and other entertainment venues.

Similarly, if you take High Street south of downtown, visitors find two other popular gathering areas, the ***Brewery District*** and ***German Village***. Read more about German Village in the spotlighted feature above. As for the Brewery District, the nook of Columbus just west of German Village is home to dining options, entertainment, bars with local beers, and America's largest resident theater company, Shadowbox Live.

Columbus has more than its share of quirky and unusual museums. Offerings include the ***Early Television Museum***, which features hundreds of pre–World War II American and British TVs, including mechanical televisions from the 1920s and 1930s. Other displays include a collection of antique picture tubes and early television studio production equipment and a 60-line flying spot TV scanner camera from the 1930s. Visitors can see themselves as they would have appeared on a 1930s mechanical television system.

The Early Television Museum is at 5396 Franklin St., Hilliard (a suburb northwest of Columbus); (614) 771-0510; earlytelevision.org. Open Sat, 10 a.m. to 6 p.m., and Sun, noon to 5 p.m. No admission charge, but donations welcome at $5 for adults and $2 for children (ages 12 and under).

Another intriguing small museum is the ***Motts Military Museum*** in suburban Groveport, which is dedicated to preserving the memory of all who have served in the U.S. military. Exhibits and artifacts span from the Revolutionary War to modern times, many associated with a particular soldier or group of soldiers. For example, the Civil War Union coat on display was worn by a Major Thomas Henry at Gettysburg in 1863. And the Civil War Colt .44 revolver was donated to the museum by a relative of the soldier who carried it in 1860. Other exhibits include one of Columbus native Eddie Rickenbacker's medals, a World War II Landing Craft, and a corncob pipe owned by General Douglas MacArthur.

The Motts Military Museum is at 5075 S. Hamilton Rd., Groveport; (614) 836-1500; mottsmilitarymuseuminc.com. Open Tues through Sat, 9 a.m. to 5 p.m.; Sun, 1 to 5 p.m. Adults $12; senior citizens $10; students $7.

Gahanna has become part of the Columbus metropolitan area, but the city also has been able to preserve some of its historic structures and with them, a unique identity. Original log homes and Victorian-influenced homes and shops still grace this city core. One way to enjoy this history on a nice day is to take a walking tour around the historic district of ***Gahanna***. The area was settled just after the Revolutionary War. The federal government gave away plots of land as payment to Union soldiers. John Clark formally founded the city in 1849.

Thurber House Stories

When he was seven years old, James Thurber and his brothers William and Robert decided to act out the tale of "William Tell." Young James was the one who stood with the apple on his head while his older brother took aim with a bow and arrow.

"His brother must have been taking too long to shoot so James turned around and the arrow hit him in the left eye," said Anne Touvell. "He lost his eye and had a glass eye from the age of seven. Eventually he ended up going blind (at age 47) because the stress was too much on his good eye."

As former deputy director at the Thurber House in Columbus, Touvell said she sometimes wonders "if James Thurber would have become the prolific writer and humorist if he hadn't gone blind."

As it was, Thurber became a beloved writer and cartoonist whose works are considered American classics. Thurber wrote thirty-two books including *The Secret Life of Walter Mitty* and *The Catbird Seat*. He was also the creator of numerous *New Yorker* magazine cover cartoons.

Born December 8, 1894, in Columbus, James Grover Thurber was the son of Charles, a civil clerk, and Mame, an eccentric woman who would influence many of her son's stories. "The family moved often and rented places to live all over the city," Touvell said.

The Thurber House is where the family lived from 1913-1917 when Thurber was a student at Ohio State University. Walking through the Victorian house is like seeing Thurber's stories come alive. The living room is where Thurber's Grandmother Fisher was convinced that "electricity was dripping invisibly" all over the house.

You could start your tour at the ***Lily Stone Bed & Breakfast*** at 106 S. High St. This building began its life as the Stone family home and was built around 1900. The Stone family that settled here were descendants of Thomas Stone, one of the signers of the Declaration of Independence. The Gahanna Historical Association owns the B&B, and volunteers keep the four-guest-room operation going. Rates are $110 per night or rent the whole house for $330 per night. Call (614) 475-3342; gahannahistory.com.

Almost directly across the street is the home of the city's founder, John Clark. Just to the north of the ***John Clark House*** is one of the original log homes build in the Gahanna area. This house was originally built in 1840 and was relocated to this spot by the Historical Society in 1968.

If you head farther north on High Street, you will find the ***Sanctuary***. This late Gothic revival–style building is on the National Register of Historic Places. Built as a Lutheran church in 1895, the impressive brick structure has become a popular place for wedding receptions. If you do not see a bride and groom posing for wedding photos there, you may see them at Creekside Park.

Thurber's story "The Car We Had to Push" detailed the room where Grandmother Fisher contested that electricity "leaked out of empty sockets if the wall switch had been left on." Off the living room is a small alcove where Thurber's father often slept with the family dogs when his three sons got to be too much for him.

In the kitchen, Thurber's mother made special gifts as an apology for their dog Muggs who liked to bite people. Muggs was immortalized in Thurber's story "The Dog Who Bit People."

The small bedroom where the future humorist and cartoonist slept has the Underwood #5 typewriter that Thurber used while at *The New Yorker* magazine. The Wall of Fame closet in the bedroom is filled with signatures of authors who have given readings at the Thurber House.

The dining room is where Thurber first heard footsteps of the ghost in "The Night the Ghost Got In." Thurber hid in the bathroom when he heard the ghost running up the back stairs.

Visitors are invited to touch anything in the house except the Underwood typewriter. Play the piano, listen to the Victrola, skim the magazines, photograph anything, sit in a comfy chair, and even use the old-timey bathroom.

"Make yourself at home," the docents say. "We think that's what James Thurber would have wanted."

James Thurber died November 2, 1961, of pneumonia after a stroke and was buried in Columbus. He was 66 years old.

Thurber House is located at 77 Jefferson Ave., (614) 464-1032, thurberhouse.org

Walk west on Town Street toward the river and turn south or left on Mill Street. Town Street and Granville Street bound the park, where an old mill once labored. Now a waterfall graces the former millrace. This park is one of the centerpieces of an effort to preserve and rejuvenate the historic district.

Along your walk through the historic district you will find shops offering handicrafts, antiques, and other collectibles.

If you are still hankering for a little more Gahanna history, take a little drive down Johnstown road to what the locals call the "Moosesonian." While scarcely displaying the wealth or breadth of collections of the Smithsonian, the ***Ohio State Moose Association Museum*** will be of special interest if you, or a family member, belong to the Loyal Order of Moose or the Women of the Moose. While modest, this collection of pictures, documents, and Moose memorabilia is one of only two such collections in the country.

The Ohio State Moose Association Museum is at 335 W. Johnstown Rd., Gahanna; (614) 476-9103; ohiomoose.net. Open Mon through Thurs, 3:30 to 11 p.m.; Fri and Sat, noon to midnight; Sun, 12:30 to 8:30 p.m. Admission: free.

Roses Are for Romance

Romance off the beaten path could mean treating your special someone to—not a dozen roses—but hundreds of dozens! You can't pick them and take them home, but the two of you can share the sweet smell of romance as you stroll through the rose gardens of Whetstone Park in Columbus.

The park is home to ball fields and to wooded paths and ponds, but the highlight of the area is the impressive display of rosebushes, especially during the month of June, when the park hosts the rose festival. Rose fanciers love to walk among the varieties and see their favorite flowers. The casual gardener will appreciate the rows and rows of roses just for their broad spectrum of colors and light, inviting fragrance.

If you wander the Park of Roses on summer weekends, don't be surprised to see a wedding party using this as a floral background for their most romantic day. The park also hosts many concerts and poetry readings in the spring and summer months.

The poet Robert Burns wrote, "My love is like a red, red, rose . . ." The park can't guarantee love, but a romantic ramble through the roses could be a good beginning.

The rose festival is held in early to mid-June at Whetstone Park, 3293 N. High St., Columbus. Call (614) 645-3330 or visit the Columbus Parks and Recreation website at columbus.gov for information.

The Hanby family and the work done at the ***Hanby House*** touched the lives of many Americans during the mid-1800s. This house, built in 1846, served as a stop on the Underground Railroad, helping slaves in their flight from the South to freedom. Benjamin Hanby was a minister, teacher, and an abolitionist.

Hanby also was famous as a composer. Among his works are "Darling Nellie Gray" and "Up on the Housetop." The Hanby House contains many family belongings, including the original printing plates for "Darling Nellie Gray" and the composer's flute.

Bishop William Hanby, Benjamin Hanby's father, was a United Brethren minister and cofounder of Otterbein College. Hanby House has been designated a United Methodist shrine.

The Hanby House is located at 160 W. Main St., Westerville; (614) 891-6289, (800) 600-6834; westervillehistory.org. Open March through December Tours by appointment. Admission: adults $3; senior citizens $2.50; children (ages 5 to 17) $1.

Gentlemen, start your engines. That's what visitors to the ***Motorcycle Hall of Fame Museum*** no doubt would like to do . . . start up the many powerful and exotic bikes on display. Enshrined in the Hall of Fame are more than 200 motorcyclists who have made major contributions to the sport—from

HELPFUL WEBSITES

Ohio Division of Travel and Tourism
ohio.org

Columbus Convention and Visitors Bureau
experiencecolumbus.com

Columbus Dispatch
dispatch.com

early twentieth-century racing champ Ralph Hepburn to modern-day enthusiast Jay Leno. In addition to the Hall of Fame, the museum consists of three large exhibit areas.

One favorite exhibit is the Heroes of Harley-Davidson, which features many great Harley bikes. But the focus of this exhibit is the people who have built Harley-Davidson into one of the world's great commercial brands.

For example, you will see a painstaking re-creation of the famous Milwaukee backyard shed where William Harley and Arthur Davidson created their first motorcycle in 1903. And you'll learn about Bessie Stringfield, the 1940s African-American "Motorcycle Queen of Miami" who broke color and gender barriers as a competitive rider. Whether your interest is racing or cruising, any motorcycle enthusiast will be in hog heaven here.

The Motorcycle Hall of Fame Museum is at 13515 Yarmouth Dr., Pickerington; (614) 856-2222; americanmotorcyclist.com. Open daily 9 a.m. to 5 p.m.; closed holidays. Admission: adults $10; senior citizens $8; children (ages 12 to 17) $3.

Places to Stay in West Central Ohio

BELLVILLE

Wishmaker House Bed & Breakfast
116 Main St.
(419) 886-9463
wishmakerhouse.com

COLUMBUS

The Blackwell Inn & Pfahl Conference Center
2110 Tuttle Park
(614) 247-4000
theblackwell.com

BrewDog DogHouse Columbus Hotel & Brewery
96 Gender Rd.
(614) 908-3054
brewdog.com

50 Lincoln Short North Bed & Breakfast
(614) 299-5050
50 E. Lincoln St.
columbus-bed-breakfast.com

Hotel LeVeque, Autograph Collection
50 W. Broad St.
(614) 224-9500
marriott.com

The Timbrook Guesthouse
5811 Olentangy River Rd.
(614) 634-2166
timbrookguesthouse.com

DELAWARE

Winter Street Inn
185 W. Winter St.
(740) 990-8695
winterstinn.com

GREENVILLE

Downtowner Bed & Breakfast
201 E. Third St.
(937) 997-2000

Wayman's Corner Bed & Breakfast
633 Central Ave.
(937) 316-6074
waymanscorner.com

MANSFIELD

The Safe House Bed & Breakfast
219 N. Stewart Rd.
(419) 961-1098
destinationmansfield.com/venue/safe-house-bed-breakfast/

Spruce Hill Inn & Cottages
3230 Possum Run Rd.
(419) 756-2200
sprucehillinn.com

RUSSELLS POINT

Oak Island at Indian Lake
accessible only by boat from Russells Point
(614) 560-3859
indianlake.com/cottages-hotels

SPRINGFIELD

Colonial Manor Bed & Breakfast
3774 Urbana Rd.
(937) 390-3949
colonialmanorbnb.com

Emma's Bed and Breakfast
4200 E. National Rd.
(937) 505-3602
emmasbb.com

Simon Kenton Inn
4690 Urbana Rd.
(937) 399-9950
simonkentoninn.com

URBANA

Cobblestone Hotel & Suites
170 Ohio 55
(937) 652-7828
staycobblestone.com

Scioto Inn
205 Scioto St.
(937) 508-4546
sciotoinn.com

VERSAILLES

Hotel Versailles
22 N. Center St.
(937) 526-3020
hotelversaillesohio.com

The French House Bed & Breakfast
7660 Burns Rd.
(937) 526-3100

Places to Eat in West Central Ohio

BELLVILLE

Buckeye Express Diner
810 Oh 97 W
(419) 886-2900
buckeyeexpressdiner.com

Der Dutchman Restaurant
720 OH 97
(419) 886-7070
dhgroup.com/restaurants/der-dutchman-bellville-oh

River Rock
7 Main St.
(419) 886-2599
riverrockbellville.com

Wishmaker House
116 Main St.
(419) 886-9463
wishmakerhouse.com
Lodging is also available.

COLUMBUS

Barcelona Restaurant & Bar
263 E. Whittier St.
(614) 443-3699
barcelonacolumbus.com

Figlio
1369 Grandview Ave.
(614) 481-8850
figliopizza.com

Hyde Park Prime Steakhouse
569 N. High St.
(614) 224-2204
hydeparkrestaurants.com

The Guild House
624 N. High St.
9614) 280-9780
theguildhousecolumbus.com

J. Gilbert's Wood Fired Steaks & Seafood
1 E. Campus View Blvd.
(614) 840-9090
jgilberts.com

Lindey's
169 E. Beck St.
(614) 228-4343
lindeys.com

Marcella's
615 N. High St.
(614) 223-2100
marcellasrestaurant.com

Martini Modern Italian
445 N. High St.
(614) 224-9259
martinimodernitalian.com

Milestone 229
229 S. Civic Center Dr.
(614) 427-0276
milestone229.com

The Refectory Restaurant
1092 Bethel Rd.
(614) 451-9774
refectory.com

Rooh
685 N. High St.
(614) 972-8678
roohcolumbus.com

Schmidt's Sausage Haus
240 E. Kossuth St.
(614) 444-6808
schmidthaus.com

Watershed Kitchen + Bar
1145 Chesapeake Ave.
(614) 357-1936
watersheddistillery.com

DELAWARE

Amato's Wood Fired Pizza
6 S. Sandusky St.
(740) 369-8797
amatoswoodfirepizza.com

Bun's Restaurant
14 W. Winter St.
(740) 363-3731
bunsrestaurant.com

Old Dog Alehouse & Brewery
13 W. Williams St.
(740) 990-4506
olddogalehouse.com

1808 American Bistro
29 E. Winter St.
(740) 417-4373
1808americanbistro.com

Typhoon Asian Fusion Bistro
10 N. Sandusky St.
(740) 362-9227
ohtyphoon.com

GREENVILLE

The Merchant House
406 S. Broadway St.
(937) 459-4405
tmhgreenville.com

Montage
527 S. Broadway St.
(937) 548-1950
montagecafe.com

Tolly's Gastropub
644 Wagner Ave.
(937) 459-5225
tollysgastropub.us

LIMA

The Met
306 N. Main St.
(419) 999-9463
themet306.com

Old City Prime
215 S. Main St.
(419) 227-7463
oldcityprime.com

MANSFIELD

Hudson & Essex
51 E. Fourth St.
(419) 513-5151
hudsonandessex.com

Oak Park Tavern
2919 OH 430
(419) 589-2637
oakparktavern.com

MARION

Sansotta's Fresh Italian
1292 Delaware Ave.
(740) 751-6596
sansottasitalian.com

SPRINGFIELD

Cecil & Lime
227 E. Cecil St.
(937) 322-7950
cecilandlime.com

The Hickory Inn
652 N. Limestone St.
(937) 323-1779
thehickoryinn.com

Speakeasy Ramen
365 Ludlow Ave.
(937) 324-3722
speakeasyramen.com

Stella Bleu Bistro
20 N. Fountain Ave.
(937) 717-0478
stellableubistro.com

TROY

The Caroline
5 S. Market St.
(937) 552-7676
thecarolineonthesquare
.com

Lincoln Square Restaurant
1320 Archer Dr.
(937) 332-0222
lincolnsquare5.com

Los Pitayos Mexican Restaurant
2317 W. Main St.
(937) 440-8999
mexicanrestauranttroyoh
.com

Sakai Japanese Bistro
2303 W. Main St.
(937) 440-1302
sakaijapanese.com

Smith's Boathouse Restaurant
439 N. Elm St.
(937) 335-3837
smithsboathouse.com

UPPER SANDUSKY

The Steer Barn
1144 E. Wyandot Ave.
(419) 294-3860
thesteerbarn.com

VAN WERT

Mi Ranchito
865 N. Washington St.
(419) 238-0123
miranchitomexican.com

The Edition
139 E. Main St.
(419) 771-1234
editionvw.com

VERSAILLES

Silas Creative Kitchen
21 W. Main St.
(937) 526-3020
hotelversaillesohio.com
Lodging is also available.

Winery at Versailles
6572 OH 47
(937) 526-3232
wineryatversailles.com

WAPAKONETA

La Neta Mexican Grill
1262 Bellefontaine St.
(567) 356-5226
lanetamexicangrill.com

The Side Rail
17 E. Auglaize St.
(419) 738-6593
thesiderailrestaurant.com

Northwest Ohio

Historic Plain

Surrounded by cornfields in the plains of northwest Ohio is a unique historical village—***AuGlaize Village***. Seventeen reconstructed or restored buildings (ca. 1860 to 1920) have been gathered from the surrounding area and provide visitors with a glimpse of life a century ago in this flat farming region of the state. Self-guided tours of AuGlaize allow you to explore at your own pace.

In Dr. Cameron's office, built in 1874 in Jewell, there are old medical journals and catalogs advertising medical products such as foot and ankle braces and the "Harvard Physician's Chair" that rural doctors used for surgery, adjusting it to one of dozens of positions depending on the particular procedure to be performed. Dr. Cameron owned one of these chairs, and it is in the back room of his office.

The Chapel of Crosses Church, which the congregation of Saint John's Lutheran Church in Sherwood built in 1875, is a one-room frame structure containing an antique wooden pump organ. The Story and Clark Company of Chicago manufactured this ornately carved instrument in 1892.

NORTHWEST OHIO

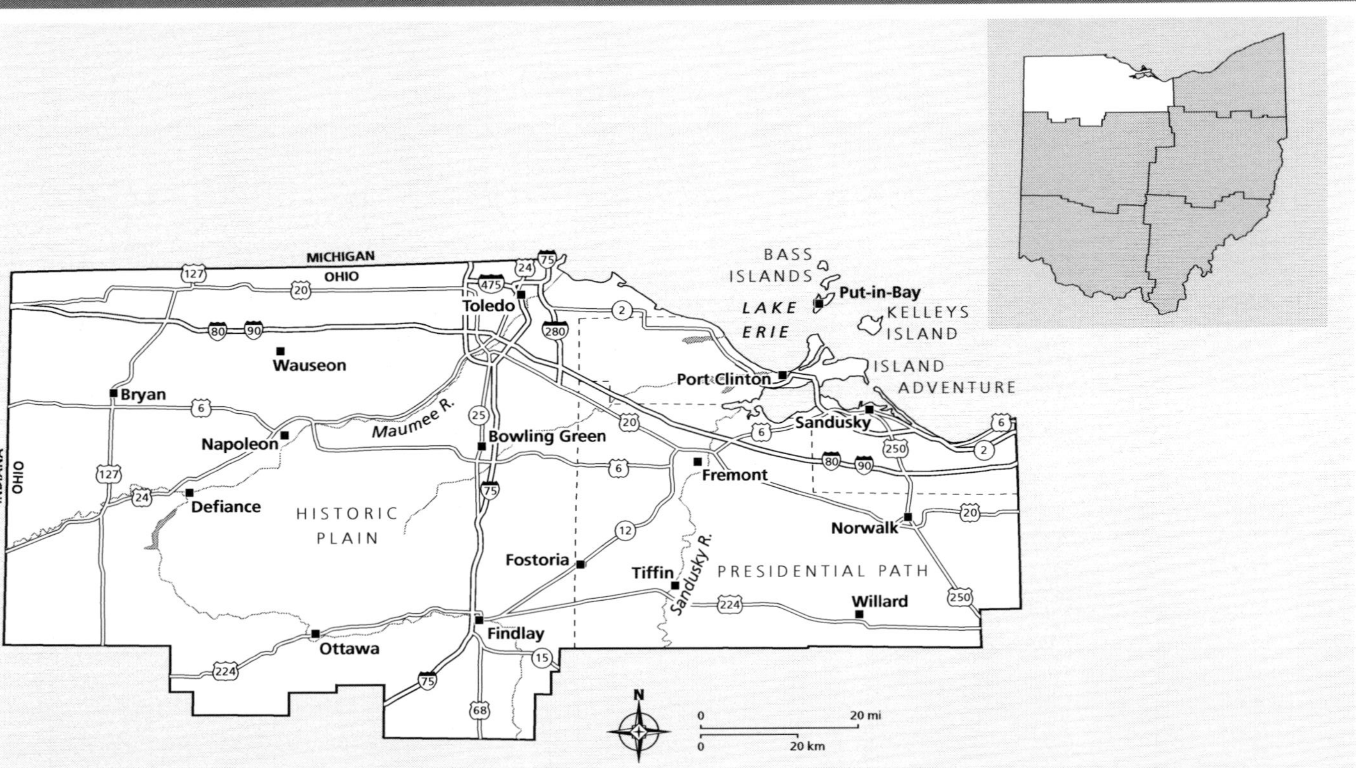

The Sherry School has textbooks from the mid-1800s, including McGuffey's *Eclectic Spelling Book*, teacher Mable Carroll's attendance records from the 1882 school year, and a student's certificate of promotion from 1896. The mailboxes in the front room of the old post office from Mark Centre still have mail in them—a 1906 copy of the *Saturday Evening Post* and a postcard dated 1899 notifying a Defiance man that he owes the Farmer Mutual Fire Protection Association another 25 cents on his insurance policy.

Other restored buildings include a completely equipped 1903 dentist's office (containing some grisly-looking instruments), the Ayersville Telephone Company with its old-fashioned switchboard and telephones, a blacksmith's shop, the Minsel Barber Shop, a sawmill, a gas station, a railroad station, an operating smokehouse, and a broom factory.

AuGlaize Village's two museums hold a varied collection of pioneer items. One building has an extensive assortment of antique farm implements, such as an elaborate, horse-drawn straw baler, and numerous fruit and tobacco presses.

BEST ATTRACTIONS

- AuGlaize Village
- Fort Defiance
- Independence Dam State Park
- Historic Sauder Village
- Barn Restaurant
- Toledo Museum of Art
- Tony Packo's Cafe
- Wildwood Preserve Metropark
- Fallen Timbers State Memorial
- Isaac Ludwig Mill
- Fort Meigs
- Schedel Arboretum and Gardens
- Heineman's Winery and Crystal Cave
- Perry's Cave
- Mon Ami Winery
- Marblehead Lighthouse
- Glacial Grooves
- Cedar Point
- Merry-Go-Round Museum
- Wagner's 1844 Inn
- Captain Montague's Bed & Breakfast
- Edison Birthplace Museum
- Old Prague Restaurant
- Rutherford B. Hayes Presidential Center
- Firelands Museum
- Historic Lyme Village
- Mad River & NKP Railroad Society Museum
- Seneca Caverns

Also in the museum is a 1936 farm tractor, a 1937 four-wheel-drive tractor, and a rare 1919 Defiance Motor Company truck. This local auto and truck manufacturer assembled vehicles for six years until the company failed in 1925. For military buffs, a separate building contains military equipment and hardware, including Civil War uniforms, cannons and mortars, and a variety of pistols and muskets (including a 1763 "Brown Bess" flintlock). Model railroad enthusiasts will enjoy the building filled with small trains.

Throughout its season, AuGlaize Village hosts special events days, such as the annual Harvest Demonstration and the Johnny Appleseed Festival. Craft experts show the old-fashioned way to dip candles and weave rugs, and demonstrate other pioneer skills.

AuGlaize Village is south of US 24 on Krouse Road, 3 miles west of Defiance at 12296 Krouse Rd.; (419) 990-0107; sites.google.com/site/auglaizevillage museum. The village is open for about seven event weekends May through Oct, Sat, 10 a.m. to 5 p.m.; Sun, 10 a.m. to 4 p.m. Check the website for list of events. Admission: adults $5; children (ages 5 and under) free.

A quiet residential neighborhood in nearby Defiance is the site of a former fortification that played a significant role in this region's history. The bluff at the confluence of the Maumee and Auglaize Rivers was where General "Mad" Anthony Wayne's American troops built ***Fort Defiance*** in 1794. Wayne launched his campaign against the Native Americans and British in the area from this fort, which consisted of four blockhouses and a tall stockade fence around the perimeter. It was erected in five weeks, and General Wayne, admiring the completed fortification, is reported to have said, "I defy the British, the Indians, and all the devils in hell to take it!" Upon hearing that, a fellow officer suggested, "Then call it Fort Defiance."

It was from here that Wayne's forces marched against the Native Americans, defeating them at the Battle of Fallen Timbers. Two cannons, one facing each river, are all that remain of the fort

fountaincity

Bryan was known as "Fountain City" because of its artesian wells. It all started in 1841 when Daniel Wyatt was digging a well next to his log cabin. He stopped digging at the end of one day; when he awoke the next morning, water was pouring out of the hole. Water would flow from just about any hole dug in the area, and this liquid abundance attracted settlers to Bryan.

But the spouting water was not completely a blessing. In the 1880s a New Yorker claimed the fountains violated a patent he held, and he demanded $10 from each well owner, a claim described locally as the "Great Swindle." And some of the fountains resulted in litigation, as neighbors were flooded out by the spewing discharge. The flow gradually subsided, with the last fountain petering out in 1971.

today. When you stand on that hill, however, at the junction of these great rivers, the strategic importance of this spot is readily apparent.

The Fort Defiance Memorial is at the end of Washington Avenue in Defiance. It is open during daylight hours, and no admission is charged.

East of Defiance in nearby Independence is another historic site. ***Independence Dam State Park*** is a long, narrow green space between the swift Maumee River and a now-idle section of the old Miami and Erie Canal. This canal, which was built between the 1820s and the 1840s, connected Toledo (and Lake Erie) with Cincinnati (and the Ohio River). As part of the canal construction boom in Ohio early in the nineteenth century, the Miami and Erie provided cheap transportation for goods and new settlers, stimulating the economic development of the region. Nevertheless, by as early as the 1850s, the speed and flexibility of the railroad signaled the beginning of the end of the canal era.

Independence Dam was built to divert water from the river to the canal, and this section of the Miami and Erie holds water to this day. The massive wooden gates of Lock 13 at the entrance to the park are the only such gates still in existence on this canal. In sharp contrast to the boom years, today the banks are overgrown, and the former towpaths have been erased by time.

Visitors to the park can take advantage of the hiking trails, picnic areas, and primitive campsites. Fishing and boating are popular on the wide Maumee River, and the park has boat-launching ramps.

Independence Dam State Park is at 27722 OH 424, 3 miles east of Defiance; (419) 956-1368; ohiodnr.gov/go-and-do/plan-a-visit/find-a-property/independence-dam-state-park. Open year-round; no admission charge.

Erie J. Sauder always had an interest in the history of northwest Ohio. First, he collected antique woodworking tools to display for his customers at the Sauder Woodworking Company. From woodworking equipment, his collection expanded to include farm tools and household items used in this section of the state in the late 1800s. These were the humble beginnings of the ***Historic Sauder Village*** near Archbold. This part of the state was one of the last to be settled because of the 2,000-square-mile Black Swamp. Only after massive drainage and land reclamation in the 1850s was this unhealthy muck transformed into fertile farmland.

Historic Sauder Village is a well-organized, carefully presented living museum. The village actually consists of three major areas: the restored farmstead, the pioneer craft village, and the museum.

Period pieces furnish the farmhouse, which was built in 1860. Wood cooking and heating stoves, rope-spring beds, and a wooden pump organ are typical of the items found in the two-story home. Costumed guides in each room explain the history and demonstrate the utility of the furnishings and equipment—how to use a hand-crank apple peeler, for instance. The last stop on the farmhouse tour is the root cellar, where the farm family stored its fruits and vegetables during the winter months. Horses, sheep, turkeys, ducks, geese, and chickens roam the farmyard.

The craft village consists of a cluster of rustic buildings set in a circle, each housing an expert in a particular craft. Brooms are made the old-fashioned way in the broom shop and are available for purchase, while the blacksmith busily forges candleholders, ladles, gates, and railings. One of the most popular shops belongs to Mark Matthews, the village glassblower. Taking 2,000°F glass from the bottom of the furnace, Mark adds color chips to the clear glass, then blows and hand shapes the soft, hot glass into beautiful spheres and paperweights. As with the other craftspeople in the village, Mark explains each step of the process. Other craft demonstrations at Sauder include woodworking and pottery. The village also has a cooper, a spinner, a weaver, a tinsmith, and a basket maker who demonstrate their crafts.

The village museum contains an impressive collection of tools, machinery, and household items used by early settlers in this region. A large number of old farm wagons, buggies, and carts are on display, as are farm craft tools, such as woodworking tools, and farm implements, including an 1886 potato digger and an 1860 cultivator. The museum's Conestoga wagon, first designed in 1755 in Conestoga Valley, Pennsylvania, once transported newcomers to the area. Countless meat grinders, butter churns, wood-burning stoves, and foot-powered sewing machines fill this vast exhibit space. A quilting demonstration also takes place there. If you need more time to see it all, spend the night at the 98-room Sauder Heritage Inn, or in the 48-site campground, and make it a two-day visit.

florida, in ohio?

The town of Florida may or may not be on the site of a Native American village named Snaketown. The tribe of Shawnee Chief Captain Snake did occupy a village in this part of the state from about 1786 until 1794, when confronted by the army of General "Mad" Anthony Wayne. But was it where Florida stands today? An archaeological dig in 1984 sponsored by the Ohio Humanities Council attempted to answer this question, with mixed results. Although the dig did uncover arrowheads, animal bones, and a 40-foot canal boat, no conclusive evidence of Snaketown was discovered. One thing is certain: jokes about the name Florida, especially during an Ohio winter, are guaranteed.

Historic Sauder Village is located at 22611 OH 2, northeast of Archbold; (419) 446-2541, (800) 590-9755; saudervillage.org. Open May, Wed through Fri, 10 a.m. to 3:30 p.m.; Sat, 10 a.m. to 5 p.m.; June through Labor Day, Wed through Sat, 10 a.m. to 5 p.m.; Sept and Oct, Wed through Fri, 10 a.m. to

3:30 p.m.; Sat, 10 a.m. to 5 p.m. Closed Nov through late Apr. Admission: adults $24; senior citizens $22; children (ages 4 to 16) $18.

If you have worked up an appetite touring the Historic Sauder Village, stop in next door at the ***Barn Restaurant***. This restaurant is housed in an actual poplar barn, which was originally built 2 miles northeast of its present location in 1861. Sauder saved the barn from being razed and had it moved in 1974. Country cooking is the order of the day here, where you can find family-style dinners of chicken, ham, and beef. Other menu items include a selection of steaks, shrimp, and perch. The menu also offers a variety of sandwiches and salads. There are always two fresh soups warming in the large pots, including unusual ones such as Kneppley soup—a ham broth with dough drops. A generous salad bar is loaded with just about every type of salad imaginable, plus a myriad of salad fixings.

The exposed rough beams of this structure, the antique farm implements mounted on the walls, and the period costumes worn by the waitresses all enhance the rustic atmosphere of the Barn Restaurant. All breads and pastries at the restaurant are made fresh daily at the Doughbox Bakery, which is next door.

The Barn Restaurant is at Sauder Village on OH 2, northeast of Archbold; (419) 445-2231, (800) 590-9755; saudervillage.org. Open year-round Tues through Sat, 11 a.m. to 7 p.m.

A walk along the trails in ***Goll Woods State Nature Preserve*** takes you through the best living example of the Great Black Swamp forest that covered much of this region of postglacial lake plains, located to the south and west of Lake Erie. Native American people and settlers tended to avoid this swampy area, as the old-growth forest combined with the swampy floor imbued the area with a certain eerie and foreboding atmosphere. The Great Black Swamp is one of the few remaining virgin, old-growth forests in the state, with some trees estimated to be 400 years old. This area of swamp forest and wetlands was part of the Goll family farm from the early 1800s. The state purchased the land from the family in the 1960s to preserve this rare and well-preserved piece of Ohio's natural history, and the preserve was opened to the public in 1975. The pioneer-era cemetery of the Goll family remains as part of the park.

In the approximately 40-acre forest, white oaks, chinquapin oaks, burr oaks, and cottonwoods create a magnificent canopy in the warmer months, and some have trunks more than 4 feet in diameter. Ohio Department of Natural Resource officials estimated that one crusty burr oak might be 500 years old. You can also find specimens of big tooth aspen, rock elm, black gum, black maple, dogwood, ironwood, bitternut, and pignut hickory trees. Though many of these giant trees remain in this 321-acre preserve, gone are the population of wolves, beaver, bobcats, cougars, black bear, and elk that once found a home in the preserve. Along with the forest, this natural area also has swamp meadows. This forest and wetland provides a refuge for many animals, including deer, red-tailed fox, and squirrels, and many species of birds, including the red-headed woodpecker, barred owl, scarlet tanager, and the rose-breasted grosbeak. Besides being a popular haunt for birders, the preserve attracts wildflower enthusiasts who visit each spring looking for a glimpse of spotted coralroot or three-bird orchids.

The preserve also boasts a wide array of amphibians, such as salamanders, turtles, and frogs, and is a bit too well known for mosquitoes. While summer brings warmer weather and the magnificent tree canopy, it also brings swarms of mosquitoes. If you are interested in hiking and exploring the preserve, consider an early spring visit, before the mosquitoes hatch. If you come later, be warned to slather on a good coating of strong repellent.

There are roughly 3 miles of trails through the preserve. Trailheads can be found off the main parking lot. The Burr Oak trail is the most popular and is about 1 mile long.

Goll Woods State Nature Preserve is north and west of the city of Archbold; ohiodnr.gov/go-and-do/plan-a-visit/find-a-property/goll-woods-state-nature-preserve. From Archbold, go north on OH 66 for 1½ miles to Township Road F, go west for 3 miles to the junction with Township Road 26, then go south about 0.25 mile to the preserve parking lot located on the east side of the road. Open one-half hour before sunrise to one-half hour after sunset daily.

If you are traveling in northwest Ohio from the spring to early fall, a visit to the ***Butterfly House in Whitehouse*** could provide a colorful addition to the day's travels. More than 1,000 butterflies waft around this indoor environment to the delight of the visitor. The broad range of North and South American and Asian butterflies and moths appear like little flying jewels, with colors ranging from a striking cobalt blue to sunny yellows. Generally around 100 species play hide-and-seek with the visitors to the butterfly house.

ALSO WORTH SEEING

Toledo Zoo

Toledo Museum of Art

COSI, Center of Science and Industry, Toledo

Maumee Bay State Park, Oregon

The indoor greenhouse provides an enjoyable environment for people as well as these showy insects. Feeders, filled with sugar water, are a popular gathering point for the colorful insects. A variety of plants and an indoor water feature provide a relaxing setting as you try to spot as many of the species as you can.

There are special programs, presentations, and events that highlight the life cycle, migration, and other facets of butterfly life, so you might want to check the website for dates and times. One very special event takes place in September when hundreds of locally raised monarch butterflies are released into the wild to begin their fall migration to Mexico.

The Butterfly House in Whitehouse is located at 11455 Obee Rd., Whitehouse; (419) 877-2733; wheelerfarms.com. Open May through Aug, Mon through Sat, 10 a.m. to 4 p.m.; Sun, noon to 4 p.m.; Sept, Thurs through Sat, 10 a.m. to 4 p.m.; Sun, noon to 4 p.m. Open weekends in Oct, Sat, 10 a.m. to 4 p.m., Sun, noon to 4 p.m. Admission: adults $10; senior citizens $9; children (ages 4 to 11) $8.

One of the finest art museums in the nation is in Toledo—the ***Toledo Museum of Art***. Founded in 1901, the museum is a privately endowed nonprofit arts institution with extensive collections of glass, American and European paintings, sculpture, decorative arts, and graphic arts.

In an hour or a day, browse and discover treasures from ancient Egypt, Greece, and Rome; riches within a medieval cloister; and the splendors of a room from a French château. Marvel at great works by such masters as El Greco, Rubens, Rembrandt, Gainsborough, Turner, van Gogh, Degas, Monet, Matisse, Picasso, Remington, Hopper, and Nevelson.

The Toledo Museum of Art is at 2445 Monroe St., Toledo; (419) 255-8000, (800) 644-6862; toledomuseum.org. Open Wed and Thurs, 11 a.m. to 5 p.m.; Fri and Sat, 11 a.m. to 8 p.m.; Sun, 11 a.m. to 5 p.m. No admission charge.

The first Libbey Glass factory was founded in Cambridge, Massachusetts, in 1818, a long way from Toledo. But abundant natural gas lured the factory to Toledo 70 years later, helping to make Toledo the "glass capital of the world." Long a pioneer in the development of modern glassmaking, Libbey Glass made its mark internationally in 1893, when the company constructed a house completely built of glass for the World's Columbian Exhibition in Chicago. Many of the other pieces created specifically for the exhibition are now displayed at the Toledo Museum of Art.

But it's not art that draws crowds to the ***Libbey Glass Outlet***; rather it's bargains. Here you will find stemware, fountain ware, tumblers and mugs, plates and bowls, canisters and ashtrays, plus L.E. Smith handcrafted glassware, all at factory outlet prices.

The Libbey Glass Factory Outlet is at 205 S. Erie St., Toledo; (419) 254-5000. Open Mon through Fri, 9:30 a.m. to 5:30 p.m.; Fri and Sat, 8 a.m. to 5 p.m.; Sun, 10 a.m. to 5 p.m.

Tony Packo's Hungarian hot dogs have been scarfed down by Toledoans for more than eighty years. Billing itself as the place "where man bites dog," ***Tony Packo's Cafe*** was made famous outside Toledo by Jamie Farr, who, as M*A*S*H's Corporal Klinger, yearned for the spicy food of his favorite hometown eatery.

Farr and other celebrity visitors to Tony Packo's engage in a local tradition—signing a hot dog bun, which is then mounted and displayed for all to enjoy. In addition to hot dogs, diners find spicy pickles and peppers, steaming hand-rolled stuffed cabbage, spicy chili, Hungarian hamburgers, and homemade chicken soup with Hungarian dumplings.

Tony Packo's Cafe is at 1902 Front St., Toledo; (419) 691-6054; tonypacko.com. Open Mon through Thurs, 10:30 a.m. to 9 p.m.; Fri and Sat, 10:30 a.m. to 10 p.m.; Sun, 11:30 to 9 p.m.

Lucas County also is the location of one of the state's most scenic parks—***Wildwood Preserve Metropark***. These 500-plus acres of lush natural beauty, with hardwood forests, ravines, meadows, and the serene Ottawa River, contain wildlife such as deer, fox, mink, muskrat, opossum, and raccoon. Owls, hawks, and pheasant nest here, and wildflowers such as bittercress, buttercups, and wild hyacinth are abundant.

The five primary hiking trails allow visitors to explore the high ridge and the cottonwood and sycamore trees in the river floodplain. The prairie trail leads hikers through one of the last tallgrass prairie remnants in the state, where some of the grasses reach a height of 10 feet. The newest area features a boardwalk trail, a covered bridge, and a historic one-room schoolhouse.

The elegant Manor House, a Georgian colonial brick mansion, is nestled in a clearing and surrounded by deep, cool woods. This stately former residence has twenty-two rooms, with tours offered Jan through Mar, Sun from noon to 5 p.m.; Apr through Oct, Wed through Fri, and Sun from noon to 5 p.m. Note that the manor is closed the first week of each month Apr through Oct and all of Nov and Dec (except during holiday events). Other facilities in the park include picnic tables, barbecue grills, shelter houses, and playground equipment.

Wildwood Preserve Metropark is at 5100 W. Central Ave. (OH 120), east of I-475 and west of downtown Toledo 43615; (419) 407- 9718, (419) 407-9718; metroparkstoledo.com/explore-your-parks/wildwood/. Open daily, 7 a.m. to dark; no admission charge.

The desire to preserve and honor the traditions and memorabilia from a century and a half of service in a proud profession led to the creation of the ***Toledo Firefighters Museum***. This museum is only open on Saturday afternoons, so plan ahead if you want to visit the 1920s-vintage firehouse, Old Station Number 18. The impetus for starting this historical center was to have a permanent home for "Neptune." Neptune is the nickname for a wooden hand pumper that was shipped to the city of Toledo via the Erie Canal. The museum also displays a range of historic firefighting equipment from equipment used by the first bucket brigades to an 1895 Ahrens Steamer, a 1929 Pirch Pumper, a 1936 Schecht ladder track, and a 1948 Buffalo Pumper. One particularly striking and romantic vehicle is the horse-drawn steamer, a shiny red, black, and brass wagon. Also red, and quite rare, is the more modern and utilitarian-looking 1969 Willey's Fire Jeep. The story of more than 150 years of Toledo firefighting also is told in timelines, newspaper stories, pictures, toys, vintage uniforms, and historic documents. The center also helps to educate children about fire emergencies. One display replicates a child's bedroom. Fire prevention bureau staff uses this area to help children role play and learn how to react if a fire were to break out.

The Toledo Firefighters Museum is at 918 W. Sylvania Ave., Toledo; (419) 478-3473; Open Sat, noon to 4 p.m. Admission: free, but donations are welcomed.

Part of the Toledo area Metropark system, ***Oak Openings Preserve*** encompasses nearly 4,000 acres. The preserve has been hailed by the Nature Conservancy as one of the "200 last great places on earth." Oak Openings is basically a huge beach that once bordered a lake, but a lake that has long since receded into history. As the huge glaciers moved across Ohio, they created these glacial lakes and thick sandy beaches along their shores. This thick sand now creates an unusual natural area that provides a home to many plant and animal species.

The preserve area is so large that it is a good idea to start off your explorations at the Buehner Nature Center, where you can get an overview of the history of the area through interactive displays. After learning about the formation and current importance of this region for wildlife, you can use the center's maps and information to plot your strategy for exploring the preserve. The park offers more than 50 miles of trails ranging in length from about ½ mile to more than 17 miles. Many trailheads are easy to access from the nature center, and their names suggest the varied habitats you can experience. Enjoy a hike on the Ridge Trail (2½ miles), the Horseshoe Lake Trail (1½ miles), the Sand Dunes Trail (1.7 miles), the Ferns and Lakes Trail (blue) (2.9 miles), the Lake Circuit Trail (0.6 mile), or the Evergreen Trail (1.9 miles). Some trails are designated for bikes, and there are 26 miles of horse trails, too. Cross-county skiing is also permitted on all trails in the winter.

Bowling Green Ghost

Those attending a theater production at Bowling Green State University may, according to university legend, meet the theater department's resident ghost—Alice.

This ghost is Ohio's version of Phantom of the Opera, for Alice must, according to the superstitious, be invited to every theater performance. This must be a formal invitation issued by the stage manager, who must be alone on stage. If Alice is not consulted or not thanked after the performance, actors report that Alice is given to shows of temper, such as knocking over set pieces.

Just who Alice is—or was—also is a matter of legend. According to one of the most popular stories, Alice was a Bowling Green student and a budding actress. She was on her way to the theater to receive an honor as "Actress of the Year," but was killed in a car crash before collecting her prize. Another tale is that she actually was killed in the theater when a falling object cut short her performance as Desdemona in Shakespeare's *Othello*.

Those students and staff who have communed with Alice say she sometimes appears as a shadowy figure with long, flowing hair. She has also returned in full costume when *Othello* is being performed, perhaps to finish the performance that she began so many years ago. So, if you attend a Bowling Green State University theater production, just be warned—there is always the possibility of a very special guest appearance by the famous Alice.

Throughout much of the preserve, it is easy to see the sandy beaches and sand dunes. There are also other types of habitats, such as wetland areas, savannahs, and prairie. Between the sand and the wetland conditions, it is difficult for large trees to take root. Settlers nicknamed the region "Oak Openings" because the soil conditions were such that trees grew far apart here so it was easy to find openings through which to drive wagons.

The preserve provides a haven for many rare and endangered species. Moths and butterflies, such as Edward's hairstreak—brown with touches of blue and orange—and the brown Persius dusky wing have been spotted here. Exotic plant species found in the dunes and oak savanna areas include the strange-looking and rain-loving earth star (fungi) as well as sand cherry bushes, prickly pear cactus, and goat's rue, which was once employed as a medicine to fight the plague. As you walk the dune, you might spot a glimpse of red as a scarlet tanager flies by. Bluebirds, indigo buntings, whippoorwills make the preserve their home, and migrating songbirds use the wetlands as a refueling stop on their annual journeys north and south. In the wetlands and prairie areas, look for spotted turtles as well as a host of interesting plant species. In late summer the yellow sneezeweed, with yellow petals surrounding a huge center, will be in bloom. Always worth the hunt for the enthusiast of the exotic are the bug-digesting sundews. The grass pink orchids and the fringed orchids are delicate additions to this landscape, but the wildflower photographer will find plenty of other subjects with coneflowers, asters, and a host of others dotting the somewhat soggy ground.

Oak Openings Preserve is located at 4139 Girdham Rd., Swanton; (419) 360-9179; metroparkstoledo.com/explore-your-parks/oak-openings-preserve-metropark/. Open daily, 7 a.m. until dark. Admission is free.

On August 20, 1794, General "Mad" Anthony Wayne's army engaged a Native American war party led by Chief Little Turtle at the battleground known as Fallen Timbers, so called because a tornado felled a grove of trees here. Today, more than two centuries after the battle, ***Fallen Timbers State Memorial*** is a peaceful reminder of that pivotal conflict—one that shaped the future of Ohio's settlement by whites from the East. Wayne's defeat of the natives here, on a bluff above the north bank of the Maumee River, led to the signing of the Treaty of Greenville in 1795, under which the Native Americans surrendered their claims to most of Ohio.

Turkey Foot Rock, a large boulder at Fallen Timbers, is the subject of native lore. According to legend, Chief Turkey Foot of the Ottawa tribe stood at this rock to rally his warriors against General Wayne's troops. The chief was later killed on this spot, and for years after the battle, Ottawa braves would come to Turkey Foot Rock and offer tobacco to the Great Spirit for their deceased leader.

Fallen Timbers State Memorial is on US 24, west of Maumee at 6601 Anthony Wayne Trail; (419) 535-3050, (800) 860-0149; metroparkstoledo.com/explore-your-parks/fallen-timbers-battlefield-fort-miamis-metropark/. Open 7 a.m. until dark; no admission charge.

A friendly rivalry between Gilead (now Grand Rapids) and Providence—just across the Maumee River—lasted for generations. The Howard family settled at the site of Grand Rapids in 1822, attracted to the location by its great natural beauty and the potential for commerce, thanks to the river.

On the other side of the Maumee, Peter Manor constructed a sawmill in 1822, and Providence took an early lead as the center of development for the area. That original sawmill was razed to make room for the Miami and Erie Canal.

In 1865, a much larger mill went up, and almost 150 years later, the ***Isaac Ludwig Mill*** still operates, if only for demonstration purposes. Most of the mill's equipment is more than seventy-five years old, and some dates back to pre–Civil War days. River water diverted to a canal falls through two turbines, creating a combined force of 230 horsepower.

TOP ANNUAL EVENTS

Historic Port Clinton Walleye Fest
Port Clinton, May
(419) 734-5503

Put-in-Bay Pooch Parade
Put-in-Bay, June
putinbay.com

Annual Founder's Day Celebration
Put-in-Bay, June
(419) 285-2832
visitputinbay.org

Crosby Festival of the Arts
Toledo, June
(419) 720-8714
crosbyfest.com

Key West Days at Put-in-Bay
Putin-Bay, Aug
(419) 625-5009
shoresandislands.com

Maumee Summer Fair
Maumee, Aug
maumeesummerfair.com

National Tractor Pulling Championships
Bowling Green, Aug
(888) 385-7855
pulltown.com

Milan Melon Festival
Milan, Sept, Labor Day Weekend
(419) 504-8664
ohiotraveler.com/milan-melon-festival

Heritage Days of Mt. Blanchard
Findlay, Aug
(800) 424-3315
visitfindlay.com

Tiffin Seneca County Living History Festival
Tiffin, Sept
(419) 447-4141
tiffinfestival.com

Johnny Appleseed Festival
Defiance, Oct
(419) 782-0739
visitdefianceohio.com

The canal era in this part of Ohio peaked in the 1850s, and when the railroad arrived here, it arrived in Gilead, renamed Grand Rapids, shifting commerce back across the river. An 1848 fire nearly wiped out Providence, and the great cholera epidemic of 1854 took a particularly heavy toll on the town, which today consists of only the mill, a church, a building that once served as a hotel for canal travelers, and a lone home.

Although the Isaac Ludwig Mill survived the fire of 1848, a blaze a century later, in 1940, destroyed the top floors of this historic structure. The mill bears the name of its second owner, who acquired it in 1865. Isaac Ludwig died in 1906 and is buried in the township cemetery at Mount Pleasant.

Carefully restored and listed on the National Register of Historic Places, Isaac Ludwig Mill today offers a glimpse of Ohio's past. The mill produced flour, meal, and livestock feed commercially until the 1940 fire, and it continues to grind corn into cornmeal and wheat into flour as it has for decades. Visitors not only observe the art of water-powered milling, but also may purchase the results. Waterpower also drives drills and saws and demonstrations of lumber being cut. The canal boat the *Volunteer* transports visitors through a restored 1-mile stretch of the original canal, including Lock 44.

Isaac Ludwig Mill is on US 24 at OH 578, across the Maumee River from Grand Rapids; (419) 407-9718; metroparkstoledo.com/explore-your-parks/providence-metropark/. Open May through Oct, Wed through Sun, 10 a.m. to 5 p.m. No admission charge to the mill. Canal boat rides: adults $7; senior citizens $6; children (ages 3 to 12) $4.

After your mill tour, come across the river to charming Grand Rapids, a town that has overcome considerable adversity. Fire has destroyed nearly every building at one time or another during its century-and-a-half history, and spring flooding has done serious damage, especially the floods of 1903 and 1913. As recently as 1957, floodwaters filled downtown in a mere five minutes, sending residents scrambling to rooftops.

Serious restoration of Grand Rapids began in 1975, and what started slowly has picked up momentum, with most structures now in pristine condition. Special events throughout the year, from the spring flood watch, which attracts thousands to view the surging power of the scenic Maumee, to the October Applebutter Fest, add to the town's interest. Intriguing shops line both sides of Front Street.

Standing in the Grand Battery of ***Fort Meigs***, with its three 12-pounder cannons aimed across the Maumee River, you can almost hear the blast of cannon fire and feel the rain of falling earth and timber from shells exploding nearby. The fort was under siege for nine days and nights in May 1813, but the American forces in the fort held off the British attack and repelled them again when the British launched a second invasion three months later.

Ohio's role in the War of 1812 is not given much space in the history books, but the American forces, commanded by General William Henry Harrison, twice turned back British offensives at the fort that Harrison named for Ohio's governor at the time, Return Jonathan Meigs. Harrison's forces constructed the fort in early February 1813, and this fortification became the base for 3,000 troops. On April 28, British forces began to construct a camp and gun batteries opposite Fort Meigs; four batteries across the river and two east of the fort. The British siege began May 1, 1813, and lasted until May 9.

The entire Fort Meigs fortification has been carefully reconstructed, including the seven blockhouses and the 2,000-yard stockade wall. A flat-topped mound of earth built against the inside of the wall forms a banquette (or firing step), where the soldiers stood to fire musket rounds at the invaders attacking the 10-acre fort. Some of the blockhouses contain museums describing the history of the battles here, while others contain twelve-pounder cannons as they

blanchardriver inspiration

"Down by the Old Mill Stream," Tell Taylor's famous song, was inspired by the Blanchard River. Taylor was born in nearby Vanlue and grew up in Findlay.

He moved to New York City in 1897, opening one of Tin Pan Alley's first music publishing houses. During a visit home in 1908, Taylor spent some time along the Blanchard at the Misamore mill. It was this visit that inspired the song, published in 1910.

Taylor returned to Findlay for good in 1922 and is buried along the river he made famous.

did in May 1813. Signs aid visitors taking a self-guided tour of the fort by explaining the significance of various locations inside the stockade. On weekends, costumed soldiers set up camp at Fort Meigs, further enhancing the sensation that one has stepped back in time to the early nineteenth century. Just outside the stockade walls are picnic tables and barbecue grills.

Fort Meigs is at 29100 W. River Rd., on OH 65 west of the intersection with OH 25, in Perrysburg; (419) 874-4121, (800) 283-8916; fortmeigs.org. Open Apr through Oct, Wed through Sat, 9:30 a.m. to 5 p.m.; Sun, noon to 5 p.m. The visitor center and museum are open year-round with those same hours. Admission: adults $10; senior citizens $8; children $5; children (age 5 and under) free.

You can step back into the early 1800s as you visit the ***Wolcott House Museum Complex***. James Wolcott and his wife, Mary, a Miami Indian, boarded a dugout canoe and followed the Maumee River down to the foot of the rapids at Maumee City. This part of Ohio was becoming an important shipping point and offered entrepreneurs like Wolcott an opportunity to build a business. Wolcott built warehouses and steamships to transport merchandise during an era of bustling lake and canal trade.

James and Mary also purchased 300 acres of land to build their impressive home, which is a blend of classic and federal architecture. As you stroll through the museum complex, you can visit this home and also an 1840s saltbox-style farmhouse, a log home, a country church, a Greek revival–style home from the mid-1800s, and a railroad depot complete with caboose and boxcar.

If you have a chance to call ahead, ask about special events. Throughout the year, the complex plans craft classes for children and festivals to tempt all members of the family out on the lawns for some old-fashioned fun.

The Wolcott House Museum Complex is at 1035 River Rd., Maumee; (419) 893-9602. Open Apr through Dec, Thurs through Sun noon to 4 p.m.; guided tours Sat and Sun at 12:30 and 2:30 p.m. Admission: adults $5; senior citizens $4; students $2.50.

As you are driving around Wood County, you just might pass part of the ***Snook's Dream Cars Automobile Museum*** out on the open road. "Long time car guy" Bill Snook created the expansive collection. His son Jeff Snook is curator of the museum and since he keeps all the "exhibits" in working condition, Jeff just can't help occasionally taking one of the vintage cars for a spin.

This is a living museum where vintage cars are not only displayed but also repaired. The Snooks have re-created a 1940s-era Texaco station, complete with service bays and a variety of the pieces and parts you would have seen on display in a pre-war filling station. There is also an interesting collection of promotional items that would have delighted customers asking for a fill-up some 70 years ago. A collection of coin-operated games will please the children (and the adult children as well).

The cars in the collection cover the 1930s to the 1960s. You will see coupes, convertibles, sedans, roadsters, and race cars. American carmakers from the past and present are represented, such as Cadillac, Ford, Chevrolet, Buick, Pontiac, Packard, Kaiser, as well as some foreign dream cars, among them models from Jaguar, Triumph, MG, and Lotus.

Snook's Dream Cars Automobile Museum is at 13920 County Home Rd., Bowling Green; (419) 353-8338; snooksdreamcars.com. Open Mon through Fri, 8 a.m. to 5 p.m.; Sat and Sun, "by appointment or by chance." Admission: adults $8; senior citizens $6; children $5.

Island Adventure

Gardens, especially traditional Japanese gardens, are havens for contemplation and peace. The ***Schedel Arboretum and Gardens*** welcomes guests into such a quiet place. An extensive 17-acre arboretum surrounds a gracious home that was formerly the residence of Joseph and Marie Schedel.

The home, built in 1882, and the gardens were the beneficiary of the Schedels' loving attention and now serve as their living memorial. They created a foundation to support the home and grounds after their deaths in the 1980s. The home features many unusual items purchased by the couple on their world travels. These include Japanese silk embroideries, Persian rugs, and a Hereke silk prayer rug, as well as carved antique jade and bronze pieces that are more than 3,000 years old.

The grounds are home to a wide variety of native and exotic plantlife. The Japanese garden tends to draw the visitor's attention to its stone lanterns, bridges, and a stupa—a stone memorial tower shaped like a pagoda. The landscaped grounds also host sixteen species of pine trees, including the bristlecone pine, which is believed to be the oldest living tree species on earth.

Waterfalls, pools, and two lakes add the relaxing sounds of water to the landscape. They also provide a home for fish, ducks, blue herons, and white egrets. The gardens also host an annual outdoor sculpture exhibit featuring the work of nationally prominent sculptors.

The Schedel Arboretum and Gardens is located at 19255 W. Portage River South Rd., Elmore; (419) 862-3182; schedel-gardens.org. Open April through Oct, Tues through Sat, 10 a.m. to 4 p.m.; Sun, noon to 4 p.m. Admission: adults $12; senior citizens $11; children (ages 6 to 13) $6.

The ***Magee Marsh Wildlife Area***, adjoining Crane Creek State Park, is a 2,000-acre wildlife area. This wetland is both home to a wide variety of birds and animals, and a resting and feeding place for migratory waterfowl, making it a particular favorite with birders. Bring binoculars and look for warblers and waterfowl, and maybe one of Ohio's small but growing number of bald eagles. More than 300 bird species have been sighted at the marsh, and 143 species are known to nest there. Turtles, frogs, and toads are also residents of the marsh, along with muskrats, mink, raccoons, rabbits, and white-tailed deer.

Visitors can enjoy three walking trails, each about a mile long. You can also take a drive down the road to the beach to get a flavor of the marsh environment. The Crane Creek State Park beach is open for swimming and picnicking in the summer months.

The Magee Marsh Wildlife Area is at 13229 West OH 2, Oak Harbor; (419) 898-0960; ohiodnr.gov/go-and-do/plan-a-visit/find-a-property/magee-marsh-wildlife-area. Open dawn to dusk. The Sportsmen's Migratory Bird Center is open year-round, Mon through Fri, 8 a.m. to 5 p.m. Open from 11 a.m. to 5 p.m. on weekends in the summer.

A half dozen islands are sprinkled in Lake Erie just north of Catawba and Marblehead peninsulas. Easily accessible by air or ferry, Put-in-Bay is the center of activity on South Bass Island. A large, protected harbor attracts boaters, who often dock their vessels overnight.

This safe harbor also attracted Commodore Oliver Hazard Perry in 1813. His fleet lay at anchor here before defeating the British fleet commanded by Captain Robert H. Barclay in the Battle of Lake Erie on September 10, 1813. To commemorate Perry's triumph and pay tribute to the subsequent decades of peaceful relations between the United States and Canada along their lengthy, unfortified border, a monument was constructed at Put-in-Bay. This 352-foot-tall column, built of pink granite from Milford, Massachusetts, has a 45-foot-diameter base. It was built between 1912 and 1915 and is the world's largest Doric column. The observation deck at ***Perry Victory and International Peace Memorial*** is open to the public daily from mid-May through Sept, daily 10 a.m. to 6 p.m. The park at 93 Delaware Ave. is open the first week of Oct through May daily from 10 a.m. to 5:30 p.m. Admission to the memorial and observation deck is $10 for adults (ages 16 and up). All special events and admission to the visitor center and memorial grounds are free. Check the website for more information: www.nps.gov/pevi/index.htm.

After a walking tour of the town of Put-in-Bay, it's time to explore other points on this small, wooded island. Bicycles and golf carts are two of the most enjoyable ways to survey South Bass, and rentals are available. Trams, buses, and taxis also transport visitors around the island.

About halfway across the island from Put-in-Bay (10 minutes by bicycle) on Catawba Road is ***Heineman's Winery and Crystal Cave***. Heineman's offers tours of both a unique geode cave and its winery and sells wine by the glass, bottle, or case. The cave, 40 feet beneath the surface, is actually an unusually large geode. Geodes (stones with a cavity lined with crystal) are relatively common in nature, but they are normally no larger than a baseball or softball. The Crystal Cave geode is large enough to hold thirty people. It was created under pressure over 4.5 million years. The cave remains a cool 52 degrees year-round, and guides explain the history and geology of this unique formation.

After the cave tour, join another guide for a tour of the winery. Heineman's grows approximately 50 percent of the grapes they need, purchasing the rest from other island vineyards. From twelve kinds of grapes, Heineman's produces almost twenty wines, plus fresh grape juice, with an output of 30,000 gallons of wine and juice annually. The Lake Erie islands are ideally suited for vineyards because of the soil's high limestone content and a relatively late frost, thanks to the warming influence of Lake Erie.

On the winery tour, visitors can see large presses that squeeze 180 gallons of juice from each ton of grapes. The grapes ferment in oak barrels, some holding as much as 1,680 gallons, or in stainless-steel tanks. Other stops on the winery tour include the bottling, labeling, and packing areas.

After your tour, enjoy a glass of Heineman's wine in the wine garden, which has picnic tables and nicely kept gardens. Cheese plates are also served.

Heineman's Winery and Crystal Cave tours are given from May through Sept, 11 a.m. to 5 p.m. daily, Sun, from noon to 5 p.m. The winery is open daily from mid-Apr to late Oct, 11 a.m. to 7 p.m.; Sun, noon to 7 p.m. The winery and cave are at 978 Catawba Ave., Put-in-Bay; (419) 285-2811; heinemanswinery.com. Admission for the combined tour is $10 for adults and $5 for children (ages 6 to 11), and it includes a complimentary glass of wine or grape juice.

Across the street from Heineman's is another cave—a much larger one—known as ***Perry's Cave***. Commodore Oliver Hazard Perry is credited with the discovery of this limestone cavern, which measures 208 feet by 165 feet and is 52 feet below the surface. Perry used water from the cave to fill the water kegs for his ships prior to the Battle of Lake Erie in 1813.

Along the north wall of the cave is a large lake of crystal-clear water, which rises and falls with the level of Lake Erie. The luxurious Victory Hotel, once the largest hotel in the world, pumped water from this lake for its drinking water. The hotel burned down in 1919, and its ruins are on the south side of the island on the grounds of South Bass Island State Park. Also on the park's grounds are gemstone mining areas where you can sift for semiprecious gemstones, an antique car museum, butterfly house, human maze race, 25-foot-tall climbing wall, and a miniature golf course.

Perry's Cave is open weekends in spring and fall, daily during summer months, Sun through Fri, 11 a.m. to 5 p.m.; Sat, 10 a.m. to 6 p.m. The cave is located near Put-in-Bay at 979 Catawba Ave. (419) 285-2283; perryscave.com. Admission for three of the attractions is $24 for adults and $14 for children (ages 6 to 12). A super combo packet for all five attractions is $35 for adults and $22 for children (ages 6 to 12).

English Pines Bed and Breakfast provides quality overnight lodging for visitors not ready to ferry back to the mainland. This home, within walking distance of "downtown," dates from the island's early settlement in the mid-1800s and features ornate flourishes. The inn's twelve guest rooms each can accommodate up to four people and have private baths. A continental breakfast is included.

English Pines Bed and Breakfast is at 182 Concord Ave., Put-in-Bay; (419) 285-2521; englishpines.com. Rates: $90 to $205 per night.

Traveling to South Bass Island is relatively easy most of the year, with Miller Boat Line, providing ferry service from the Catawba peninsula to the south end of the island; (800) 500-2421; millerferry.com. The company ferries both autos and passengers, though reservations are sometimes required for automobiles. Ferry service to the island is available only from March through November, because the island is iced-in during winter months.

The fastest boats from Port Clinton to downtown Put-in-Bay are Jet Express's hydrojet catamarans, which make the trip in 22 minutes. These 3,500-horsepower, super-modern vessels run circles around the older ferry boats as they zip you to and from South Bass Island. For more information call Jet Express at (800) 245-1538; jet-express.com.

Are you dreaming of a walk along a beach, away from cars and the bustle of life? Rather than hop a plane to the Caribbean you can hop on a ferry and spend some relaxing days at ***St. Hazards Resort*** on Middle Bass Island. The resort has villas, cabins, and campsites. Cabins sleep up to four people, and the villas can sleep up to six. Both have refrigerators and microwaves; the villas have a full kitchen. You will have to bring your own towels and linens. For water enthusiasts, there is a heated pool and Jacuzzi, along with 200 feet of private beach. The complex also features an on-site store, restaurant, and bike rentals. Call in advance for reservations and ferry information.

St. Hazards is at 1223 Fox Rd., Middle Bass; (800) 837-5211; sthazards.com. Campground rates: $50 to $75 per night; lodging rates: $109 to $259.

The ***Scenic Rock Ledge Inn Cottages*** offers four cottages available from March through October. The cottages all have fully equipped kitchens, including a microwave, coffeemaker, and tableware, plus cable TV and air-conditioning. The cottages are surrounded by shade trees with a direct view of Lake Erie and beautiful sunsets. Steps near the cottages lead down to the lake for swimming or just relaxing. For that outdoor cooking experience, cottage guests also have outdoor grills and picnic tables. The cabins are more rustic than the romantic inn rooms. Cabins, like inn rooms, do have air-conditioning, and they vary in size and floor plans. Some cottages have one bedroom; others have two. All can sleep four people (but some on a sleeper sofa). Two bathrooms are also available in some units.

Scenic Rock Ledge Inn Cottages is located at 2772 E. Sand Rd., Port Clinton; (419) 734-3265, (877) 994-7625; scenicrockledgeinn.com. All rooms have a two-night minimum stay. Rates start at $205 for two nights, double occupancy.

Not far away is one of the most popular public beaches on Lake Erie—the lengthy stretch of sand at ***East Harbor State Park***. Lifeguards watch swimmers during summer months, and there are snack bars and bathhouses (with showers).

In addition to the lakefront beach, the park contains 800 acres of water in three protected harbors. Middle Harbor, with its restriction on motorboats, offers an ideal environment for the thousands of resident and migratory waterfowl attracted to the lush acreage, making bird-watching a favorite pastime. East Harbor State Park is the home of many black-crowned night herons, and a large great blue heron nesting ground is nearby.

Boat-launching ramps are in the park, and a park naturalist conducts nature programs during the summer. Winter sports at East Harbor include ice fishing, iceboating, skating, sledding, and snowmobiling.

East Harbor State Park is at 1169 N. Buck Rd. off OH 269, near the junction of OH 269 and OH 163, Marblehead; (419) 734-4424; ohiodnr.gov/go-and-do/plan-a-visit/find-a-property/east-harbor-state-park.

Standing guard at what is known as the "roughest point in Lake Erie," the ***Marblehead Lighthouse*** is the oldest continuously operating lighthouse on the Great Lakes. The shallow water in this part of the lake, along with 200 miles of open water between Buffalo and Marblehead, allows howling northeasters to generate waves 10 to 15 feet tall.

The crash of those waves against the rocks around the lighthouse often shoots spray all the way up to the beacon 67 feet above the water. The Marblehead Lighthouse, built of native limestone in 1821, originally used candles for its light. The candles were replaced by oil-burning lamps, which in turn were replaced by an electric light and a 300-millimeter glass lens, which make the beacon visible for 7 miles.

Although rough water often bashes this peninsula in the spring and fall, peaceful days prevail in the summer. Picnic tables near the lighthouse make this an excellent place to stop and relax as you explore the Lake Erie shoreline. The Keepers House contains displays relating to the lighthouse and the peninsula's history, plus a small gift shop.

The Marblehead Lighthouse is off OH 163 in Marblehead, marbleheadlight houseohio.org. The lighthouse and museums are open daily from noon to 4 p.m. Memorial Day weekend through Labor Day. Park grounds are open year-round. The last tower tour begins at 3:40 p.m. No admission charge to tour the Keeper's House or Lifesaving Station. Tours to climb the tower cost $3 for adults and children age 6 or older. The tower has 77 steps to the top. Children under age 18 must be accompanied by an adult.

Four miles north of Marblehead and 9 miles northwest of Sandusky is ***Kelleys Island***. It was originally called Cunningham Island, named for the island's first white inhabitant, who lived here from 1800 to 1812. But Native Americans visited the island sometime between AD 1200 and 1600 and created the inscriptions (or pictographs) pecked into the 32-by-21-foot flat-topped slab of limestone known as ***Inscription Rock***. The rock rests on the water's edge on the south side of the island, and its pictographs have nearly been erased by erosion. Fortunately, a visitor here in 1850, U.S. Army Captain Seth Eastman, made a permanent record of the inscriptions. He carefully measured and drew in detail the pictographs, and from his drawings, reliefs have been made of the inscriptions. These reliefs, including the one exhibited at Inscription Rock, clearly reveal at least eight human figures wearing headdresses etched in the rock, plus bird and animal figures.

Inscription Rock is near the intersection of Water Street and Addison Road on the south side of Kelleys Island; (419) 797-4530; ohiohistory.org/visit/browse-historical-sites/inscription-rock-petroglyphs/. Open daylight hours; no admission charge.

The quarries on 2,800-acre Kelleys Island once supplied 500 one thousand–ton boatloads of limestone annually, and vineyards, wineries, and fruit and vegetable farms flourished. At the turn of the twentieth century, the island had a year-round population of 1,700. Today the quarries have closed and farming activity has declined, but the island, with a year-round population of approximately 300, offers restaurants, lodging, bicycle and boat rentals, and tram tours to visitors.

The site of the ***Glacial Grooves*** is on the north side of Kelleys Island. A glacier moving down from Labrador, Canada, scoured these grooves into the limestone bedrock. The grooved limestone is a trough 400 feet long, 25 to 35 feet wide, and 10 to 15 feet deep, and it's one of the most accessible examples of such grooves in the world.

These grooves were formed at a time when this part of the earth was much colder and wetter than today. Snow and ice would not completely melt during the short summers 30,000 years ago, so an ever-deeper mass of frozen snow accumulated. As the weight of this mass increased, the glacier crept southward at the rate of an inch or two per day, taking 5,000 years to arrive at the site of the Glacial Grooves. The pressure of that mass, which was up to a mile deep, carved the grooves still visible in the island's limestone. Even more spectacular grooves once existed in this area, but they were destroyed by a nearby quarrying operation.

The Glacial Grooves are at the north end of Division Street, Kelleys Island; (419) 797-4530; ohiohistory.org/visit/browse-historical-sites/glacial-grooves-geological-preserve/. Open daylight hours; no admission charge.

Just across the road from the Glacial Grooves is Kelleys Island State Park. The park offers campsites (rented on a first-come, first-served basis), a sandy swimming beach, and boat ramps; (419) 746-2546; ohiodnr.gov/go-and-do/plan-a-visit/find-a-property/kelleys-island-state-park.

The ***Kelleys Island Ferry Boat Line*** provides daily ferry service between Kelleys Island and Marblehead from Apr through Dec; (419) 798-9763, (888) 225-4325; kelleysislandferry.com. The Griffing Flying Service provides air transport to the island from the Griffing-Sandusky Airport; (419) 734-5400; flygriffing.com.

If you aren't ready to take the last ferry back to the mainland, stay overnight on Kelleys at the ***Eagle's Nest Bed & Breakfast***. Three rooms are available in the guest house, which is separate from the residence of owners Mark and Robin Volz. The upper unit is a one-bedroom apartment with a living room (and queen-size sofa bed), bedroom, small kitchen, private bath, and sundeck. The two downstairs units each have a microwave and refrigerator, a private bath, and plenty of country charm.

Eagle's Nest Bed & Breakfast is at 216 Cameron Rd., Kelleys Island; (419) 746-2708; eaglesnestbnb.com. Rates: $110 to $180 per night. A full breakfast is no longer served but coffee, tea, juice, and pastries are available on the porch where breakfast was traditionally served.

Back on the mainland, amusement park aficionados will definitely want to visit one of Ohio's most popular parks, ***Cedar Point***. Situated at the tip of a long, narrow peninsula jutting out into Lake Erie, this 364-acre park delights guests with a wide assortment of rides, more than 100 entertainers performing in live shows, and an 18-acre waterpark. However, it is the park's unmatched collection of roller coasters that attracts visitors from all over the country. Eighteen in all, they range from junior coasters to the Millennium Force, which drops 300 feet at 93 miles per hour, and the 420-foot-tall, 120-miles-per-hour Top Thrill Dragster, the tallest and fastest roller coaster in the world. New in 2018, the Steel Vengeance is said to be the tallest, fastest, and longest hybrid roller coaster in the world. The Steel Vengeance offers a surprisingly intricate wood structure below with smooth steel track above. Check the website at cedarpoint.com for more information.

For those needing accommodations at Cedar Point, the park has its own three hotels, an RV campground, two marinas, and the Lighthouse Point upscale camping complex with cabins, cottages, and luxury RV sites. Hotel Breakers offers 669 guest rooms and suites in addition to two outdoor pools, outdoor water playground, and indoor pool and restaurants. Hotel rooms range from $135 to $695 per night. For 2018, Cedar Point introduced twenty-five new ultimate RV sites with patios at Lighthouse Point. Each of the new full hookup sites feature a stylish, private patio area, dining table with chairs, built-in charcoal grill and firepit with comfy furniture. Four of the new sites also include a glider swing with views of Lake Erie. A new restroom facility and bathhouse are planned to open adjacent to the expansion. Standard cabins, deluxe cabins, and cottages are available at Lighthouse Point.

A short drive away from Cedar Point is the 419-room value-priced Cedar Point's Express Hotel. The rooms have a mini-fridge and microwave. The hotel also offers an outdoor pool, sprayground, and complimentary Wi-Fi. Another option within driving distance is Cedar Point's Castaway Bay, an indoor waterpark oasis offering a variety of rooms and suites. The 38,000-square-foot water paradise includes an outdoor pool, daily visits from Snoopy, a fitness room, complimentary Wi-Fi, a restaurant, snack shack, and Starbucks. For reservations, call (419) 627-2106. Cedar Point also has two marinas with slips available for day rental.

Cedar Point is on the Cedar Point Causeway, north of Sandusky; (419) 627-2350; cedarpoint.com. Open May through Aug plus weekends in Sept and Oct.

On the square in the heart of downtown Sandusky, in a magnificent 1920s neoclassical building that once housed the city's post office, is the unique ***Merry-Go-Round Museum***. The centerpiece of the museum is a fully restored and operational Allen Herschell carousel; a ride on this indoor gem is an absolute must. But there is much more to discover in this fabulous structure, now listed on the National Register of Historic Places.

Stop by and watch carousel carvers at work. They will explain and show you what it takes to restore neglected pieces, returning them to their full beauty. The museum includes a series of restoration workshops. Also on display are many examples of classic carousel animals, including those of Gustav Dentzel. A replica of his Philadelphia Carrousel Builder shop, which opened in 1867, is authentic down to the sign over the door, the tools on the wall, the workbenches, and the partially carved animals.

The Merry-Go-Round Museum is at the corner of West Washington and Jackson Streets at 301 Jackson, Sandusky; (419) 626-6111; merrygoround museum.org. Open Feb, Sat, from 11 a.m. to 4 p.m., Sun, from noon to 4 p.m.; Memorial Day through Labor Day, Tues through Sat, 10 a.m. to 4 p.m.; Sun, noon to 4 p.m. Open Oct through Dec, Wed through Sat, 11 a.m. to 4 p.m.; Sun, noon to 4 p.m. Admission: adults $6; senior citizens $5; children (ages 4 to 14) $4. Admission includes one ride token.

For tranquil accommodations in the heart of Lake Erie vacation country, try a comfortable Sandusky bed and breakfast, ***Wagner's 1844 Inn***. This fine old structure features three guest rooms, each with a private bath, a Victorian parlor with an antique Steinway piano, a living room with a wood-burning fireplace, and a screened porch and enclosed courtyard.

Innkeeper Barbara Wagner decided the time was right for a bed and breakfast after her child moved away from home. Barbara gave up her full-time nursing career to operate her own business. As she puts it, "Since I love to cook, entertain, and decorate, a bed and breakfast was a logical choice."

Breakfast is served in the formal dining room in the winter and on the porch in summer. A typical morning meal includes fresh fruit and juice, baked rolls or muffins (perhaps the popular pecan rolls), muesli cereal, or a German pancake. Once the home of grocer and dry goods store owner William Simpson, one of the founders of Sandusky, the 1844 Inn is today loaded

huron's shipbuildingera

Lake Erie's coastal communities boomed during the early nineteenth century as trade along the lake expanded. Villages located at the mouths of rivers feeding the lake often had natural harbors, and Huron was no exception.

Here shipbuilding flourished, including the construction of the mighty steamships—the royalty of lake vessels. The steamer *Walk-in-the-Water* kicked off the steamship era on Lake Erie in 1818, but met a tragic end when it went down off Buffalo. Huron's shipbuilding dominance ended with the construction of the canal at nearby Milan.

with antiques. Its style is Italianate, and it is listed on the National Register of Historic Places.

Wagner's 1844 Inn is at 230 E. Washington St., Sandusky; (419) 626-1726; wagnersinnsandusky.com: $125 per night, double occupancy, including continental breakfast. Reservations recommended.

The achievements of Ohio-born Thomas Edison are staggering—he invented the phonograph, the incandescent light, the motion picture camera, the fluoroscope, and the nickel-iron-alkaline battery. In fact, at the time of his death Edison held 1,093 different American patents.

The Edison Birthplace Museum in Milan provides an opportunity for visitors to learn more about this prolific inventor. Edison's father, Samuel, was involved in the Papineau-Mackenzie Rebellion, an unsuccessful Canadian counterpart to the American Revolution. Samuel migrated to Milan in 1839, attracted by the boom in shipping created there by the canal linking Milan, an inland community, with Lake Erie. In fact, in the 1840s, Milan was one of the world's major grain ports and shipbuilding centers. For example, in 1847, 918,000 bushels of grain were shipped from Milan, and fourteen warehouses loaded as many as twenty schooners per day—amazing statistics for a town 8 miles from the lakefront. Milan's boom was short-lived, however, for the coming of the railroad and the flood of 1868 ended the town's brief heyday as a port.

The small, redbrick house where Thomas Edison was born on February 11, 1847, is just up the hill from the former location of Milan's warehouses and port. The Edison home and adjacent small museum contain a number of his inventions—an early mimeograph machine (which Edison sold to the A.B. Dick Company in 1887), phonographs, telegraph equipment, dictating machines, motion picture cameras—and a model of Edison's 1893 movie studio, called the "Black Maria," which rotated and had an adjustable opening in the roof to allow sunlight to illuminate the stage.

Pictures of Edison with family and friends like Henry Ford adorn the walls of the home, and Edison's hat, cape, cane, and slippers are displayed, as is an unusual pig-shaped footstool. Edison bought his birthplace from his sister's family in 1906 and was shocked to find on a visit here in 1923 that this house did not yet have electric lights, a situation he quickly remedied.

The Edison Birthplace Museum is north of OH 113 at 9 N. Edison Dr., Milan; (419) 499-2135; tomedison.org. Feb., March, and Apr, Fri through Sun, noon to 5 p.m.; May, Thurs through Sun, noon to 5 p.m.; June through Aug, Tues through Sat, 10 a.m. to 5 p.m., Sun 1 p.m. to 5 p.m.; Sept and Oct, Thurs through Sun, noon to 5 p.m.; Nov and Dec, Fri through Sun, noon to 5 p.m. Closed Jan. Also open on Feb 11–Thomas Edison's birthday. Admission: adults $15; senior citizens $10; children (ages 5 to 18) $10.

Two blocks from Edison's birthplace is Milan's central business district, which was built around a 1-square-block park. Century-old buildings house many of the town's shops, and the shady park makes Milan a pleasant stop.

Vermilion is perhaps Ohio's most picturesque Lake Erie coastal town, with quaint homes set on meandering lagoons, sumptuous sail and power pleasure craft, and fine dining. Vermilion exudes an atmosphere of peacefulness and prosperity, and attracts visitors with sun, seafood, and recreation.

One Vermilion restaurant warrants special attention—***Old Prague Restaurant***. Set in a delightful cedar structure in the center of Vermilion's shopping district, this distinctive establishment serves both Old World recipes and American favorites. The large, open dining area offers a homey, comfortable setting, and the friendly people at Old Prague make guests feel almost like family.

The specialties at Old Prague are "Nationality Favorites," which include Bohemian goulash, chicken paprikash (farm-fresh chicken in zesty sour cream sauce), and wiener schnitzel. Two other popular entrees are roast duck and roast pork, which are served with sauerkraut. All meals come with traditional egg dumplings or spaetzles.

American dinner entrees include Boston strip steak, ham steak, grilled chicken breast, and roast chicken with stuffing. Those who favor fish can choose from a half dozen dinners such as fresh Lake Erie perch, scallops, broiled salmon, or a fisherman's platter. Lighter fare includes sandwiches, vegetarian risotto, cabbage rolls, salads, and appetizers. Two homemade soups are served daily.

The Old Prague Restaurant is at 5586 Liberty Ave. (US 6), Vermilion; (440) 967-7182; sites.google.com/view/oldprague/home. Open June through Oct. Thurs and Fri, 5 p.m. to 1 a.m.; Sat, 4 p.m. to 1 a.m.; Sun, noon to 6 p.m. Hours vary the rest of the year. Call Old Prague or check the website for times.

Presidential Path

Rutherford B. Hayes (or "Ruddy," as he was known to his friends) was president of the United States exactly 100 years before Jimmy Carter. For a glimpse at the politics and lifestyle of that era, visit the ***Rutherford B. Hayes Presidential Center*** in Fremont. The center, on a lush 25 acres known as Spiegel Grove, consists of a stately Victorian mansion, the expansive Hayes museum, and a presidential library with more than 70,000 volumes.

The museum contains exhibits from Hayes's early career as a lawyer, first in Fremont (which was then known as Lower Sandusky) and later in Cincinnati. Hayes, in fact, was instrumental in having the name of Lower Sandusky changed to Fremont. With nearby towns named Sandusky, and Upper

Sandusky, the residents of Fremont gratefully accepted the change, as did the U.S. Post Office.

It was in Cincinnati that Hayes became involved in politics, and old party tickets indicate his first race was in 1859 for city solicitor. At the outbreak of the Civil War, Hayes enlisted in the Union army, and a letter from his wife, Lucy Webb Hayes, written to him while he was in the army, is on display. Hayes was wounded several times during the war, seriously at the Battle of South Mountain.

Nominated for a seat in Congress before the war's conclusion, Hayes refused to leave active duty service to campaign. After his four years in Congress, he was elected governor of Ohio in 1867 and 1869, and again in 1875. The museum's campaign relics include political cartoons, newspaper clippings, hats, and banners. Hayes's favorite chair, which he used while governor, is also there.

Hayes's election to the presidency took place in 1876, but a dispute over 20 electoral votes was not resolved until March 2, 1877—three days before the inauguration. By an electoral vote count of 185 to 184, Hayes became the 19th U.S. president, defeating New York governor Samuel Tilden. Photographs of Hayes's inauguration are in the museum, as is the Haviland china used by the Hayes White House. A magnificent sideboard carved by Cincinnatian Henry L. Fry for use in the private White House dining room, and the presidential glassware used by presidents from Andrew Jackson through Hayes, are also displayed.

A short walk from the museum across the shady lawn brings you to the elegant Hayes Mansion. This enormous home has thirty-one rooms, and a large front porch faces the towering trees of Spiegel Grove. Members of the Hayes family lived in the mansion until 1965, when it was opened to the public for guided tours.

President and Mrs. Hayes used many of the furnishings now in the home when they returned to Fremont from Washington in 1881. Many of the pieces were gifts from around the world that they received while in the White House. Although each room has lavish appointments, the dining room, with its massive table for twenty-four guests, is exceptional. Fourteen fireplaces warmed the spacious residence, some with mantels of Italian marble, others of hand-carved hardwoods with tile insets. The 13-foot ceilings in the drawing room are just tall enough to accommodate the life-size portrait of Hayes and its ornate frame. Throughout the home are the original gas lighting fixtures, which have been converted to electricity.

The Rutherford B. Hayes Presidential Center is at the corner of Buckland and Hayes Avenues in Fremont; (419) 332-2081; rbhayes.org. The museum and residence are open Mon through Sat from Apr through Dec, 9 a.m. to 5 p.m., Sun, 12:30 p.m. to 5 p.m. Tues through Sat from Jan through Mar, 9 a.m. to 5 p.m., Sun, 12:30 p.m. to 5 p.m. Admission for museum or residence: adults $13; senior citizens $11; teens (ages 13 to 18), and children (ages 6 to 12) $3. A combination ticket to tour both the museum and the home is adults $20; senior citizens $18; children teens (ages 13 to 18) $10, and (ages 6 to 12) $5. The library is open Mon through Sat, 9 a.m. to 5 p.m.; no admission charge.

The Firelands region of Ohio takes its name from the Revolutionary War period. While the British held New York City, they made frequent raids against the coastal towns in Connecticut, burning homes, barns, and stores. After the conflict, the citizens petitioned the new state of Connecticut for compensation for their losses, and in 1792 the "fire-sufferers" were awarded land on the western edge of Connecticut's Western Reserve lands in Ohio—the Firelands.

The ***Firelands Museum*** is operated by the Firelands Historical Society, the second-oldest such society in the state. The museum was described by the society's first members as merely a "cabinet of curios," but today hundreds of items are on display in the two-story Preston-Wickham House, which local newspaper editor Samuel Preston built in 1835 as a wedding present for his daughter, Lucy, and her husband, Frederick Wickham. The extensive gun collection includes dozens of weapons: pistols, rifles, and muskets, some made before the American Revolution, plus military swords and knives. In the Native American exhibit, moccasins, beads, baskets, and tomahawks, as well as ancient points, gouges, and hatchets are displayed.

The basement is filled with an impressive group of pioneer tools, such as a 6-foot blacksmith's bellows, a yarn winder and spinning wheel, butter churns, farm implements, and game traps. On the second floor is a marvelous wooden Indian (ca. 1860) that once stood in front of a local tobacco shop, and the bell clapper from the old Norwalk courthouse that burned down in 1913 (the bell melted in the heat). Period clothing and personal items from early residents of the region are exhibited, as is the first organ manufactured by Norwalk's A.B. Chase Company in the 1870s.

The Firelands Museum is at 4 Case Ave., Norwalk; (419) 668-6038; firelands museum.com. From June through Aug, the museum is open Tues through Sat, 10 a.m. to 3 p.m.; Sun, noon to 4 p.m. Open Thurs through Sun, 11 a.m. to 3 p.m. in June, July and Aug; May through Oct, Sat and Sun, 11 a.m. to 3 p.m. Admission: adults $5; senior citizens $4; children (ages 13 to 18) $3.

The elegant exterior of the ***Georgian Manor Inn*** reflects the civility and elegance of another era. The Georgian revival home, built in 1906 by a local dentist, is now an elegant bed and breakfast located on 1.4 acres and surrounded by a number of large historic homes and estates. Each of the four guest rooms in the 27-room mansion is decorated with antiques and reproductions. The sunroom, the library, the living room with its oak-manteled fireplace, and the parlor offer comfortable indoor surroundings, but guests are often drawn to the tranquility of the gardens and two porches. A patio looks out over a 3-foot waterfall and small stream that flows into a lovely pond. In spring and summer, the gardens are filled with the color and scent of a variety of herbs and flowers.

A full breakfast is served at 9 a.m. For those wishing to dine earlier, the serving is a fruit melon plate, cereal, toast, orange juice, tea, or coffee.

The Georgian Manor Inn is at 123 W. Main St., Norwalk; (419) 663-8132, (800) 668-1644; georgianmanorinn.net. Lodging rates: $140 to $225 per night.

When John Wright arrived in America in 1843, a young man of 20, he dreamed of one day building a vast estate similar to those in his native England. Forty years later, after acquiring 2,400 acres, he established a sawmill and kiln to prepare lumber and brick for what is today known as ***Wright Mansion***.

When listed on the National Register of Historic Places in 1974, the Wright family home was declared significant as "an unusually substantial and stately example of the Second Empire–style mansion found as a relatively isolated farmhouse rather than an urban residence." But for a "farmhouse," Wright's home was constructed with many surprisingly modern conveniences, thanks to his ingenuity. For example, he installed two bathrooms with running water and flush toilets that were supplied with water pumped by a windmill to a large tank on the third floor. This at a time—the 1880s—when most rural residences still used water pitchers and chamber pots.

Piped natural gas was unheard of in this country setting before 1900, but Wright developed his own gas system, making acetylene in a small brick building at a corner of his front yard and routing it to chandeliers on all three floors of his home. And a central heating plant in the basement sent hot steam to radiators throughout the house.

The Wright Mansion is the centerpiece of ***Historic Lyme Village***, a 16-structure collection of historic buildings. Tours of Wright Mansion take visitors past magnificent woodwork used throughout this expansive residence: beams and rafters of oak, and intricate interior trim of walnut, curly maple, and cherry.

After walking past the huge parlor doors, visitors find room after room of period furnishings, including Wright's piano. A graceful staircase ascends to the second floor, which has eight bedrooms. Most of the third floor is a huge ballroom, with a stage set directly under the central tower at the front of the home.

More rustic structures make up the rest of Lyme Village. Ohio settler pieces, such as a rope bed, spinning wheel, and wood cooking stove, furnish

Annie Brown's log home, built in 1851 in Seneca County. Ms. Brown occupied this modest house from 1869 to 1951.

Spinning and weaving exhibits (and occasional demonstrations) can be found in the Schriner Log House, an 1870-vintage structure that was used as a residence until 1947. Other occasional Lyme Village demonstrations include blacksmithing and woodworking at the North Adams Barn, built more than a century ago.

Antique farm implements fill the Biebricher Centennial Barn (erected in 1876), a Gothic board-and-batten building with unusual louvered windows. The Seymour House, moved to Lyme Village in 1976 to save it from demolition, is one of the oldest homes in this part of Ohio, and it served as the Seymour family home for more than a century (1836–1948). It likely was a stop on the Underground Railroad. Today it houses country furnishings typical of the early nineteenth century, including a fabulous old pump organ. Other structures of note include the Merry School House, built in the 1860s and used as a school until 1935; the Detterman Church, built in 1848 and believed to be one of only two known remaining original log churches in Ohio; and Schug Hardware, the hardware collection from Bellevue's C.W. Schug Hardware, which was in business from 1927 until the 1980s. Visitors may also explore the Cooper-Fries General Store, filled with displays and merchandise, and the Greenslade Cobbler's Shop.

Lyme Village also includes a unique museum—the Postmark Collectors Club Museum. Formerly housed in private homes, a converted schoolbus, and in a building that twice served as the Lyme, Ohio, post office, the museum has found a permanent home in the Groton Township Hall. Millions of postmarks—the "cancels" used by postal authorities to show where mail originated and to void stamps—fill the museum, the most extensive such collection in the world.

Historic Lyme Village is at 5001 OH 4, just east of Bellevue; (419) 483-4949; lymevillage.com. Tours are given June through Aug, Wed through Sat, 11 a.m. to 5 p.m. Closed Sept through May except for special functions and scheduled tours. Admission: adults $12; senior citizens $11; children (ages 6 to 12) $6.

Railroad buffs, youngsters, and anyone who has ever dreamed of being the engineer on a fast-moving freight train as it streaks across the countryside will want to climb aboard the many trains displayed at the ***Mad River & NKP Railroad Society Museum***. On self-guided tours of the rail yard, you'll discover a number of intriguing locomotives, passenger cars, and even cabooses. Many of these are open, permitting you to virtually walk through railroad history.

Those who are knowledgeable about trains especially appreciate some of the Nickel Plate Road additions to the museum's collection, including Alco

RSD-12 Diesel and Dynamometer Car X50041. But anyone will enjoy visiting the RPO Post Office Car, complete with mail sacks, sorting bins, and mail crane. Inside the Nickel Plate Box Car and Fruit Growers Refrigerator Car are extensive displays of railroad models, lanterns, locks, timetables, signs, photos, badges, and the like.

And when you climb into the cab of the museum's Wabash F Diesel, you can't help but imagine yourself racing along the main line from New York to Chicago or crossing the Rockies on your way to deliver freight to the West Coast. From the cupola of a caboose, you get a feel for the working environment at the other end of a long freight train, while tours of America's first dome car demonstrate how trains treated their passengers in days gone by.

An old section house serves as the welcome center for the museum. It's staffed by volunteers, many of them current and former railroad workers who enjoy answering questions and explaining life on the rails. Be sure to ask about upcoming railroad excursions on Ohio tracks.

The Mad River & NKP Railroad Society Museum is on Southwest St., just south of US 20, Bellevue; (419) 483-2222; madrivermuseum.org. Open daily, noon to 4 p.m., Memorial Day to Labor Day; weekends only in May, Sept, and Oct. Admission: adults $10; senior citizens $9; children (ages 5 to 12) $5.

Widely known as the "Earth Crack," ***Seneca Caverns*** was designated a Registered Natural Landmark in 1997. Discovered in 1872, the cave was opened to the public by the Bell family in 1933.

A one-hour tour takes visitors through seven rooms or levels, the deepest 110 feet below the surface to the Ole Mist'ry River. Fossilized fish, shells, and corals are visible throughout the limestone cavern, which remains a cool 54 degrees year-round. Comfortable walking shoes are a must. Visitors also may pan for gemstones and minerals at the cavern or browse the gift shop.

Seneca Caverns is off OH 269, 4 miles south of Bellevue; (419) 483-6711; senecacavernsohio.com. Open daily Memorial Day to Labor Day, 9 a.m. to 7 p.m.; weekends only in May and from Sept to mid-Oct, 10 a.m. to 5 p.m. Rates: adults $22; senior citizens $20; children (ages 4 to 11) $10; also for children (ages 4 to 11) $15 for cave tour and Paydirt Gemstone Bag.

Places to Stay in Northwest Ohio

DEFIANCE

The Second Story
210 Clinton St.
(419) 980-0327
secondstorydefiance.com

FINDLAY

Findlay Inn
200 E. Main Cross St.
(419) 422-5682
findlayinn.com

Hancock Hotel
631 S. Main St.
(419) 423-0631
hancockhotel.com

GRAND RAPIDS

Grand Kerr House
1777 Beaver St.
(419) 610-8138
thegrandkerrhouse.com

Mill House Bed & Breakfast
24070 Front St.
(419) 832-6455
themillhouse.com

HURON

Captain Montague's
229 Center St.
(419) 433-4756

Sawmill Creek Resort
400 Sawmill Creek Dr. W.
(419) 433-3800
sawmillcreekresort.com

KELLEYS ISLAND

Eagle's Nest Bed & Breakfast
216 Cameron Rd.
(419) 746-2708 (summer)
eaglesnestbnb.com

Kelley's Island Venture Resort
441 W. Lakeshore Dr.
(419) 746-2900
kiventureresort.com

Water's Edge Retreat
827 E. Lakeshore Dr.
(419) 746-2333
watersedgeretreat.com

MIDDLE BASS ISLAND

St. Hazards Resort
(800) 837-5211
sthazards.com

NORWALK

Georgian Manor Inn
123 W. Main St.
(419) 663-8132
georgianmanorinn.com

PORT CLINTON

Four Seasons Bed & Breakfast at Catawba Point
5078 E. Water St.
(614) 499-5126
4seasonsbandb.com

Our Sunset Place Bed & Breakfast
2803 E. Sand Rd.
(419) 732-3875
oursunsetplace.com

Scenic Rock Ledge Inn Cottages
2772 E. Sand Rd.
(419) 734-3265,
(877) 994-7625
thescenicrockledgeinn.com

HELPFUL WEBSITES

Ohio Division of Travel and Tourism
ohio.org

Toledo Convention and Visitors Bureau
visittoledo.org

Toledo Blade
toledoblade.com

Ottawa County Visitors Bureau
shoresandislands.com

Cedar Point
cedarpoint.com

PUT-IN-BAY

Anchor Inn Boutique Hotel
500 Catawba Ave.
(419) 285-5055
anchorinnpib.com

Ashley's Island House
557 Catawba Ave.
(419) 285-2844
ashleysislandhouse.com

Bird's Nest Resort
1371 Langram Rd.
(419) 285-6119
birdsnestresort.com

Bodee's Bungalow Boutique Hotel
385 Dollar Ave.
(419) 705-0804
bodeesbungalow.com

Chapman House
50 Chapman Rd.
(419) 631-1404
chapmanhousepib.com

English Pines Bed and Breakfast
182 Concord Ave.
(419) 285-2521
englishpines.com

Getaway Inn at Cooper's Woods
210 Concord Ave.
(419) 285-9012
getawayinn.com

Harriet's House
247 Erie St.
(419) 341-2191
harrietshouse.com

Put-in-Bay Resort Hotel
439 Loraine Ave.
(419) 285-7427
putinbayresort.com

SANDUSKY

Farrell House Lodge
1104 Fremont Ave.
(419) 625-8353
farrellhouselodge.com

Hotel Breakers
1 Cedar Point Dr.
(419) 627-2106
cedarpoint.com

Hotel Kilbourne
223 W. Water St.
(844) 373-2223
hotelkilbourne.com

Kalahari Resorts
7000 Kalahari Dr.
(877) 525-2427
kalahariresorts.com

Millsite Lodge
5712 Heywood Rd.
(419) 706-7442
millsitelodge.com

Wagner's 1844 Inn
230 E. Washington St.
(419) 626-1726

TOLEDO

Casey-Pomeroy House
802 N. Huron St.
(419) 243-1440
caseypomeroy.com

The Kings Throne
2040 Collingwood Blvd.
(567) 318-3581

Scottwood Inn
2335 Scottwood Ave.
(419) 242-4551
scottwoodinn.com

Places to Eat in Northwest Ohio

ARCHBOLD

Barn Restaurant
22611 OH 2
(419) 445-2231
saudervillage.org

Casa Vieja
1230 S. Defiance St.
(419) 445-0141
casaviejas.com

The Home Restaurant
218 N. Defiance St.
(419) 445-6411
thehomerest.com

Samuel Mancino's Italian Restaurant
106 S. Defiance St.
(419) 446-4600
samuelmancinosarchbold.com

BOWLING GREEN

The Clay Pot Bistro
182 S. Main St.
(419) 373-6050
theclaypotbistro.com

El Zarape
1616 E. Wooster St.
(419) 353-0937
el-zarape.com

Kermit's Family Restaurant
307 S. Main St.
(419) 354-1388
places.singleplatform.com/kermits/menu

Pagliai's
945 S. Main St.
(419) 352-7571
pagliaisbg.com

SamB's Restaurant
146 N. Main St.
(419) 353-2277
sambs.com

CATAWBA ISLAND

PORT CLINTON

Bistro 163
1848 E. Perry St.
(419) 734-9887
bistro163.org

Casa Las Palmas
4000 E. Harbor Light Landing Dr.
(419) 734-6593
casalaspalmas.m.takeout7.com

Ciao Bella
3880 E. Harbor Light Landing Dr.
(419) 734-2426
ciaobellaohio.com

1812 Food & Spirits
2590 E. Sand Rd.
(419) 960-7588
1812foodandspirits.com

Orchard Bar & Table
3266 NE Catawba Rd.
(419) 797-7324
orchardoncatawba.com

SANDUSKY

Bay Harbor
1 Cedar Point Dr.
(419) 625-6373
bayharbordining.com

The Club Restaurant & Bar
1220 Sycamore Line
(419) 625-3776
theclubsandusky.com

Crush Wine Bar
145 Columbus Ave.
(419) 502-9463
sanduskywinebar.com

J Bistro Downtown
129 W. Market St.
(419) 502-2280
jbistrodwtn.wixsite.com

Vine & Olive
4917 Milan Rd.
(419) 502-4000
vine-olive.com

TOLEDO

The Beirut
4082 Monroe St.
(419) 473-0885
beirutrestaurant.com

The Chop House—Toledo
300 N. Summit St.
(419) 720-4335
thechophouserestaurant.com

Fowl & Fodder
614 Adams St.
(419) 214-1588
fowlandfodder.com

Georgio's Café International
426 N. Superior St.
(419) 242-2424
georgiostoledo.com

Kengo Sushi & Yakitori
38 S. St. Clair St.
(419) 214-0574
kengotoledo.com

Mancy's Steakhouse
953 Phillips Ave.
(419) 476-4154
mancyssteakhouse.com

Registry Bistro
144 N. Superior St.
(419) 725-0444
registrybistro.com

Rockwell's
27 Broadway St.
(419) 243-1302

Schmucker's Restaurant
2103 N. Reynolds Rd.
(419) 535-9116
schmuckersrestaurant.com

Souk Mediterranean Kitchen & Bar
139 S. Huron St.
(567) 777-7685
soukkitchenbar.com

Tony Packo's Cafe
1902 Front St.
(419) 691-6054
tonypacko.com

VERMILION

Chez Francois Restaurant & Touche Bistro
555 Main St.
(440) 967-0630
chezfrancois.com

Lucky Chinese Restaurant
4793 Liberty Ave.
(440) 967-8883
luckyvermilion.com

Martino's International Café
4415 Liberty Ave.
(440) 967-3463
martinosinternationalcafe.com

Old Prague Restaurant
5586 Liberty Ave.
(440) 967-7182
sites.google.com/view/oldprague/home

Rudy's Bar & Grill
5665 Liberty Ave.
(440) 967-4534
rudysbarandgrillvermilion.com

Salvatore's Ristorante Italiano
4560 Liberty Ave.
(440) 967-0777
salvatoresvermilion.com

Woodstock Café & Coffee
665 Main St.
(440) 967-7687
woodstockcafeandcoffee.com

Index